# Adventure Capital

The publisher and the University of California Press Foundation gratefully acknowledge the generous support of the Ahmanson Foundation Endowment Fund in Humanities.

# Adventure Capital

*Migration and the Making of an African Hub in Paris*

Julie Kleinman

UNIVERSITY OF CALIFORNIA PRESS

University of California Press, one of the most distinguished university presses in the United States, enriches lives around the world by advancing scholarship in the humanities, social sciences, and natural sciences. Its activities are supported by the UC Press Foundation and by philanthropic contributions from individuals and institutions. For more information, visit www.ucpress.edu.

University of California Press
Oakland, California



Library of Congress Cataloging-in-Publication Data

Names: Kleinman, Julie, author.
Title: Adventure capital : migration and the making of an African hub in Paris / Julie Kleinman.
Description: Oakland, California : University of California Press, [2019] | Includes bibliographical references and index. |
Identifiers: LCCN 2019014743 (print) | LCCN 2019019829 (ebook) | ISBN 9780520304406 (cloth : alk. paper) | ISBN 9780520304413 (pbk. : alk. paper) | ISBN 9780520973084 (ebook)
Subjects: LCSH: West Africans—France—Paris. | Immigrants—France—Paris. | Gare du Nord (Paris, France). | Racism—Economic aspects—France—Paris.
Classification: LCC DC718.A34 (ebook) | LCC DC718.A34 K55 2019 (print) | DDC 944/.361004966—dc23
LC record available at https://lccn.loc.gov/2019014743

Manufactured in the United States of America

28 27 26 25 24 23 22 21 20 19
10 9 8 7 6 5 4 3 2 1

Dòw b'a fò olu ma *"clandestin"*

Anw dun ko olu ma tunkannaden

*Some call them "illegals"*

*We call them children of adventure*

—FATOUMATA DIAWARA, *CLANDESTIN*

# CONTENTS

# ACKNOWLEDGMENTS

Writing this book has been an adventure, and like the Gare du Nord it brings together paths both beaten and less explored. It is a product of encounters across many boundaries. It has been shaped through ongoing conversations with research participants, friends, and mentors—and several people who have been all three. At the end of the day, I had to sit down and write, a practice I often experienced and heard described as isolating and painful. Yet thanks to this long journey, I have created many ties, and they are the kind that give life meaning and that lift us from isolation. This book is a profoundly social product, a product of many adventures.

"The adventure is hard work." This refrain of many West African migrants in Paris came to me often as I was writing, as did their imperative to avoid getting stuck, to keep moving. My deepest gratitude goes to the people who give this project its life and its source. Without Baha Niakate, it may have never gotten off the ground. More than a key informant, he has also acted as research assistant, friend, and brother. His generosity and insight into the social world of the Gare du Nord allowed my research to take flight. His family in France and in Mali—Mina, Silima, Bakary, and Tene—has taken me in and traveled with me, and I will keep trying to find ways to reciprocate their hospitality. The group of West African men I met at the Gare du Nord let me into their community, amiably put up with my intrusive questions, shared their stories, and taught me more than I could contain in this book.

I was able to research and write this book thanks to the support of several institutions and grants. These include the Mellon International Dissertation Research Fellowship of the Social Science Research Council, the Krupp Foundation Dissertation Research Award of the Minda de Gunzberg Center for European Studies, the

Frederick Sheldon Traveling Fellowship of Harvard University, the Harvard Center for Middle Eastern Studies, the Harvard Department of Anthropology, the Harvard Weatherhead Center for International Affairs, the Harvard Committee on African Studies, the Cora Du Bois Trust, the Mellon Postdoctoral Fellowship in the Humanities, the Oberlin College H. H. Powers Grant, Penn State University, the Penn State Center for Global Studies Career Development Award, and Fordham University. I wrote and revised much of the manuscript thanks to a Macmillan-Stewart Fellowship at the W. E. B. Du Bois Research Institute of the Hutchins Center at Harvard University. I thank these institutions and the many people who administer these grants and fundings for their support and work. Parts of chapter 4 appeared in "Adventures in Infrastructure: Making an African Hub in Paris," *City & Society* 26(3): 286–307 (2014); parts of chapter 5 appeared in "The Path Between Two Points," *Transition* (113): 25–43 (2014) and "From Little Brother to Big Somebody: Coming of Age at the Gare du Nord," in *Affective Circuits: African Journeys and the Pursuit of Social Regeneration*, edited by Jennifer Cole and Christian Groes, 245–68, Chicago: University of Chicago Press (2016). I thank the publishers for the permission to reprint this material.

The folks in Paris who made this research possible are too numerous to list here. I would like to thank Catherine Avice and the SNCF workers at the TGV-Escale Gare du Nord, Patrick Cabaniols and Yann Lorquin, for welcoming me as a summer intern and making me feel like part of the cheminot family. The Gare du Nord railway police team (SUGE) generously allowed me to intrude upon them on several occasions, as did the Equipe Assistance Rapide team. Thanks to Etienne Tricaud and Daniel Claris for offering their time and insight about redesigning the station. The Association pour l'Histoire des Chemins de Fer en France (AHICF) and its director, Marie-Noëlle Polino, offered railway resources and many great contacts. The staff at French archives and libraries were enormously helpful, and I would like to extend my gratitude to the Archives de Prefecture de Police in Paris, where Commissaire Françoise Gicquel and Olivier Accarie helped me access many documents I may never have seen otherwise. Thank you to the brilliant Sorélia Kada for providing rigorous research assistance. Among the many scholars and experts who gave me their time and insight in Paris, I would like to thank Julien Artero, Karen Bowie, Beth Epstein, Christian Lallier, Léna Mauger, Anne Monjaret, Steve Rhinds, Stephanie Sauget, Sylvie Tissot, and Stéphane Tonnelat. Jonathan Friedman was my official host at the Ecole des Hautes Etudes en Sciences Sociales (EHESS), but also provided much in the way of community and lively exchange. The intellectual comradeship I found in Paris kept me going on even the darkest days, and for that I would like to thank Lauren Elkin, Erin Schlumpf, Barbara Karatsioli, Rebecca Johnson, Nadim Audi, and Anna Weischelbraun. In Bamako, thank you also to my many hosts, friends, and Malian families, in particular Chérif Keita, Aminata Cissé, Rosa and Chérif Cissé, Bruce Whitehouse, and Katarina Höije; as well as Phil Paoletta and the whole team at the Sleeping Camel. My appreciation goes to Brema Ely Dicko at the University of Bamako and the members of the Association Malienne des Expulsés (Amadou Coulibaly, Ousmane Diarra, Alassane Dicko, Souhad Toure, and the late Mamadou Keita, *Allah ka hin a la*), who taught me what the adventure means.

This project has had many interlocutors along the way, and it begins with my intellectual roots at Haverford College. My deepest thanks to Mark Gould for nearly two decades of support and mentorship, and for, as he likes to say, rewiring our brains. The brilliance, criticism, and dedication of Laurie Kain Hart, Maris Gillette, and Zolani Ngwane have inspired me, pushed me, and provided the best exemplars of scholar-teachers that I still try to emulate. The seed of this project came from my work at the EHESS with Marc Abélès, who spurred me to take risks. Paul Silverstein has been a long-standing source of intellectual support and inspiration.

Four amazing women have shaped my intellectual trajectory. Ajantha Subramanian has paved the way for combining intellectual, political, and social commitment. Jean Comaroff has been my model of generosity and brilliance in mentorship and scholarship, and has provided insight and counsel at many stages of this project. Since the time I was working on my dissertation, the careful reading and criticism of Joan Wallach Scott has made this a better book. I cannot thank Jennifer Cole enough for offering extra-institutional support and mentorship, and I strive to meet her high standards and emulate her ability to cut through all the pretense and mess to the heart of things.

In my graduate days at Harvard, I benefitted from the mentorship of Vince Brown, Steve Caton, Caroline Elkins, Bill Granara, Susan Kahn, Michael Herzfeld, and Michèle Lamont. I first started writing about the Gare du Nord in Engseng Ho's graduate seminar Mobilities, and he and the members of that seminar offered the generous antagonism that one hopes for in grad school. Camille Robcis, Christian Groes, Trica Keaton, Sasha Newell, Charles Piot, Jason Throop, and Henrik Vigh have offered help, intellectual community, and opportunities to present my work.

Writing and our whole intellectual enterprise has been much less lonely thanks to the incredible people I have met on this journey. I am humbled and inspired by Louisa Lombard, who has read almost all of the manuscript in many of its stages, and has offered the best kind of intellectual, moral, and emotional support and insight, from integrating theory and ethnography and navigating life after the field to navigating the field with a toddler. I have the pleasure of being in writing groups and partnerships that have offered more than only great criticism, and would like to thank Cal Biruk, Jatin Dua, Jonathan Echeverri Zuluaga, Claudio Sopranzetti, Anand Vaidya, and Rebecca Woods for reading my stuff and for sharing their brilliant work with me, sometimes over cocktails and often across several time zones.

I would also like to thank my extended cohort in the PhD process: Naor Ben-Yehoyada, Kerry Chance, Namita Dharia, Alireza Doostdar, Alex Fattal, Anush Kapadia, Darryl Li, Jennifer Mack, Lilith Mahmud, Federico Perez, Laurence Ralph, Erin Schlumpf, and Dilan Yildrim. Orkideh Behrouzan has been an inspiration and a dear friend when I most needed it. For helping me make a new intellectual home for a brief period in Cambridge, England, I thank Anastasia Piliavsky, Nadia Marx, Robert Priest, Michal Murawski, and the Cambridge Anthropology Division.

I was fortunate to begin writing this book at Oberlin College on a Mellon Postdoctoral Fellowship in the Humanities, where Grace An and Libby Murphy were wonderful hosts, interlocutors, and friends. I could not imagine a more ideal place to think and write, and would like to thank my people of the Lady's Grove, and in particular Laura Baudot, Cal Biruk, Erika Hoffman-Dilloway, Vange Heiliger, Bridget Guarasci, Daphne John, Julie Keller, Silvija Koschnick, Greggor Mattson, Kristen Sutcliffe, and Sarah Waheed. Victoria Fortuna was an inspiring writing partner and provided insight and a sunny place to write. Brandon County is our formidable Oberlin *jatigi* and an endless source of knowledge about African history, Bamako, and beer. I have learned so much from Vange Heiliger, thanks to whom this world is a brighter place. To my Penn State family: thank you for making State College livable. I could not imagine two more brilliant and generous women to navigate the first tenure-track years with than Tracy Rutler and Magalí Armillas Tiseyra. Jonathan Marks offered books, critique, and hospitality, and conversation bested only by his daughter Miranda. Alicia Decker was my sister in the African Studies program from our early days of motherhood, and Gabeba Baderoon and Dorn Hetzel welcomed our family and inspired us. Thanks to Bill Dewey, Kevin Thomas, and my other colleagues in African Studies. In the French and Francophone Studies department, thanks to Jennifer Boittin's mentorship and friendship, to Bénédicte Monicat's support, and to Heather McCoy who gave me the *fou rire* every day.

My deepest gratitude to Henry Louis Gates Jr., Krishna Lewis, and Abby Wolf at the W. E. B. Du Bois Research Institute of the Hutchins Center at Harvard University, to Jean and John Comaroff, as well as to my fellow fellows, especially Cassi Pittman Claytor and LaFleur Stephens-Dougan. Much of this book was completed at the Nantes Institute for Advanced Study where my partner had a fellowship and I was welcomed as part of the community. Thank you to Françoise Rubellin, Alain Supiot, and to Claire Mony-Laffay who went above and beyond providing me books and a friendly space to write. Thank you to Fordham University and the department of Sociology and Anthropology, and particularly to my colleagues Hugo Benavides, Orit Avishai, Daisy Deomampo, Natalia Mendoza, and Aseel Sawalha for welcoming me and for your support, and especially to Rosa Giglio. In New York, I am grateful for our hosts Greg Mann, Oumou Sidibe, and Kadiatou, for Josh Schreier, and for my writing buddy and photographer Rachel Fish. My thanks to the wonderful people at Coffee Mob in Ditmas Park, where many of these pages were written, and Common Good in Harlem, where they were finished. My hilarious and brilliant anthropologist friends Brooke Bocast and Anna West made the writing process much, much better.

This book would be much worse off were it not for fantastic editors and readers. Thanks to Chris Lura, who had a knack for drawing out clarity from muddled phrasing, to Laura Frader for her help on the introduction, and to Gary J. Hamel's excellent copyediting. Cal Biruk, Kerry Chance, Jennifer Cole, Brandon County, Andrew Konove, Caroline Melly, Sasha Newell, Andrew Newman, Chrystel Oloukoï, Josh Schreier, Ryan Skinner, Claudio Sopranzetti, and Anand Vaidya offered invaluable comments and criticism on chapter drafts. Chrystel Oloukoï and Alexandra Rallo provided first-rate research assistance. This book exists thanks to the smart stewardship of my editor Kate Marshall, Enrique Ochoa-Kaup, and the team at the University of California Press. Thank you to Paul Stoller and the two anonymous reviewers for thorough and generous criticism of the first draft of the manuscript. I am responsible for any remaining inaccuracies.

I dedicate this book to my two grandmothers, Alwina Wittenzelner O'Brien and Marcia Fanny Kaplan Kleinman (Nana), both benevolent matriarchs and forces of nature. My parents, Patricia O'Brien Kelley and Stephen Kleinman, instilled in me an early passion for books and conversation and have been there for me wherever I ended up. Kevin Kelley has been a source of much-needed comic relief, and Arthur Kleinman has given me an example to follow when it comes to doing anthropology with a purpose.

This book is the product of the path I share with my partner and fellow migrant, Isaïe Dougnon. He has shown me the meaning of intellectual rigor, of loyalty to family and community, and of building a purposeful life. He has made me an optimist. Last and most, to Alexis Amaseru, whose constant questions, ebullient energy, and love of hugs reminds me what matters and keeps us striving to create a more just world where adventures can flourish. May he also learn from the ancestors.

# Introduction

On a breezy spring day in 2010, Lassana Niaré[1] and I sat sipping espressos at a café across the street from the Gare du Nord railway station in Paris. We gazed at the station's glass-walled entrance, where groups of young West African men stood chatting as people brushed by them on their way into the busiest rail hub in Europe. Originally from a village in rural western Mali, Lassana had been living and working in France for almost a decade. He and his West African comrades met most evenings at the Gare du Nord, which they passed through on their evening commute.

I had first met Lassana the previous fall in the station's front square. At the time, he sported neat cornrows in his hair and wore baggy jeans, a jersey emblazoned with "The Bronx," and a backwards Yankees cap. He had come to France in 2001 on a three-month commerce visa and spent the better part of his twenties barely getting by as an undocumented cleaner and construction worker. He and many other West African workers came to the station for various reasons: to catch up with friends and discuss the news, find better jobs, get loans, and meet new people. For them, the station is more than a simple transit site.

"We are adventurers here," Lassana used to say—not foreigners, guest workers, refugees, or migrants. Many West Africans I met in France used the terms *l'aventurier* (adventurer) and *l'aventure* (adventure) to describe themselves and their situation. It was not just an attempt to romanticize difficult journeys and hard times.[2] These terms and their equivalents have long been used among West Africans to signify that migration is an initiatory journey, a rite of passage.[3] Seeing their voyages as part of a broader tradition helped to maintain connections to their families across long distances. It gave migrants a way to find meaning in risky travels and misfortune abroad.[4] "Soninke are the greatest adventurers," Lassana once bragged, referring to his ethno-linguistic group that comprises about two million people in the Western Sahel (a semi-arid region just south of the Sahara including parts of Mali, Senegal, Mauritania, Guinea, Gambia, and Burkina Faso) but which also has a significant global diaspora. His father and uncles all had left on adventures in their youth; most of his brothers and cousins were on their own adventures in central Africa and Spain. The notion of migration as an "adventure" was widespread among migrants at the Gare du Nord as it is with migrants from this region living across the globe.[5]

Lassana's vision departed from the assumptions of so-called "economic migration" applied to migrants like him, which assumes that migration is a relatively new phenomenon where poor people are forced to leave underdeveloped villages in Africa and go to work in European capitals.[6] Lassana, rather, saw migration as a necessary stage of life and the continuation of a long tradition. He was not alone. Many West African migrants come from places where "not migrating is not living," as anthropologist Isaie Dougnon puts it.[7] The idiom of adventure is a way for Lassana and other West Africans to conceptualize their journeys. It also provides a new perspective for understanding migrant lives and struggles more broadly.

The notion of migration-as-adventure challenges the nation-state definition of immigration, which presumes that the migrant moves from one bounded entity into another with the goal of settling and attaining citizenship, and often, in the xenophobic imaginary, of relying on state subsidies. Instead, adventurers live by the ethic of mobility, producing social and economic value by creating new networks for exchange, and making the most of what anthropologist Anna Tsing calls "encounters across difference."[8] Lassana and his friends see the Gare du Nord as the ultimate place to carry out their adventures. Instead of remaining within the well-trodden paths of kinship and village ties, they use the station to meet people outside of their communities, people who might help enable their onward mobility and realize future-looking projects. Adventurers have transformed the largest rail hub in Europe, and the Gare du Nord has changed their life course.

On the day we met for coffee across the street from the station, Lassana asked me how my research on the station was going. "Bit by bit," I responded, some of the discouragement coming through in my voice.

"It's good you're writing a book. This is what matters," Lassana replied reassuringly. "The important thing is to have projects, to think of the future, keep moving. Avoid getting stuck." This advice reflected Lassana's adventure ethos, which sought constant forward movement: he told me that he hoped to meet a German woman at the Gare du Nord, move to Germany, and find something better than underpaid construction jobs in France. Now that he had the resident permit, he wanted to go elsewhere.

As we sat at the café, a small TV set above the bar drew Lassana's attention, interrupting our conversation. The screen showed a few white people on a boat throwing life-vests toward hundreds of black people in the water. The disembodied journalist's voice intoned: "In the Mediterranean Sea between Africa and Europe, a boat filled with migrants has sunk. The nearest coast guard mounted a rescue, saving some, but many have drowned."

"We already know this story," Lassana said.

He was right: the sinking of unseaworthy vessels "filled with migrants" was frequently reported in the media in this way. In this saga linking two sides of the Mediterranean, we knew the tragedy's denouement: survivors would bring the terrible news to their villages, and families would try to locate their kin from afar. In the days that follow, bodies would wash up on pristine European beaches, or would be tugged out of the water by Frontex (European Union border control) ships. Many would never be found.[9]

Lassana narrowed his eyes at the screen, furrowing his brow. It was as if he were trying to see whether he recognized anyone. I learned later that he was trying to see if he could tell where the surviving "Africans" had come from by looking at them. But the camera panned over the migrants, returning to focus on the people in the boat as they pulled men, women, and young children aboard.

We already knew this story, as Lassana said, because of how dangerous Africa to Europe migration routes have become. European Union and member-state policies have criminalized migration by shutting down legal pathways to Europe, reinforcing border control, and detaining and deporting undocumented migrants.[10] Rather than dissuading people from migrating, these policies have led migrants to seek more perilous routes, such as crossing the Mediterranean in ill-equipped and unseaworthy vessels. Between 2000 and 2014, it is estimated that 22,400 people died attempting to enter Europe; more than 5,000 people died trying to cross the Mediterranean in 2016 alone.[11]

For Africans who have made it to Europe and have been living there for years or even decades, the tragedies in the Mediterranean strike close to home. Their brothers and sisters are taking grave risks to go abroad. Like Lassana, many West African migrants in France come from places where migration abroad is a rite of passage for young men: to remain at home is to feel stuck forever.[12] When they are denied visas at the consulate in their home countries, as most poor migrants from the global South now are, they will set out for the desert and march toward the sea, paying smugglers and joining the many refugees fleeing conflicts in Syria, Iraq, and Afghanistan.

As many scholars and activists have shown, the EU could prevent these deaths in border zones (such as the Mediterranean and the Saharan desert) by providing legal paths for those who migrate. Instead, EU policies make migrant death more likely as European border control creeps further into the African continent.[13]

Those who make it across face detention, deportation, and perilous onward journeys. Even those who get papers feel trapped, unable to return to their villages for fear that their temporary resident permits would not allow them to reenter Europe.[14] Some migrants will make their way further north with the hopes of gaining passage to England. They set up makeshift camps, a few around the Gare du Nord and others in northern French towns like Calais, which get periodically torn down. Several people have died trying to get to the United Kingdom via the underground tunnel built for the Paris-London Eurostar train.[15]

The Gare du Nord has become part of these border zones and the violence they enact. Despite being thousands of kilometers from the Mediterranean, and three hundred kilometers from France's northern border, the station operates the Eurostar rail line that takes passengers through the Channel tunnel to London. As a result, there is a legal border within the Gare du Nord that passengers to the United Kingdom must pass through before they board. In May 2017, an unidentified refugee was electrocuted and died at the station while trying to jump onto a London-bound train. He was not the first to die this way. The trappings of the border and those who enforce it are everywhere in the rail hub, including military patrols and customs agents, British immigration officers, two types of the French national police, railway police, and private security.

Like many railway stations across the world, the Gare du Nord has also been a magnet for those who exist on society's margins, often excluded from full participation in urban citizenship. More than any other Parisian railway station, the area is known as a site where homeless people, sex workers, teenage runaways, petty criminals, and drug users congregate alongside the throngs of passengers taking international trains. Since 2009, the Gare tended to be in the news for one of two reasons (based on tracking Google alerts): a police action following "gang fights," drug trafficking, or youth delinquency; or the arrival of an international celebrity on the Eurostar train. French literature and filmmaking represent it as a site of encounter, danger, and/or criminality.[16] The neighborhood around it has been formed by successive waves of migrants, from rural French to southern Europeans to North and sub-Saharan Africans to South Asians, leading tourist brochures to describe it as "exotic" and "colorful."[17]

The station has been used as an example of France's urban ills, a dangerous and seedy locale where African immigrants and their descendants were accused of taking over Parisian public space. "You arrive at the Gare du Nord, it's Africa! It's no longer France!" exclaimed Nadine Morano, former French government minister and congresswoman, while being interviewed on French television. In a similar vein, I heard several white French people refer to it as "*la Gare des Noirs*" (the Noir/Black Station) instead of the Gare du Nord (the North Station). I will return later in the book to both of these racialized representations, which are interpreted differently in the station's social world. According to the head of John Lewis, one of the biggest

English department store chains, the station is "the squalor pit of Europe." In the popular imaginary of many commuters from the Paris region I spoke to, the Gare is an unavoidable nuisance that they must pass through to get where they are going.

But the violence of the border and the presence of society's excluded does not define the station. In the social imaginary of many migrant communities, it has taken on other meanings. For example, for the Algerian-French novelist Abdelkader Djemaï and the *chibanis* (Algerian retirees) in his novella *Gare du Nord*, the station is a symbol of warmth and connection holding the promise of distant lands: "As soon as they approached the Gare du Nord," Djemaï writes of the *chibanis*, "They felt attracted by its warm atmosphere, its feminine forms, and by the soft light that had the color of a good beer. It was the port where they debarked depending on their mood and their imagination." Although the station also reminds them of their precariousness, their "fear of ending up homeless like all of those on the sidewalks of the Gare du Nord," it remains a mobile home-away-from-home, fitting to lives woven in the interstices of urban life in France.[18] Or as writer Suketu Mehta speculates, "Maybe what keeps the immigrants in the area, is the knowledge that the first door to home is just there, in the station, two blocks away. The energy of travelers is comforting, for it makes us feel that the whole world, like us, is transient."[19] These narratives anchor the station to the immigrant history of northeast Paris where it is located. They evoke the aesthetic of movement as one of the factors that draws so many to the station.

Lassana and his adventuring peers often used the word "crossroads" to describe what they appreciated at the station; unlike segregated spaces of the Paris capital region so often studied in the scholarship on migration, it brings together people from all backgrounds.

"We all started out in the immigrant dormitory," Lassana used to say, referring to the *foyers* built in the 1950s in France to house foreign workers. "But we didn't stay there very long, we didn't want to put ourselves on the sidelines."

His friend Mahmoud, an older Pakistani man who had been in France for decades, agreed. "You don't want to be on the sidelines, so you come to the Gare du Nord," he said.

Many migrants saw the station as a site of convergence and social potential. Lassana and his peers also said that it helped them to understand and live in the "real France": the one hidden by media representations and invisible from the "sidelines" of suburban housing projects and immigrant dormitories.

## BEYOND BORDERS

By examining the intersection of West African adventures with the Gare du Nord, we can disrupt the "story we already know" about migration and integration, and offer other stories too often obscured by the focus on border violence, detention, and deportation in the media and in scholarship.[20] Even when intended as critique, the media spectacle of migrant death and the emphasis on the repressive tactics of policing and security often end up enhancing the visual impression of states' power to exclude undesirable populations. The focus on borders, camps, and the security apparatus enacting dramatic forms of exclusion at entry points and in transit zones tends to neglect the way that migrant experience is also defined by the more banal functioning of a capitalist market system in which migrants are included but as subordinate members of a social, economic, and political system that offers them few rights and privileges while requiring their labor, a process anthropologist Nicholas De Genova calls "inclusion though exclusion."[21] The focus on repression also tends to ignore the failures and gaps in state-made exclusionary measures and the ways that migrants have contributed to the making of Europe and its urban spaces.

Lassana and other West African adventurers use the station to challenge "inclusion through exclusion" and build an alternative form of meaningful integration via urban public space. I have chosen to use the controversial word *integration* not as an analytical concept but as a provocation and to displace some of the commonsense ways of thinking about what integration means and what it could look like, especially since rural migrants from West Africa are often presented as refusing to integrate. The term is used in French state immigration policy (including the now defunct "High Council of Immigration") and political speech, usually to imply that certain communities—most often Muslims and people of color—have failed to "integrate" in an acceptable way.[22]

At the Gare du Nord, migrants develop new strategies to work around the restrictions placed on their mobility by French policies and migration restrictions put into place since the 1970s, policies that created the category of the "clandestine" migrant.[23] The 2008 economic crisis and the 2015 "migration crisis" have created further obstacles to migrant livelihoods by fueling nationalist political movements and making it more difficult for migrants to find jobs and secure legal status.[24] When their sojourns abroad started to extend to over a decade and the signifiers of status and success escaped their reach, migrants began to seek new ways to attain their goals in France.

It was in this quest that West African adventurers have developed what they call the "Gare du Nord method," a set of practices and an overall moral orientation through which they seek to create new channels to produce value abroad. This approach is based on combining the lessons of courage and discipline taught in their village upbringing with the strategies they learned on the road across West and Central Africa, and the knowledge they gain in France. Through it, they seek to create value through social relations and systems of exchange and reciprocity. The result of their labor, I argue, is the creation of an African hub: not a cultural enclave of "Little Africa," but a hybrid node of communication and exchange in which the material infrastructure of the French state becomes entangled with the social relationships and economic practices of West African adventurers.

Given immigration restrictions that lead migrants to stay longer in French territory, yet policies that exclude them from French public life, West African migrants are using the station to build a pathway toward a more dignified form of integration and mutual belonging that resonates with their adventure. Given their status, the limited form of integration and success they achieve is often provisional and symbolic. The material conditions of their lives, the discrimination they face, and their exclusion from a decent labor market bars them from achieving their plans abroad. Their experiences reveal that French ideals of "social mixing" and positive coexistence (often called *le vivre ensemble,* or "living-together") are inflected with what Jean Beaman calls "France's racial project" based on white supremacy.[25] Adventurers offer their own implicit and explicit critiques of that project. Their Gare du Nord method comes much closer than French institutions at actualizing the promise of mutual belonging encapsulated in *living-together.*

## STORIES WE TELL

I am writing this book at a time when we need new models for understanding migrants' lives and the structures that constrain them. Political ideologies of populist nationalism and economic imperatives that govern migration policy in the global North have created a broken system that is leaving tens of thousands dead at sea and on other perilous migration routes, while also leading to worsening economic and social outcomes for migrants and their descendants who arrive at their destinations. The current modes of managing migration are not working. Liberal models of tolerance celebrate multiculturalism but cover up structural inequalities and state policies of deportation and exclusion. The economic imperative of the capitalist system to maintain an available but restricted pool of migrant labor leads to precarious jobs and hardship. The global management of migration, spearheaded in Europe and the United States, creates avoidable suffering. It is what kills migrants each day. In this context, adventurers recognize that their options for futures abroad are getting thinner. Yet they are spending more and more of their lives far from home, in a permanent state of transit. As their time on the road lengthens to cover the greater part of their adult life, they also become wary of the futures proposed to them by their kin: of settling in their village as a household head in an arranged marriage.

The stories and narratives that we impose on migration play a key role in formulating how we imagine the problems it presents, and, thus, which solutions are possible. A typical narrative, bolstered by a long history of French sociology, from Emile Durkheim to Pierre Bourdieu and Abdelmalek Sayad, highlights that migration is produced by the inequalities of a capitalist market world system that forces people living in collectivist communities to be uprooted and then transplanted as wage laborers to a context where they suffer on the margins.[26] Sayad used his sociology of Algerian immigrants in a powerful critique of French modes of integration and immigration management, but French xenophobic rhetoric has recycled the uprooting thesis to blame sub-Saharan African immigration for many problems in French society, from the national debt and rising unemployment to crime and insecurity.[27] The infamous 2005 banlieue "riots"? According to several politicians and intellectuals, African family structure and polygamy was to blame.[28] The problem, they said, was not with "African culture" but rather with its importation into France. According to this logic, cultural practices became problems and explanations for violence when they left their acceptable place in the "African village" and came to occupy French urban spaces and public housing.[29]

Another story about migration, used to describe European immigrants to the United States and recently applied to African migration, imagines that migrants are heroic individuals realizing their dreams by breaking away from oppressive conditions and social constraints.[30] Both of these stories begin from the assumption that migration is defined by a breaking away that ruptures kin relationships and can lead to social pathology. In both cases, the problem is located in the sending country (it is underdeveloped or uncivilized, or perhaps the social environment is stifling), and so the solution must be focused on migrant culture and sending countries, removing European responsibility for reproducing inequality.

Where will new models and narratives come from? I propose that they come not from academic and policy debates but from the migrants themselves, from the way they see the world through their notion of adventure and the way they configure themselves as adventurers through the public space of the Gare du Nord. From this perspective, they are not ethnographic objects providing *evidence* of the effects that capitalist market logics and French/EU migration policy have on West African migrants, but rather offer new *theorizations* of migration and French urban public space, and predictions of what the future might hold.[31] If migration is recognized instead as a potential form of social continuity, a normal part of the life course, then the problems that migrants face today in France can be exposed for what they are: produced by French and EU policies that arrest and constrain the mobile pathways of migrants. The solution, then, needs to help enable these pathways instead of further limiting them or making them more dangerous.

The frame of adventure has become a way for West African migrants to make sense of and act in a world of enduring risk, where migrant death on the road has become an ordinary occurrence. Where they could go from employed and "legal" to jobless and "illegal" overnight.[32] Where their own capacity to meet their needs and their social obligations to their family are tenuous. Where they are marked by the color of their skin as threatening and fundamentally unlike white French citizens. In the face of border deaths and precarious existences, the Gare du Nord has become a key site in their efforts to make meaningful social ties to help them not only survive in Europe, but to "become somebody," as Lassana put it, against the odds.

Across the world, migrants are using new strategies to confront difficult circumstances. Much recent work has explored how migrant communities create social networks and community among co-nationals or co-ethnics. Such strategies play into what the French state deplores as "communitarianism," by which they mean the ways that migrants create enclaves that bar their integration into "French" ways of life.[33] Adventurers suggest that this version has it backwards. Instead of building their networks of "co-ethnics" and extended kin in France, West African migrants at the Gare du Nord depart from their kin and village communities to create social ties and families across national, racial, ethnic, and class boundaries. Meanwhile, it is rather the French state that promotes communitarianism through racial profiling, urban redevelopment, and regulations aimed at curbing marriages between French citizens and non-nationals. The adventurer imaginary and Gare du Nord method offer a critique of the French politics of difference and the marginalization it produces, as well as an alternative model for what migration management, migrant integration, and the elusive goal of urban living together might look like.

## WHY THE GARE DU NORD?

My attention first turned to the Gare du Nord during the French presidential election campaigns of 2007, when the French nightly news reported that a riot had taken place there following the violent arrest of a Congolese man who had entered the commuter rail area without a ticket. Politicians and news media used the event as evidence that an incursion had taken place: from their perspective, African residents of suburban housing projects had succeeded in bringing the "disorder" of their worlds to the international train station, a vital center of French capitalism. The event sparked a debate over what kind of order the French state should maintain and who could legitimately occupy French public spaces. It helped to confirm right-wing candidate Nicolas Sarkozy's victory a few weeks later by bringing the themes of insecurity and immigration back to the center of political debate.[34]

As I began to examine the station and its history, I found that the Gare du Nord, operating as a critical urban space and border zone within Paris, provides an extraordinary site for the exploration of the way borders, state policy, urban

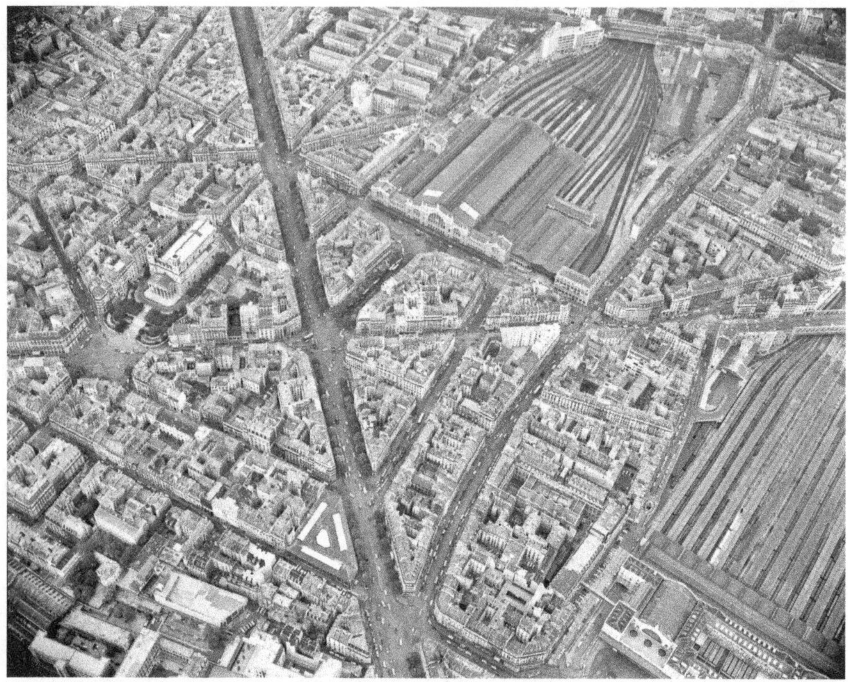

FIGURE 1. Aerial photo of the Gare du Nord and surrounding area, 1960. Archives de la Préfecture de Police.

public space, and migration intersect in France. Since its construction in the mid-nineteenth century, the station has hosted the political struggles of workers and migrants, as well as state experiments in control and policing. In addition to the meanings it has for many immigrant communities in Paris, the history of the station and its many renovations reveal how racial inequality has been built into urban spaces from their inception. It plays a pivotal role as a site for the government's efforts to police migration within Paris, connecting the policing of what anthropologist Didier Fassin calls the "internal boundaries" of France to the policing of its territorial borders.[35] It is an important site in the social and professional lives of many adventurers and migrants—from nineteenth-century provincial workers arriving in the capital to West Africans like Lassana today. The station is an alternative place for "migrant city-making," the apt term that Ayse Çaglar and Nina Glick Schiller use to describe how urban areas are produced through the ways migrants build connections across scales (local, regional, and global) when subject to inequality and power differentials.[36] There are many railway stations in Paris, but none of them—according to West Africans I met there—provided such a distinctive "international crossroads."[37]

The station's name designates potential: it proclaims that from here, you can get to the north. All of the trains that leave the station will first pass through Paris's 10th and 18th districts, both gentrifying areas with halal butchers, sidewalk cafés, a West African market, trendy bars, Turkish sandwich shops, Sri Lankan restaurants, and art deco apartment buildings. The rails then cross under the circular highway that separates city from suburbs and proceeds to traverse the Seine-Saint-Denis, a district that combines high-modernist public housing projects with old town squares. The vast majority of the station's passenger traffic comes from the commuter rail, built in the 1970s, which brings suburban traffic into the city center. Those train lines include the exurbs or *grande banlieue*, where picturesque towns and single-family homes give way to rolling farmland. The high-speed lines race through that whole stretch in a blur to arrive in the provincial northern capital of Lille, one hour away, now in commuting distance to Paris. From there, it is one hundred kilometers northwest to the English Channel, where the Eurostar trains will pass through an underwater tunnel, before traversing the English countryside on their way to London. The northeastern route through Lille connects the Gare du Nord to northern European cities of Brussels, Antwerp, Amsterdam, and Cologne. By the 1990s, over five hundred thousand people passed through the Gare du Nord each day, making it the busiest station in Europe. Today, that number may be closer to one million on some days.[38]

As a node created by multiple transportation infrastructures coming together, the Gare du Nord has also become a central point of exchange in unsanctioned economic networks and urban hustling, from commerce in stolen cell phones, personal check fraud schemes, and pirated DVD sales to the formalized structures that enable the sale of illegal drugs arriving on the train from Belgium and the Netherlands.[39] Networks of Eastern European immigrants have mobilized transportation and related tourism infrastructure to make money from begging practices, which have joined the ranks of "uncivil" offenses (*les incivilités*) punished by the railway police.[40]

The station's social environment has also been produced through the changing legal economy. The establishment of West and North African networks there occurred when migrant settlement patterns in Paris met the process economists call the flexibilization of labor: agencies specializing in temporary day-labor work placements sprang up around the station in the 1970s, and in the morning would recruit construction workers at the entrance. Around that time, African migrants were moving to the cheaper housing in the area and also to the new public housing in suburbs served by the Gare du Nord rail lines. The work agencies are still in the area, though they no longer recruit at the Gare. But many West Africans still meet at the station and use it to find work.

It was no coincidence, Lassana told me, that they ended up at Europe's busiest rail hub. "It's an *international* railway station here," as he often put it. The potential for movement suffused the station, with fifteen hundred trains coming and going each day and passengers from the world over pouring out of the station's doors. It is the "true wilderness," as Bakary, a Senegalese migrant put it, referring to the Gare du Nord as that liminal space of possibility in his migratory rite of passage where, away from his family, he would prove his ability to overcome obstacles and danger.

## NEW ADVENTURES: REDEFINING THE MIGRANT'S JOURNEY

When I first asked Lassana what he meant when he referred to his departure from his home village as "leaving on adventure" (*partir en/à l'aventure*) and to himself and his comrades as adventurers (*aventuriers*),[41] he explained it this way: "We're all looking for a way to get out of struggle (*la galère*) and into happiness (*le bonheur*). But some are not cut out for adventure, and they stay in *la galère*. But I'm an adventurer. My father was an adventurer. My father was poor. My mother was poor. But my father told me, if you're born in misery you can end up with happiness, but if you're born with wealth you can end up in misery. And he told me my pathway would take me far from our home." The notion of adventure helped Lassana connect his struggles to a tradition passed down from father to son. It offered a framework for interpreting hard times abroad as well as a sense of belonging to a larger community of adventurers.

Adventure was not just another word for migration: it contained a whole world of West African migrant histories.[42] Precolonial trading empires and colonial rule have helped shape a flexible cultural idiom for West Africans voyaging abroad. Like all idioms, it is not a deterministic cultural pattern but rather a malleable resource that migrants draw on in different contexts, transforming it as they do so. As Lassana taught me, it provided a template for those who left their families for lands unknown. Sylvie Bredeloup, an anthropologist who has long studied the notion of adventure among West Africans, calls it a form of "moral experience" in which migrants seek personal and social fulfillment through migration.[43] Examining how West African migrants understand and express their life course through this idiom sheds light on critical aspects of migratory pathways that are often ignored in policy debates. The adventurer outlook offers a cultural logic and moral template for how life should unfold, and for how people ought to relate to one another.

Seeing migration as adventure does not mean seeing it as a romantic or thrilling odyssey that exists outside of the social realm. "*L'aventure*" and "*l'aventurier*" are rather loose French translations of terms from Mande languages spoken by West Africans in France (including the languages Soninke, Bamanakan, Malinke, Mandingo, Jula/Dyula, and Khassonke). The space of this journey is called the *tunga/tunwa*, an unknown or foreign place, a "space of exile."[44] In Soninke, the word *adventure* is also translated as *gunne* ("wilderness/bush") and *adventurer* is a translation of *gounike/gudunke* and other similar terms meaning "the man of the bush" or "the man of the wilderness."[45] These terms point to what makes the West African migratory adventure specific and remarkable: Migration in this case is a rite of passage in which the migrant must confront risk and the unfamiliar to ensure his social becoming. Becoming a marriageable man meant undertaking an initiatory journey during which the migrant is supposed to accumulate wealth before returning home to marry and settle in the village. Migration in this context is seen as a way of reproducing—not dismantling—peasant communities.[46]

Adventures have a long history. Well before they migrated to France, the importance of commerce and travel among Soninke had already been established through a long history of contact, exchange, and mobility, including trans-Saharan trading empires and caravans that predate European colonization.[47] Similar idioms have existed in many parts of West and Central Africa, as Jean Rouch documented in his 1967 film *Jaguar* about Nigerien migration to Ghana, and as anthropologist Paul Stoller explored in his ethnography and fiction (including his ethnographic novel *Jaguar*, narrating the present and pasts of journeying Songhay traders from Niger).[48] These notions are being updated and transformed in present contexts, such as the recent resurgence and new significations of the term "bushfalling" to describe Cameroonian migration to Europe.[49]

Islamic religious commitments shape the adventures examined in this book. They provide a moral template for how to act in foreign and fraught situations: Lassana's father guided him to use the Qur'an to "find the pathway" through Islam while abroad, in order to avoid trouble that could disrupt his voyage. It was thought that going to Qur'anic school was the best training for succeeding abroad because it provided moral discipline. Amadou and Jal referred to the importance of "*din*" (religion, from the Arabic) in helping them stay on the right path in France. Seeking knowledge and (self-) discovery through travel is based on Islamic traditions, whether in pilgrimage to Mecca and other sites of religious learning, such as Timbuktu, or in voyages to the non-Islamic world, as the writings of the great fourteenth-century traveler Ibn Battuta testify.[50]

Colonial rule did not introduce mobility, but it would transform the pathways of many adventurers as they became wage laborers.[51] Many Soninke continued their mobile traditions by seeking work across the French empire. They took grueling jobs cultivating crops in Senegal or working on the docks in Marseille not because they were forced to by the real burden of French colonial taxes or because they were desperate and disenfranchised, lacking land or wealth and seeking to escape. Rather, as historian François Manchuelle illustrates, migrants were often village nobles who left with the goal of strengthening traditional authority and their own status.[52] Voyages have long conferred prestige to migrants.[53] There is a saying that I heard several versions of in Soninke and Bamanakan that reflects this notion: "If he who has visited 100 places meets he who has lived 100 years, they will be able to discuss." In other words, knowledge gained through travel abroad can disrupt a rigid hierarchy based on age, allowing a younger man to exchange and converse at the same level as his elder.[54]

The adventure has further transformed as structural readjustment policies implemented in the 1980s led to diminished buying power and stagnated social mobility across most of the continent.[55] In rural Senegal and Mali, droughts of the 1970s and 1980s compounded the precariousness of rural communities. Transnational migrants sending remittances became "national heroes," as anthropologist Caroline Melly puts it, taking the place of the diminished state to provide new possibilities for rural communities to survive.[56] In addition to house-building, contributing to diaspora village associations to build mosques, schools, and infrastructure such as water towers and electricity in a display of what Daniel Smith calls "conspicuous redistribution" became a mark of having "become somebody" as an adventurer.[57]

The notion of migration as adventure and the personhood of the adventurer as an alternative to the abject refugee or the subjugated wage laborer offers a compelling counternarrative to state policies aimed at controlling and defining migration and migrants. Migration, in this tradition, is not a problem to be solved but a mechanism for social and economic reproduction; it is not only a choice made to combat poverty or dire circumstances, but a pathway toward social becoming.[58] As much as it has changed over time, the notion of adventure serves as a hermeneutic, guide, and moral beacon for West Africans abroad, a lighthouse that they seek in times of trouble.[59] From the perspective of adventure, migrants are embedded in a social system in which confronting risk through the migratory journey helps—not hinders—their transition to adulthood. From the perspective of adventure, migrants are not seeking settlement, citizenship, and dependence but rather the conditions of possibility for continued mobility and exploration.

## LASSANA'S PATH

Lassana was fourteen when he began making plans to leave his home. The following year, unbeknownst to his family, he jumped onto a truck and went from village to village doing odd jobs until he made his way to Bamako, the Malian capital. His father sent his brother to get Lassana to return. Instead, Lassana refused, saved up more money, and left for Côte d'Ivoire. This dramatic and secretive escape from the clutches of parental and elder sibling authority, as he tells the story, set the stage for his ensuing adventure across West Africa and into France.

He had grown up in a village I will call Yillekunda, ten kilometers from the town of Diema in the region of Kayes, the largest sending region of Malian immigrants to France. He grew up in a multiethnic and multilinguistic environment dominated by Soninke speakers. The village depended on millet and other grain harvests from collectively owned agricultural land as well as on remittances from migrants abroad, and it had experienced severe droughts in the 1970s and 1980s. As in other parts of the Senegal River Valley, his village was plagued by a lack of access to water for irrigation, as well as a lack of state presence and infrastructure.[60]

Lassana's family was part of the ruling elite in a village divided between "nobles" and those in professional castes (such as blacksmiths).[61] He was the first son of his father's second wife and had three older step-brothers (the children of his father's first wife). Lassana's position within his family would have several consequences for the trajectory his life took. As the son of a second wife, he had to do the bidding of his half-brothers and accept the beatings he got from them without complaint. His mother died when he was ten years old and his older sister left to marry a Malian living in France, leaving him and his younger brother alone to fend for themselves against them. There was a public school with instruction in French located near his village, but like most of his brothers who would be leaving on adventure, Lassana attended Qur'anic school. Qur'anic school, according to his father, would prepare them for a difficult and disciplined life on the road and help them to stay on the right path of Islam while abroad.

Lassana's departure on the truck signified his leaving of the world of lineage and his entrée into the liminal world of adventure. Far from being outside the bounds of kin reciprocity, however, he relied on help and finance from family members while on the road. Once successful, he would have to help kin with their migratory projects. Leaving has become an expensive business, entailing high fees for identification documents, visas, and travel tickets or large sums paid to traffickers. While some families may save money to help fund migration, it is often kin abroad who have the capital to help their family members depart.

To get out of West Africa, Lassana needed a national ID card, for which he would have to pretend to be over eighteen. Bamako, he intimated, was not distant enough to be part of a "true adventure," and he knew he had to move on or risk being sent back to his family. He worked odd jobs for Soninke cousins until he had enough to go to Abidjan. Lassana stayed in Côte d'Ivoire, moving to Daloa, a center of the cacao trade, until he saved enough money to get a passport and apply for a merchant visa that would grant him a temporary stay in France. He had proved himself on the road, and when he was eighteen, he got his father's blessing for the trip to France. He returned to Bamako to get his papers in order.

His father, who had ventured as far as neighboring Senegal, visited him there and taught him the secret rituals he had to practice once in Europe to avoid misfortune. His older sister in France sent him a plane ticket. He did not go back to Yillekunda before he left for Europe. Returning home would have been anathema when his adventure had barely begun. In 2001, he boarded an Air France flight with a three-month visa, imagining that he would stay for two or three years and then move on or return to Mali. He would not leave France for almost a decade.

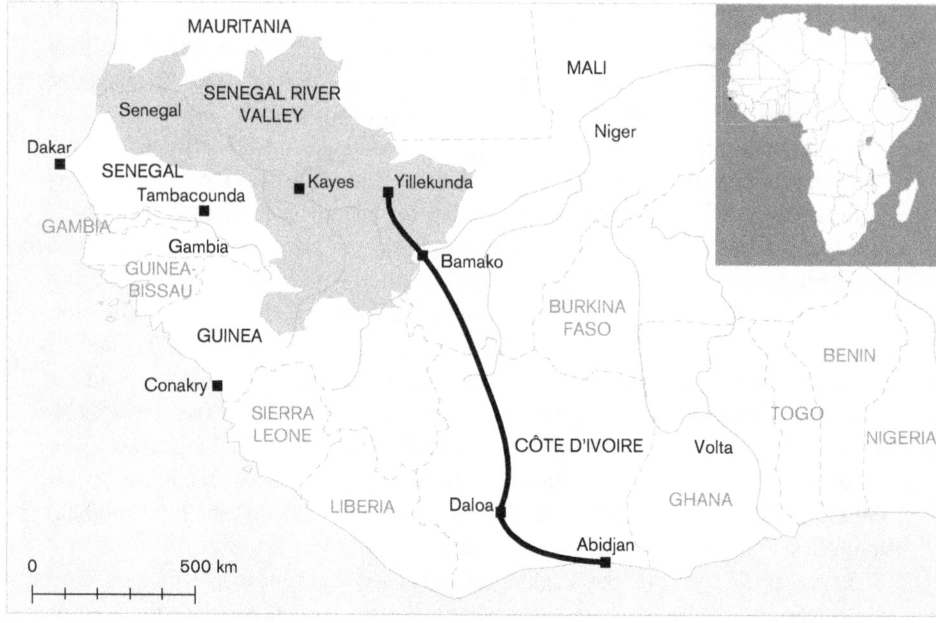


MAP 1. The West African home region of many adventurers at the station, showing the route Lassana took from Yillekunda to Abidjan before coming to France. Thomas Massin.

*Tunga te danbe don, nga a be den nyuman don:* this is the Bamanakan (Bambara) proverb of the adventure, which anthropologist Bruce Whitehouse argues is key to understanding West African migrants and which he translates as: *Exile knows no dignity, but it knows a good child.*[62] Or in other words, as Lassana's friend Dembele put it, "When you're an *aventurier*, you're nobody." An almost identical proverb exists in Soninke: *Tunwa nta danben tu, a na len siren ya tu*, which Soninke linguist Abdoulaye Sow translates as "Our identity can be ignored in foreign lands, but not our courage."[63] Migrants leave their home and go into a new world where the status they grew up with (their lineage-based identity/dignity) means very little; what matters is their own hard work. This is why, as Whitehouse points out, they can take jobs that would otherwise be shameful. The proverb is a poetic concentration of the adventurer's liminal logic, and of the notion that when they leave *en aventure* they leave the constraints of village structures behind. But their activities at the Gare du Nord suggest that they do seek both dignity and respect—not only jobs and material resources—through their time there. They hope to recover the masculine status and dignity denied by the police, their legal status, and their jobs. In this context, they suggest a new version of the proverb: *Exile that lasts for decades may yet know dignity, if you have courage.*

## DWELLING IN MOTION

Most West African adventurers in France do not end up at the Gare du Nord, and given its reputation for attracting criminals and delinquents, many even look down at their brethren who do. Those who invest in the station are seeking a pathway to success and social relationships outside the scripts of French assimilation and kin expectations. By focusing their efforts on the Gare du Nord, they cultivate an alternative version of integration into French public space. They sought to meet passengers coming from afar on high-speed trains and to form friendships with other adventurers. As in the social clubs (*grins*) of urban West Africa, they were not brothers but equals who met to chat and drink tea, sometimes developing strong social obligations of solidarity.[64] Lassana and his peers even developed a particular way of interacting with the police. Their practices—whether economic, social, romantic, or a combination of all of those—involved making connections across the station's many social boundaries, and their strategies stressed the importance of building horizontal networks and relationships more than they focused on gaining the rights of citizenship from the French state.

Those horizontal relationships and networks suggest that integration (contrary to French rhetoric on the subject) is not opposed to community, mobility, and ties to elsewhere. Adventurers at the Gare du Nord delve into French urban life—at the center, not on the sidelines—because they believe that full experience abroad is what will allow for self-realization and for the reproduction of their agrarian communities. The notion of settlement as a goal does not make sense to them; meaningful integration instead ought to create opportunities for mobility and personal growth. They are not simply "economic migrants"; they are also explorers seeking knowledge in faraway lands.

What if, adventurers ask, integration did not entail settlement? Could there be a more just model of integration based on a more mobile worldview? Instead of thinking through migration from the endpoint of settlement, we might instead see it through what Catherine Besteman calls "emplacement"—the many ways that migrants experience and engage with places where they live. Emplacement here is a form of belonging that diverges from the official paths of assimilation offered by state programs and laws.[65] Through emplacement, migrants form communities and make their mark on their dwelling places, which can also become important loci of political claim-making.[66] Unlike neighborhoods and immigrant dormitories, emplacement at the Gare du Nord has a direct connection with mobility. Emplacement in this context engages with transportation infrastructure—the channels and pathways that meet at the station. By staying put and practicing emplacement in a space meant for circulation, adventurers also challenge the prevailing logic of how the station is managed and policed. They dwell there, create networks, and try to produce value, but they do not settle. This dwelling-in-motion is rich in narrative: adventure stories are told and retold at the station, and become circulating tales that provoke debate and discussion over how migrants in France ought to act, work, and respond to hardship. By tracing adventurer strategies and pathways at the Gare du Nord, I examine how migrants make emplacement and mutual belonging through a public space designed for transience and anonymity.[67]

## MOBILITY AND FIELDWORK

My work with adventurers like Lassana and many of his friends whom I met during the years I spent researching pushed me to look beyond the media spectacles surrounding the station in the 2000s and to consider the longer history of the Gare du Nord. To understand their lives and what drew them to the station, I had to understand this complex space that hundreds of thousands of people passed through each day, a space whose history as France's largest international train station offered a crucial window into ways that ideas about racial and cultural difference had been built into French public spaces.

Carrying out an ethnography of a major transportation hub has some methodological challenges, and I experimented with approaches from urban studies, anthropology, cultural history, and geography. I needed some guiding lights of my own as I joined adventurers at the station. The corpus of urban anthropologist Setha Low offered a multifaceted approach to doing ethnography in complex public spaces, and Low illustrates how to balance political economic critique without losing the texture of lived experience and emotional attachments.[68]

Paul Stoller's ethnography of West African traders, *Money Has No Smell: The Africanization of New York City* has provided a model of what the transnational ethnography of migrant experience in urban space can contribute to our understanding of global economic transformations. Focusing on the trajectories of a small number of migrants reveals, as Stoller puts it, "how macrosociological forces twist and turn the economic and emotional lives of real people."[69] I build on Stoller's approach by examining the longer history of the Gare du Nord, seeing this site as a prism reflecting not only the migrant experience but also state projects of ordering and policing difference. The station itself offers the methodological object from which I have built this ethnography outward to answer the question: What does migration, urban space, and integration look like from the view from the tracks, from the perspective of the Gare du Nord?

The second inspiration is Lassana himself, his story, and his commitment to this project. I have tried to do justice to his story and analysis, in the process documenting how an adventurer confronts the precarious realities of contemporary migration while negotiating his own coming of age. This approach recalls the life history method, well established in African studies, that privileges narrative depth in order to show how individuals imagine and build their worlds under a set of historical conditions and constraints.[70] The innovative work on life course by anthropologists Jennifer Cole and George Meiu (among others) offers a framework to consider the continued importance of social and kin relations in changing conditions.[71] In following Lassana's adventure, I also take my methodological cue from West African modes of imagining life pathways, where aspirations for living a dignified life in tough circumstances lead to the invention of new strategies.[72]

*Adventure Capital* is based on eighteen months of intensive fieldwork in Paris between 2009 and 2011, as well as several visits between 2012 and 2018 that allowed me to follow up with the people I worked with and track changes at the station. As Peter Redfield observed, ethnographers often have more in common with Claude Levi-Strauss's bricoleur than with the engineer: fieldwork unfolds through improvisation with available materials rather than via engineered design.[73] "The subway corridors," Marc Augé suggests in *In the Metro*, "ought to provide a good 'turf' for the apprentice ethnologist," but only if she dispenses with classical methods of interview and survey, and instead is able to observe, follow, and listen.[74] I followed these improvisational approaches as I traced the many threads that led to and from the station, going where they took me instead of defining a particular (national or ethnic) group in advance. Ethnographers can learn from adventurers, as I did. I became an apprentice to the Gare du Nord method—learning to use encounters across difference to build networks and create value in a transit hub. They taught me to observe people, to discern what encounters were worthwhile, and to make new channels connecting places, displacing commonsense ways of seeing the world. They stress the importance of knowing the past from several angles, and were invested in uncovering the history of the Gare du Nord. To this end, I examined tribunal records and blueprints from the Paris Municipal Archives, North Railway Company correspondence and meeting minutes from the National Labor Archives, and blueprints and directives from Haussmann-led Paris in the National Archives.

I spent most of my fieldwork hanging out around the station and talking to a changing group of about thirty-five West African men who ranged in age from nineteen to thirty-two, and who strolled, talked, sat, and observed together in the front square and in cafés around the neighborhood. Most of these men had been in France between three and twelve years, and about half of them were undocumented, while most of the others had recently obtained resident permits. The majority came from the western Kayes region of Mali and its adjoining areas across the borders in Senegal and Mauritania, while a few others came from Côte d'Ivoire and Guinea. They spoke a mix of French, Pulaar, and several Mande languages (Soninke, Jula, Bamanakan, and Khassonke) among themselves. Almost all identified as practicing Muslims and, with the exception of the Ivoirians, they had attended Qur'anic schools and did not speak French when they arrived. They worked in subcontracted and temporary labor jobs in construction, cleaning, and food service. In the summer of 2010, I spent two months as an SNCF intern on the high-speed lines, and accompanied railway police on their patrols, offering another perspective of what it meant to see through the lens of the Gare du Nord, and to understand how adventurers were represented and imagined by station workers.

A few caveats: The population of a major city passes through the Gare du Nord each day, and this book does not attempt to offer a picture of its totality. I made the choice to seek in-depth knowledge in order to offer the "thick description" that distinguishes meaningful ethnography, even in our "multi-sited" age of mobility.[75] Most of the subjects in this book are West African *men*, in part because French policies and policing have a particular impact on them.[76] Like the adventurers documented here, West African women are also struggling to make their own pathways toward integration—just not through the Gare du Nord.[77] I also sought to explore the way that West Africans adventurers see and create a world in the station. This called for time and resources to explore all facets of their lives, including in some cases going back to their villages and meeting their families. It was after I returned from Mali and Senegal that I began to understand what was happening at the station.

I did not have the resources to do this in-depth work with all the people and worlds of the station; the book is focused on adventurers and the networks they made. It bears pointing out that although they are often represented as "Africans," adventurers are a diverse group: they are multilingual, multiethnic, and multinational. I also chose not to focus on the people involved in drug dealing or crime: they occupied an outsized place in the media and popular representations of Africans at the station, but few of the men I met there were involved in illegal activities.

Research in a public space where I had no status was challenging. For the first six months of my research, many people believed I was a police officer or informant and denounced me to their peers. I was often yelled at and accused of conspiring with the police. I came to understand that these were attempts to situate me within an unstable universe where a single bad encounter could lead to failed immigration projects, arrest, or deportation. As in much ethnography, a "key informant" enabled my provisional integration into the station social scene. Lassana took me under his wing as a social apprentice, vouched for me, and became my de facto field research assistant (a role for which he refused to accept money). In the moments when I became dejected with the feeling that I would barely scratch the surface of what was going on at the station, he would find a new person for me to meet, or a new corner of station life to discover. He knew the place, as he liked to say, like his own hand.

Our relationship illuminated some of the way gender roles played out in this male-dominated social environment. We met because he, like many of his comrades, were using the station to meet women. He approached me to ask for a cigarette—even though he did not smoke. I asked if he would talk to me for my research. He agreed, and ended up acting as my protector, an older brother figure and station guide. This relationship meant that I was rarely hassled at the station, even when he was not present.

My experiences illustrate how constrained women's roles were at the Gare du Nord: unlike men, women could not hang out and chat—it was assumed they were there to meet men. Any time I sat in a café with Lassana (or anyone else), his friends who came by to say hello and who did not know me asked him in Soninke or Bamanakan whether I was his girlfriend. They were suspicious when he said no and explained that I was writing a book about the station. I did not fit into the categories that women were supposed to occupy. If I was not someone's girlfriend, they reasoned, I must have been with the police. It was only after I went to the station in 2016 with my son, a baby at the time, that some men I had known for years admitted that up until then, they had suspected I was French and not from the United States, and that I was working with the police. My newfound status as a mother was part of what changed their opinion.

During my research, I took on multiple roles that also helped me to understand the precarious positions these men found themselves in. When they had to find new housing, I became an amateur real estate agent, looking for apartments after assessing their budget and transportation needs. When they legalized their status and decided to make a return visit, I helped them find flights using the internet. I helped edit résumés for temporary construction work and fill out applications for unemployment benefits.

Aside from formal interviews with train station personnel and urban planners, I spent the first year in the field using my tape recorder sparingly. All the men I spoke to knew about my research project and had agreed to take part. I took my cue from other urban anthropologists working among sensitive or marginalized populations and embraced the "unassuming research strategy" of participating in daily life and conversations, and then rushing away to write it all down in a notebook afterward.[78] As I built trust among some of the men, I started using my tape recorder or cell phone to record longer narratives and conversations.

Everyone I spoke to knew I was doing research, and many of them were invested in my book project. In the decade since I began, our lives all transformed. Their adventures all turned out differently than they had imagined, and the Gare du Nord could not change the realities of legal, social, and economic marginalization. But it did give them a space to discover "the France you don't see on TV," as Lassana put it—which is also what I want to illuminate here.

## TRACING BOUNDARIES

The story of the Gare du Nord and the experiences of West African adventurers there are the twin intertwining threads that structure this book. When the station was built in the mid-nineteenth century, it was part of an imperial vision imagining the melding of modern industry, infrastructure, and international exchange. But railway terminals were also feared as threatening spaces of social mixing that needed new measures to separate, control, and police the "dangerous classes" that converged there. Chapter 1, "Dangerous Classes," considers the Gare's early days to show how inequality based on ideas of racial difference has been built into this public space, as part of efforts to ensure for smooth transport and circulation while controlling the potential threats to the political and social order of bourgeois Paris. Today, migrants confront the remnants of the station's guiding imperial ideology as they reconfigure their relationship to the history of public space in Paris.

When part of the Gare du Nord was rebuilt at the dawn of the twenty-first century, it came to embody anew the contradictions between a French Republican narrative of inclusive "living together," and the policing methods used against people of color at the station. The station's rebuilding and the 2007 revolt that took place in its wake are the foci of chapter 2, "The Exchange Hub." After considering how a public space in the center of the capital became a crucible of anti-black racism and French national boundary definition, I examine how African-French young people and West African migrants used the March 2007 station revolt to defy their marginalization and make the station into a meaningful site for political action and social relationships.

The revolt trained the floodlights of the national media on the Gare du Nord and reinforced the discourse that Africans were threatening and dangerous to French public order. But there was nothing exceptional about the racialized police intervention that sparked it. In the everyday life of this transit hub, West African migrants were living out their adventures as they were confronted with new laws and policing practices. Chapter 3, "The Gare du Nord Method," explores the encounters between migrants and police. As West Africans learn to deal with the police, they also produce new survival strategies, refashion social relationships, and confront their precarious position head-on.

Adventurers engage in many kinds of work at the station, from providing services for train voyagers to building and maintaining social relationships. Chapter 4, "Hacking Infrastructures," explores how they use the station to expand their economic opportunities by seeking encounters across difference and by transforming state transit infrastructures for their own ends. As they are further marginalized by policy and by diminishing economic opportunities, West Africans use tools and knowledge gained on their adventures in an effort to produce new channels for creating value.

The Gare du Nord method is not only a practical set of tools for dealing with the precariousness of migrant livelihoods, it is also the way that West Africans who claim it attempt to forge a new pathway for their uncertain coming of age. Chapter 5, "The Ends of Adventure," examines how West African migrants seek self-realization through the station's social world while maintaining patrilineal and village ties. The station transforms their pathways to adulthood as they connect it to transnational circuits of social reproduction.

I end by considering the outcomes of the Gare du Nord method and speculating on the ways that adventurer visions displace ideologies of difference arising from colonial domination, which exclude African migrants from being seen as part of the European collective project. The Gare du Nord cannot save migrants from marginalization. Nevertheless, migrants work to reproduce a world where adventure is still possible, and in doing so, they offer an alternative pathway toward the ideal of mutual belonging, recognition, and living together.

Adventurers undermine the boundaries—between migrant and citizen, center and periphery, neighbor and stranger—that have come to define political debate and the contours of French public space. West African migrants have pulled the Gare du Nord into networks and relationships that neither the French state nor their own families could have predicted. This book is the story of how that happened and what might happen if we consider the histories of border making and difference, urban space and migration, belonging and exclusion, from the perspective of adventurers at the largest railway hub in Europe.

# 1

# Dangerous Classes

The express commuter train barrels into an underground passage beneath the *périphérique*—the circular highway that divides the suburbs from Paris. It is 6:30 a.m. on a Thursday in mid-March in winter 2010 and the rush hour has just begun. The railcar we are in is standing room only, with the passengers' bulky winter coats brushing up against one another. The train emerges from the underground tunnel and we travel through the outlying neighborhoods of Paris proper, passing the housing projects built in the 1960s that rise up above the graffitied walls of the train tracks. We enter another tunnel and a pleasant recorded voice comes on to announce our arrival at "Paris–Gare du Nord." The doors open and it seems as if the entire train will empty onto the crowded platform. We are shuffled out along with most of the other passengers. In the sea of puffy jackets, I almost lose Yacouba, an Ivoirian man in his thirties who is my guide today at the station. He finds me and gives my elbow a nudge, guiding me through the crowd toward an escalator. We step on, moving to the right to make way for people hurrying to catch another train. At the top, we arrive at the mezzanine level, still underground. We walk toward the exit, passing a long strip of clothing stores that are shuttered at this early hour.

As we exit through the turnstiles, Yacouba points out that there are no police checking IDs yet and tells me they will start after the initial rush hour ends. He is running a little late for work, so there is no time to grab a plastic-cupped espresso at the Autogrill, a chain of inexpensive cafés once ubiquitous in French train stations. We take a steep escalator up to the commuter rail area, where Yacouba will board a train to his construction worksite in another suburb north of Paris. The worksite itself is not that far from the suburb where he lives—just six miles as the crow flies—but the centralized urban transit design makes it necessary to go through the city.

When we get to the top of the escalator, we go through another set of turnstiles. This time a group of burly police wait on the other side, in street clothes except for their orange armbands. Yacouba points them out to me with a nod; perhaps it is the two years he spent undocumented before getting a resident permit through his employer that have made him hyperaware of police presence. Yacouba walks past them, toward the platform. "Those ones won't stop me," he says to me, "I see them here every day. They're a special unit, looking for drug trafficking." Like many of his peers who have spent time at the station, he knows the landscape of police forces and can categorize them by their respective clothing, habits, and location. The officers he has spotted come from an investigative unit of the national police that works out of an office within the station. I bid him farewell as he rushes to board his outgoing train to get to his worksite on time.

I meet Yacouba again that afternoon on the station platform in the quiet suburban town of Enghien-les-Bains after he has finished the day's work. The commuter train car is almost empty when we board, but it has filled with passengers by the time we reach the périphérique. We arrive at the Gare du Nord, and as we exit the train, I follow Yacouba's gaze to the three policemen waiting at the head of the platform. Two other officers, a few yards away, have stopped a young black man and are scrutinizing what looks like a French national ID card. Yacouba is walking a few steps ahead of me, and the first group of police wave him aside as we reach them. I slow down and pretend to look at my phone. I cannot hear what they say to him because of the ambient noise. I stop a few yards past them, with the officers' uniformed backs to me. I see Yacouba take out his *carte de séjour*—a resident and work permit—and place it on top of his passport as he hands it to the balding officer.

The cop scrutinizes the residency card and pages through the passport. Yacouba fixes his gaze on a point just beyond the cop's shoulder in an expressionless stare that many men adopt during these stops. The cop gives him back his card without a word, and Yacouba takes it, nods, and then catches my eye and nods toward the exit. I am unsurprised but still incensed at the blatant racial profiling and want to talk about it, but I cannot keep up as he takes off down the platform. When I catch up with him, he maintains a poker face, wordlessly dissuading me from asking any questions. On our way to the exit, he greets a few friends who are heading toward the commuter trains. I follow him to the large, atrium-like arena of the newest part of the station, and I have to hurry again to keep up as we head through the big glass doors to the small plaza outside. Instead of going to get a coffee and catch up with more friends as he often does, Yacouba bids me farewell in the front square, eager to retreat into the solitude of his train journey home. He is frustrated about what has happened, and his reaction suggests the emotional struggle that migrants confront when they are stopped on public transportation. He mumbles something about needing to get home early and then heads back into the station to take his train to the outer-city where he lives, again crossing the circular highway that serves as a boundary line between suburb and city-proper.

A few months after I accompanied Yacouba that day in 2010, the minister of the interior, Brice Hortefeux, gave a speech at the Gare du Nord, unveiling new security measures and calling the station "symbolic of violence in public transport" because of the crime, drugs, riots, and gang fights associated with it.[1] The police and security forces we saw that day embody what many journalists and scholars see as the transformation of France from a social welfare state to a "security state," a process beginning in the 1970s and accelerating in the early 2000s under Nicolas Sarkozy.[2] Changes during that time period would also restrict immigration and expand the policing of immigrant groups.

The history of the Gare du Nord reveals the longer lineage of these innovations in policing and security, which have existed since its construction in the nineteenth century, when concerns over the so-called dangerous classes—often also migrant workers—coalesced around the station and its neighborhood. This history of inequality built into French public space in general, and into the Gare du Nord in particular, is key to understanding how West African migrants today remake the station and their own adventurers in France.

Interwoven into the station's history since its inauguration in 1846 (and reconstruction in 1861) are ideologies about dangerous difference. These ideologies bolstered efforts to control migrant workers from the provinces and prevent the urban underclass from interfering with the dreams of modern progress embodied in infrastructure. Often colored by ideas about the immutable differences of the underclass, these ideologies have led to policing methods intended to limit social mixing and maintain separations through the built environment. Notions that some differences between groups were "in the blood," that some people were unassimilable, did not remain static; they were reorganized and reapplied to new groups over the course of the nineteenth century. The colonizing project in Algeria (like the station, begun in earnest in the 1840s) and the simultaneous explosion of pseudo-scientific writing about racial difference profoundly shaped this evolution, as colonial subjects (and later immigrants) would come to occupy the dangerous slot. The evolution of these ideologies would be built into the Gare du Nord and guide its subsequent management.

The imagination of racialized difference, despite being written into French policy since at least the seventeenth century, has been hidden by the homogenizing narrative of French universalism. That narrative supported the story that racial difference was banished by the French Revolution and only arrived in metropolitan France in the postwar period when immigrants came from former colonies.[3] Politicians, academics, and even casual observers contrast France's reckoning with immigrant populations to the immigrant history of the United States.[4] Unlike France, they say, the United States was founded on immigration.[5] When immigrants do appear in the French national narrative, they are predominantly white European populations that (according to the popular narrative) quickly assimilated to French norms, customs, and values.[6] This narrative promotes what Ghassan Hage calls "the White fantasy of national space."[7] In the French case, this fantasy wears the garb of universalism.

Race and racism are thus often presented as existing outside of France proper—in the colonies, in the *outre-mer* (France's overseas territories), and in the United States—and as having been imported as part of "Anglo-Saxon" cultural hegemony to disturb France's color-blind "Republican model."[8] Defining *racism*, through George Fredrickson's work, as "the conviction that an outsider group is 'innately, indelibly, and unchangeably' inferior," historians Herrick Chapman and Laura Frader have argued, on the contrary, that France has been a world center in the production of racist ideology.[9] From the Black Code laws governing slaves during the *ancien régime* to Arthur de Gobineau's pseudo-scientific nineteenth-century tome *The Inequality of Human Races* to the Dreyfus affair and beyond, the government and the public sphere have promulgated white supremacy.[10] There is much evidence to suggest that slavery and colonialism were not anomalies contradicting Republican ideals, but were fundamental building blocks of French universalism and the French nation-state.[11] Racial and cultural hierarchies have thus long been part of French law and policy, not only in overseas territories and colonies but in Paris, the center of the metropole.[12] It should not be surprising that this ideology also guided the design of public spaces and infrastructures well before the arrival of postcolonial immigrant groups seen as a "problem" and blamed for challenging the universalist model.[13]

Every aspect of my journey with Yacouba, from the train to the police to the périphérique itself, is part of the infrastructural history of Paris. The commuter rail (the RER, or *Réseau-express-regional*) that took us across the périphérique moves hundreds of thousands of passengers between Paris and the suburbs each day, a significant share of which will pass through the Gare du Nord. The RER, built in the 1970s, is one of the more recent additions to the history of transportation in this neighborhood, which has long been a transit hub—from Roman conquest–era road building to the canals and barges of the early nineteenth century that defined northeast Paris as a crossroads for goods and people.[14]

As infrastructure developed, so did measures to limit the potential threats that the mobility of a growing urban underclass posed to state and industrial development. The police who stopped Yacouba at the Gare du Nord find their forebears in early railroad expansion, when private railway companies appealed to the state to provide a special police force to guard stations and tracks. At the time, private companies that managed railroads in collaboration with the government were concerned about the potential danger of large numbers of incoming migrant workers from rural areas in France. The station's neighborhood—just a field with a few windmills and houses when the Gare was built—would also emerge as a product of worker migration from rural France and Belgium. The history of the station's nineteenth-century construction reveals how the preoccupation with "dangerous classes" shaped the way it would be built and managed. The Gare du Nord came to represent both the glory of French imperial modernity and the potential dangers that modern urban life posed to the bourgeois social order established in Paris.

The lens of the Gare du Nord reveals how inequality has been built into French public space and how the notion of a dangerous other went from signifying rural populations within France to foreign populations outside of France. The discourse about the dangerous classes emerging in the nineteenth century helped to bolster France's racial project by configuring certain populations as so morally dubious and culturally other that they could not be assimilated. In other words, this racial project is not a recent phenomenon in metropolitan France, created by immigration; rather, it is fundamental to the way Frenchness and French urban spaces have been produced.

## BUILDING MODERN GATEWAYS

In June of 1848, thousands of workers in Paris rose up against the Second Republic and were brutally repressed. At the time, Louis-Napoleon Bonaparte (Napoleon's nephew) was still in exile in London. He returned to Paris in September of that year, on the heels of the failed uprising. Legend has it that in his luggage was a map of Paris, complete with notes to restore the capital to glory and "meet the requirements of movement, hygiene, and elegance."[15] Shortly after his train came to a halt, he debarked onto what would later be transformed into an emblem of his project of making Paris modern: the train platform of the *embarcadère du Nord*. Six months later, Louis-Napoleon would be elected president. By 1851, he would suspend the constitution and name himself Emperor of France. Less than a decade after the establishment of the Second Empire, he would replace the old embarcadère du Nord with the massively expanded Gare du Nord. Fittingly, the plaza in front of the station would be called the Place Napoleon III.

When the station was first constructed, it was built just at the capital city's limit. Beyond it were fields and rolling countryside. Conceived as the gateways to Paris, nineteenth-century railway stations beckoned the train user into modern urban life. Entering the French capital often meant entering a railway station, crossing through its iron-and-glass interior to the grandiose stone façades that opened onto the city. As railways expanded in the nineteenth century, this new infrastructure became a direct representation of what Karl Marx called "the annihilation of space by time"—the possibility of increased mobility, exchange, and circulation across vast territories.[16] In addition to their technological achievement, railway stations were sites of previously unseen social mixing. They became "laboratories" in which planners and passengers experimented with modern ways of using public spaces.[17]

The triumphant narrative of railway development takes its shape from the modernist narrative of progress. This narrative, as it emerged in Western Europe in the eighteenth and nineteenth centuries, sees individual development as enabled by the development of society and industry.[18] The iron and glass architecture was designed to create a modern environment that would transform rural passengers into modern subjects, in part through their experience with rail travel.[19] Railways were one of those places in the modern cityscape that united the ideals of economic and individual development, ideals that needed to "fuse" in order for modernist dreams to be realized.[20] Like other places of modern dreams, they were also the site of what critic Marshall Berman called the "tragedy of development": the Faustian nightmare that modernity could beget by unleashing the powerful forces of steam and progress. One of the most powerful renderings of this modern tragedy is in Emile Zola's novel *La bête humaine* (The Beast in Man), in which the expanding railway forms the backdrop of moral collapse.[21]

Conversely, railways were also central to utopian visions of progress, imagined to be possible through the conquest of vast territories. The nineteenth-century ideology of the Saint-Simonians, whose ideas influenced both the development of French railways and urban planning, encapsulate this vision.[22] The Saint-Simonians sought to integrate railways into transcontinental networks by connecting them to other transport systems such as canals and maritime travel. Through infrastructure, they sought to link distant countries into a single region, connecting France not only to Europe but to Algeria and Egypt.[23] Although railways were terrestrial transport, Saint-Simonians imagined the possibility of technological progress that could create new connections by weaving together networks of communication, crossing both national and natural boundaries.[24] This Saint-Simonian vision of technology overcoming borders underlay the construction of the Gare du Nord. In 1848, the Rothschild family obtained the concession for the Northern Railway Company from the French government. Their international vision would put the Saint-Simonian ideals to work for a commercial endeavor, eventually connecting Paris to Lille and Valenciennes, with branch lines to Dunkirk and Calais, among others, soon making it possible to travel from Paris to Brussels by train and to London by train and ferry.

The railway stations that punctuated these new rail networks made abstract principles of progress into concrete forms of stone, iron, and glass. They were "cathedrals of modernity" as the poet Théophile Gautier put it, with the power to unite technological progress with social progress in a Saint-Simonian utopia. According to the Saint-Simonian devotee Léonce Reynaud, the architect of the first iteration of the Gare du Nord, railway terminals held the key to the architecture of the future because they called for large spaces with high ceilings that could contain large crowds without being stifling.[25]

Modern hopes and dreams coexisted uneasily with the fears and potential disorder brought by an infrastructure meant to create order and harmony by uniting faraway places. If stations symbolized the dreams of modern France, they also hosted the perils of speed and industry.[26] Spectacular images of derailing and trains tearing through windows magnified the dangers for the French public. Foreign sabotage was also a frequent concern, and there were quotidian reports of minor incidents—such as the train equivalent of a fender bender, when brakes applied too late would lead the train engine to bump into the track head at the terminal. On a less spectacular note, passengers complained about the noise, smoke, and bad odors of railway stations.[27]

More than physical danger, however, the railways also presented the threat of social disorder and revolt. The poor rural migrants who made their way to Paris over the course of the nineteenth century were often cast as potential corruptors of urban bourgeois morality, as illustrated in H. A. Frégier's famous 1838 treatise, *On the Dangerous Classes in Large Cities and How to Make Them Better*. He wrote it at a time when Paris had doubled in population—from five hundred forty-seven thousand in 1801 to over one million in 1846.[28] Frégier, a civil servant and political economist, warned the public and the government of the moral and criminal danger of an urban underclass composed of migrants from rural areas. He described them as "savages" whose bizarre behaviors, depravity, and unhygienic practices resembled that of a "nomadic race."[29] His tome reinforced the notion that the poor were fundamentally different from bourgeois Parisians. His account of these dangerous groups seemed to be taken from the playbook of eighteenth- and nineteenth-century explorers of "exotic" lands, such as the new French colony of Algeria.[30] Like the peoples of those locales, these "dangerous classes" would require a civilizing project to diminish the threat they posed to bourgeois order.

Railways occupied an ambivalent role in this project and would magnify the questions and divisions Frégier proposed. Railways helped grow both industry and the working class and enabled an unprecedented amount of rural inhabitants to come to the city. On the one hand, this migration might achieve the national civilizing mission to "make peasants into Frenchmen."[31] On the other hand, as trains crossed the rural/urban boundary, they became polluting agents that brought undesirable populations into the capital. The question for social policy is a classic one: Is the state to be a paternalist benefactor lifting the poor out of their purported moral turpitude and into modern life, or a repressive force treating working-class people as threats who need to be policed and suppressed? In other words, could these "savages" be assimilated into the bourgeois order of things? These concerns were shaped in early French colonization and the slave trade. They would transform through France's colonial encounter in Africa, and they resonate still with contemporary public debates on the issues of immigration. They have had important consequences for the management of public and urban space and have helped shape the way the Gare du Nord is controlled and policed.

In the mid-nineteenth century, the underlying fear was that the supposed backwardness of poor provincial migrants, combined with the cramped and unhygienic living conditions of the city, would lead to crime as well as massive revolts. Frégier and his colleagues were wrong about the causes of revolt, but their fears came true in 1848. Following the urban-based insurrection of that year, the preferred solution fell on the side of police repression and urban redesign that would enable military movement and reinforce state authority. The expansion of railway transportation in the 1860s would lead to a further influx of rural migrants, and along with them came new control and containment measures, such as a special railway police force.

Railways and their terminals were wrapped up in questions of morality and social boundaries, and they occupied an ambivalent place amid the transformative years of Paris's mid-nineteenth-century urban landscape. They were both feared and revered, holding the potential for disorder and progress. As the historian Stephanie Sauget put it, railway stations were "experienced as places of dreams, nightmares, and fantasized projections."[32] From the beginning of French railroad planning, even before the first Parisian station was opened, the new technology of rail travel brought concern about the imagined dangers and rampant crime they might bring.

More than just a site of industrial progress, the Gare du Nord reflected both the dreams of modernization and the nightmares of disorder that it also could bring. The construction of the station tells a story about the railways' role in the triumphant development of modern self and society, but also reveals how fears about the "dangerous classes" influenced early urban transportation planning, policing, and urban design. From its construction, the Gare du Nord was a place where people from all walks of life might encounter each other, from urban outcasts and vagabonds to foreign dignitaries.

The station has long been what Mary Louise Pratt calls "a contact zone"—that is, a "social space where disparate cultures meet, clash, and grapple with each other, often in asymmetrical relations of domination and subordination."[33] In other words, it is a place where different kinds of people, some privileged and others less so, encounter and confront one another. This character was what brought some migrants to the station 150 years later: many West Africans I met there described the potentiality of the contact zone when they emphasized the Gare's international character and the possibility of meeting people there who "come from everywhere." Yet, as the critics of Pratt's "contact zone" point out, this perspective tends to romanticize the possibility of interaction in these zones, give more attention to the dominant representations of colonial encounters, and deemphasize the violence and distress caused by the unequal access to power and the repressive forces that control the contact zone.[34]

The social mixing that characterizes the Gare du Nord has expanded since its construction, with the growth and confluence of several routes: international and national trains, the Paris Métro, commuter rail, and bus traffic, and this is what has attracted West African adventurers like Yacouba and Lassana to its iron-and-glass interior. Since it is also an emblem of French progress that once embodied the hopes and fears of urban modernity, it provides a lens to examine how the state and railways together created and enforced social boundaries, and how those boundaries shifted over time.

## THE GARE DU NORD: AN URBAN BORDER ZONE

The Gare du Nord has long straddled an invisible internal boundary line of modern Paris that separates working from bourgeois classes. The placement of the barricades in the June 1848 insurrection illustrates the starkness of this boundary: to the station's east, hundreds of barricades; to its west, none.[35] From the station's initial conception and placement on the north-south axis of the city, it has been a border zone between Paris's poor east and rich west. When the first version of the Gare du Nord was built in 1846, it was located on the edge of Paris, in a semirural enclave outside of the city's dominion. Under the expansive vision of Seine prefect Georges-Eugène Haussmann in 1860, such enclaves would be incorporated into Paris. Railway development would help make those areas some of the most densely populated in the world as trains brought provincial migrants to Paris in unprecedented numbers.[36]

Before the still-standing station was constructed under the private auspices of Baron James de Rothschild's North Railway Company, government engineers together with Léonce Reynaud planned the first incarnation of the station on its current lands.[37] Before the railway, it was an idyllic expanse indistinguishable from the surrounding countryside. When the first station was completed, its stone wall and manicured gardens made it more a mini-quarter unto itself than an urban building integrated into a neighborhood. By separating it from the encroaching city streets, developers sustained the utopian vision of train travel. Drawings of the station represent this vision: the inside untouched by the messiness of urban life and the potential for accidents, while a few elegant users stroll on the clipped grass. As passenger traffic increased in the mid-nineteenth century, however, it became impossible to welcome growing urban crowds without marring the structure's immaculate gardens.

FIGURE 2. Illustration of the new Gare du Nord in 1866. Artist unknown; iStockphoto.com/grafissimo.

The engineers who built the first station had been concerned that it was too small. The rise in both passenger and commodity traffic proved them to be correct, and in 1855 the state decided that the station would have to be rebuilt as a much larger structure. Rothschild seized the opportunity to build a new terminal that would represent his commercial and international vision for the North railway. He had already bought most of the surrounding real estate. He sought to create a station that would embody the greatness of his railway company without encroaching on his nearby property interests.[38] The North Railway company financed the entire project, while the government prepared the terrain to host such an enormous structure, leveling any buildings that stood in its way and expropriating their residents.

The author of the impressive structure was one of the Second Empire's favorite architects: Jacques Ignace Hittorff. The Gare du Nord would be his final major oeuvre. The new building needed to satisfy many technical demands and accommodate more passengers and freight traffic. The monumental imperial style used neoclassical columns and enormous statues, each representing a North railway destination. The smaller statues stood for French towns such as Dunkirk, Lille, and Amiens. The larger statues were the European capitals, including Vienna, Amsterdam, Warsaw, and London. The façade placed the Paris statue at the apex, signifying its role as an international capital that would host dignitaries from all parts of the world.[39]

The station's pristine neoclassical façade masked the industrial architecture of iron and glass.[40] Inside, the nineteenth century station would have been full of steam and smoke, noise and odor, and crowds of people.[41] The station's interior architecture would be guided by the goal of separating wealthier classes from the provincial working class who comprised the bulk of train passengers. As the North railway tried to bring distant places together, its terminal became a place that reinforced separations among classes and populations. These contradictions were part of the visions that guided nineteenth-century railway development.

## INTERNATIONAL VISIONS

Railways are often cited as one of those nineteenth-century innovations that helped to create modern European nation-states, uniting separate regions into a single "imagined community" of a nation.[42] This narrative can overlook the imperial and internationalist vision that also guided railway development. From the beginning, much of the excitement about the Gare du Nord was focused on its ability to connect Paris to destinations beyond France's borders, from the station's façade to the way its railway lines were conceived and built. It was open to the world.

For Rothschild's North Railway company ("La compagnie des chemins de fer du Nord"), linking Paris to the provinces was incidental to the internationalist goal of connecting European capitals to one another. This broader goal was reflected in popular media: for instance, the French magazine *L'Illustration* published an issue on the North Railway Company in the 1850s. The issue opened with a presentation of the company's flagship line connecting Paris to the northern provincial capital of Amiens. Yet Amiens is barely mentioned in the magazine, and from this description it seems that the true purpose of the railway line is to link France and Belgium, or, as *L'Illustration* refers to the two countries: "Two kingdoms, brothers through language, mores, and practices; two peoples whose diplomacy created different nations without creating a distinct nationality; two people unified by so many interests." The North Railway company lines could even alter geography from this point of view: "France and Belgium have just become closer together in space; two capitals hold hands; *Paris is in Brussels and Brussels is in Paris.* Rail, that cruel instrument of all conquest, accomplished in this moment, for the happiness of the world, the sweetest and most durable of conquests."[43]

The North railway directors aimed at turning elite Frenchmen into international citizens and creating cross-border trade and commercial networks that would benefit the company and the French state coffers. Board meeting records of the development of the company in the 1850s reveal a persistent concern with international relations, including new agreements with England, Belgium, and

Luxembourg; there is minimal discussion of French or provincial interests.[44] By the completion of this northern line, the crowning achievement would be to unite major commercial capitals of Europe and open up a new era of international travel.

Rothschild's vision was not exceptional in France: his contemporaries also emphasized the international dimension of all networks.[45] The state engineer Vallée was charged by the government in 1834 with "finding the best means to bring together the three kingdoms of France, England, and Belgium," a goal that the North Railway would achieve.[46] The southbound PLM (Paris-Lyon-Méditerrané) railroad was meant to connect to the North railway. In doing so, it would link two major trading ports, going "from the North Sea to the Mediterranean," and thus also to French colonies in North Africa. The Lyon-Avignon train line would develop French-Swiss-German trade routes.[47] This international imaginary had consequences for the way railway lines were drawn and for towns that were transformed as they became connected to international routes.

Railway companies appealed to governments to make policies that would allow for the fluid circulation of people between countries. The North Railway Company in the 1850s and 1860s sought to reduce barriers to cross-border travel. In 1856, the company reports in a board meeting that the Belgian government agreed to forgo the necessity of visas for travelers with direct tickets from elsewhere who were transiting through Belgium to get to France. The company reports making a similar request to the French government, which also agreed to allow passengers transiting from Belgium, through France, to England (or the reverse) to pass without needing to obtain a French visa.[48]

First-class travelers on those cross-border lines would have enjoyed opulent compartments like those the North railway company exhibited in the press, along with the wonders of its technological achievement that garnered accolades at the Universal and Industrial Expositions.[49] Rothschild and his company projected a world of luxury and transcontinental travel where elites would enjoy their moments of leisure on a train. As we will see, twenty-first-century transformations of the Gare du Nord into a more upscale mall echo this earlier representation and even make explicit reference to it: in 2016, a fancy brasserie called L'Etoile du Nord (the old name of the train to London) was opened in the main hall of the station, in the former locale of a police commissariat. Security personnel guard the entrance. In the mid-nineteenth century, opulence was to be found only in first-class train cars and waiting rooms.

The representation of luxury travel obscured the major sources of North Railway Company profits: freight transport and third-class passenger travel (just as the dilapidated commuter line traffic at the Gare du Nord today provides more profits for the national railway company than the high-speed TGV lines). Third-class passenger tickets comprised the bulk of passenger-derived revenues (rising from 44% of profits in 1869 to 53% in 1898, while first class tickets decreased from constituting

30% of profits to 18% in the same time period).[50] The station was less chic than nearby Gare Saint Lazare, whose trains went to fashionable Normandy; many contemporaries described the foul odor of the Gare du Nord, emanating from its transports of coal and coke produced in the north of France.[51] The international imaginary of rail transport promoted both by Rothschild and by the Saint-Simonian vision contrasted with the real use of this railway and obscured where its profits came from. Migrants and mineral transport from France's poor industrial north allowed the company to thrive. Yet third-class passengers, many of them industrial workers, were represented as dangerous populations who threatened to derail modern progress.[52]

The station was built at a time when Haussmann was implementing plans to "make the right to the city an exclusively bourgeois prerogative," as David Harvey put it—allowing workers and others to come into the city on the train in order to rebuild Paris but making it impossible for them to make any legitimate claim on urban space.[53] The expropriations and destructions of Haussmann's renovation led many lower-class inhabitants to leave the historic core, but also created workers' neighborhoods where the poor were concentrated in northeastern Paris.

Although the Gare du Nord sat on the line separating the wealthy west from poor eastern areas of the capital city, it was not a wall but a space of encounter that brought them together. Urban transit systems both separated and related sections of the city: they made the segregation that Haussmann created difficult to maintain, because they allowed people to move throughout the city. At the same time, railway tracks would also cordon off entire neighborhoods.[54] To understand how this particular attribute of transit infrastructure helped produce the Gare du Nord's social environment, it is important to consider the changing perspectives on the "dangerous classes" that would guide station architects for more than a century.

## THE DANGEROUS CLASSES: FROM BETTERMENT TO CONTAINMENT

The railways served the interests of economic growth as well as the more symbolic goals of national integration and international connections. In all cases, they were a tool meant to maximize circulation (of people, goods, trains). Michel Foucault identified this new goal in early modern French urban planning, which he used as a key example of the operation of power based on "security"—for example, unlike fortified walls that would be used to keep things either out or in, the new paradigm used techniques to maximize fluid movement while minimizing risks. Urban planning became "a matter of organizing circulation, eliminating its dangerous elements, and maximizing the good circulation by diminishing the bad."[55] These goals would be refined and transformed in the nineteenth century as French imperial and industrial growth would lead the government to confront the so-called "dangerous classes" who were seen to threaten the "good" circulation that infrastructure was meant to enable.[56]

Who were these "dangerous classes"? According to mid-nineteenth century writings about them, they were a motley crew of social marginals defined by their economic status: they were poor and propertyless. They include the jobless poor assumed to be thieves and vagabonds as well as the working poor, who were threatening the political order. They were seen as morally degenerate, prone both to criminality and to revolt. They were a societal disease, lawmakers said, dangerous because they could seduce upstanding citizens into a life of crime and immorality.[57]

As infrastructure developed, so did measures to control or limit the potential threats that the increased mobility of this growing urban underclass posed to state and industrial development. Private companies that managed railroads in collaboration with the government wanted to solve the problem of disorder and moral degeneracy that the ruling classes believed could come about as a result of the mixing between "dangerous" and bourgeois classes. Urban planning and state policies would relegate poor migrants to the periphery—areas that many nineteenth-century observers referred to as "eccentric," suggesting both their distance from the spatial center and from bourgeois social norms. This marginalizing process would be repeated and refined as French colonialism expanded in the twentieth century. The French state's control of social mixing—defined in class and racial terms—was part of infrastructural development.

Attempts to manage the dangerous classes would be built into the Gare du Nord. As we have seen, the station was a symbol of the modern imperial nation and a motor of national integration, a threshold between the "modern" city and "traditional" countryside, and a space in which public and private entities vested capital, resources, and dreams of development. As such, it demanded substantial security measures to protect it from the flipside of progress, from the accidents and crowds that threatened growth and compromised circulation. The station's construction during the Second Empire would be marked as much by the construction of borders and barriers as it would by Rothschild's focus on transnational travel and circulation.

The government's approach to the dangerous classes would change under Napoleon III and after the tumultuous events of 1848. Ten years prior, Frégier had devoted part of his treatise on the dangerous classes to proposing policies that would foster their assimilation. At that time, railways were just beginning to expand and Paris had not yet been transformed by Haussmann's renovations. The 1848 revolution that would overthrow King Louis-Philippe was a decade away, part of a string of revolutions across Europe that were the result of economic crisis and high unemployment.[58] The purported moral degeneracy of the "dangerous classes"—the urban poor, migrants to the city, and workers—would make them into scapegoats for the upheaval and increase doubts about the possibility for them to be assimilated into bourgeois social order.

Railways would develop in the wake of these revolutions, expanding to traverse the whole of France once Louis-Napoleon had installed himself as monarch at the dawn of the Second Empire in 1851. His regime sought to avoid the mistakes of the past. By the time the Gare du Nord was being planned in 1854, the ruling attitude toward the dangerous classes had shifted. Eduard de Rautlin-Delaroy, a lawyer at the imperial court of Louis-Napoléon, published a pamphlet called "Dangerous Classes and How to Contain Them." Now it was a question of containment instead of betterment and assimilation. He replaced the social policy reform proposed by Frégier with an approach focused on policing and repression.

Public works projects and new industries needed workers, but those workers were seen as dangerous outsiders invading the city. The demographic change wrought by rural-to-urban migration created a process that went against the gentrifying tendencies of Haussmannian reforms. Workers came in, not out. They built their homes in the northeast of Paris and worked throughout the capital. Once new infrastructures were in place, they required continued maintenance, renewing the demand for workers that could not be satisfied by the Parisian population.[59]

These workers were not only potential revolutionaries. As we have seen, by virtue of coming from provincial regions, they were classified as inferior on the civilizational scale: "There is a great deal of evidence to suggest that vast parts of nineteenth-century France were inhabited by savages," wrote Eugen Weber to describe how Parisians viewed much of France in the first chapter of his tome investigating the transformation of the French countryside after the advent of new infrastructures and language homogenization.[60] The label of savage applied to two main groups: the "urban poor" and parts of the "rural population." The latter appeared less dangerous to the ruling elite, Weber claims, because they were more spread out. Railways would make them more dangerous by concentrating them in provincial capitals and in Paris. The population of Paris saw unprecedented growth between the 1830s and 1856, despite the falling level of real wages.[61] "Savage" peasants transformed into the urban underclass. They also went from being backward races in need of civilization to dangerous classes who could not be assimilated but rather needed to be contained with security measures.

The distinction between difference that could be included (peasants into Frenchmen) and difference that was incommensurable (the dangerous classes) and needed to be contained was derived from a nineteenth-century ideology honed through the French conquest of Algeria, which elaborated on pseudo-scientific eighteenth-century schemas of racial difference.[62] Faced with the threat of revolt, crime, and moral degeneracy supposedly brought by the dangerous classes, the response in both Paris and in Algiers was to circumscribe the danger of the underclass by isolating it and preventing the mixing of bourgeois and dangerous classes, thus emphasizing the logic of security over that of assimilation.[63] Peasants would theoretically become Frenchmen if they learned French and had contact with the bourgeois order of the capital. But they were poor, and as they joined the urban underclass, they would be accused of moral deviation. The promise of migrating to the city to become a modern individual contrasted with the experience of many workers from the rural areas during that period. They would be accused of retrograde beliefs, inherent criminality, and immoral behavior.[64] In short, they were seen as culturally other.

Migrant workers in nineteenth-century Paris became the scapegoat of all things undesirable. As in other eras, the danger did not arise from inherent immorality, but rather from their transgression of the boundaries meant to exclude them from the bourgeois public sphere. They were exemplary "matter out of place" to use the anthropologist Mary Douglas's formulation: dirty because of their insistence on occupying spaces not meant for them.[65] Although Haussmann's renovation of Paris in the 1850s and 1860s increased segregation in some parts of the city, concurrent developments made segregation difficult. Urban transportation and the development of new social spaces, such as railway stations and department stores, blurred boundaries.[66] As physical distance diminished, new methods had to be invented to maintain social distance. The idea that dangerous classes were morally degenerate and a polluting influence on respectable ladies and gentlemen justified urban separation measures and helped to solidify bourgeois class identity.[67]

The dangerous classes seemed threatening to the very railways that enabled their mobility to Paris. As the Gare du Nord's location was being debated in the 1850s, the printer of all train schedules and train-related pamphlets sold in the stations published the essay by Rautlin-Delaroy on "containing" the dangerous classes. This publication illustrates the double goal and multiple meanings that railway infrastructure brought to Paris, helping to build an ideology that could contain the more threatening aspects of a new infrastructure while ensuring transnational circulation. Delaroy singled out two causes for what he claimed was the unprecedented growth of these dangerous classes. The first was the 1848 revolution overthrowing the monarchy. The second was the completion of the railways.

Unlike the champions of progress who would proclaim that French modernity had arrived with the rail revolution and Haussmann's urban planning, Delaroy points out that the same technology that permitted faster military troop mobilization would also lead to the arrival of dangerous groups who would threaten security and stability. "The rapidity of transportation," he claimed, "allows for organized

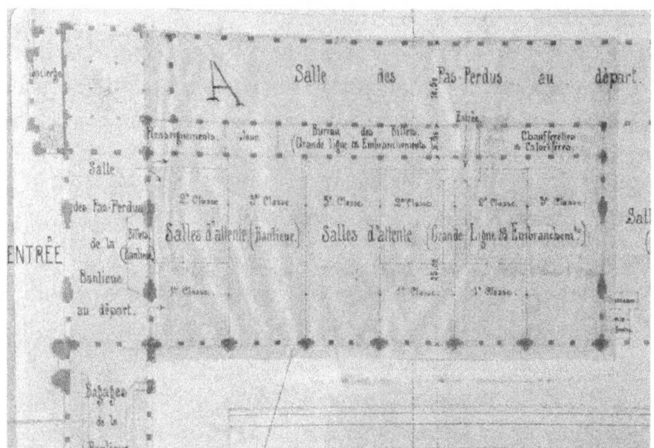


FIGURE 3. Blueprints of the Gare du Nord showing two entrances and three classes of waiting rooms, separated according to suburban ("banlieue") and long-distance ("grandes lignes") trains, 1860. Archives Nationales de France.

gangs from the provinces to arrive, at the first signal, to the capital."[68] (It is worth pointing out that 150 years later, politicians and media commentators would make the same point, when participants in the 2007 station "riot" would be referred to as "gangs"; it would also be pointed out that telephone technology (text messaging) and commuter rail transport were what enabled the quick arrival of "rioters" from the *banlieue.*) For Delaroy, thanks to the speed and transportation of the railway, the dangerous classes were more dangerous than ever. As the Gare du Nord was designed, these concerns were built into the station's interior architecture.

Blueprints of the 1860 project designing the interior of the Gare du Nord reveal a compartmentalized space in which each station function had a small room devoted to it; there was little open space. It had separate exits and entrances depending on whether one had arrived or was departing, or was coming from the suburbs or from further afield. The station was not accessible to everyone; to enter you needed a train ticket for the day in question, a platform ticket, or some other justification for your presence. The only accessible part of the station was the vestibule on the departure-side entrance. Passengers departing on trains were sorted into waiting rooms divided by destination (suburb or province). They were then further divided according to service classes—first, second, and third class, each with its own enclosed waiting room. These design solutions reinforced social boundaries through physical separations.

The dangerous classes were often seen as those who came from elsewhere to pollute Parisian blood, as Delaroy believed: they were people "of all colors and from all countries, the crazy men who come from the provinces and from abroad to find refuge in Paris" and threaten "our social order."[69] It did not matter whether they were French or foreign. They were of a different genus, and were dangerous not only because of their criminal or rebellious nature but because of their mobility.

Like many of his contemporaries, Delaroy was concerned with the issue of social mixing.[70] In order to master these undesirable yet mobile classes, Delaroy proposed a large number of elite police with military training whose main purpose would be to maintain order.[71] Such a force was necessary because dangerous classes were liable to "become confused with the honest population" when "lost in an immense city."[72] He worried about the corrupting force of mixing between mobile, vagabond populations and "the bourgeois classes," enabled by the railways. His solution was not to roll back technological progress, but rather to create an elite corps of ex-military policemen who would guard the city's bourgeois population from dangers posed by the intrusion of the masses.

His proposition had precedents. In 1837, lawmakers had proposed the necessity of new criminal laws and a separate railway police. One legislator justified the need for a new section of the penal code by explaining that "especially around Paris, we are dealing with the most destructive and degrading people [*peuple*] that exists in the world."[73] The railway police were meant to combat what lawmakers assumed would be an increase in existing crimes. They also anticipated new types of dangerous criminal and political activity ushered in by the railway, such as the potential for train sabotage or blocking trains from leaving as a part of political protest.[74] The law had special sanctions that considered it criminal for a railway employee to leave his post. Lawmakers were most preoccupied by potential attacks, such as placing something on the tracks that would lead to derailing. One section equated attacks on the railways with starting a rebellion.

Managing these "dangers" would require more than a new police force; beginning in the 1840s, they would lead to a larger series of transformations that railways and stations would require of French public space, law, and urban planning. Railway personnel were incorporated into military-style hierarchies and some were trained to monitor and keep order in the station, along with the police. Designing spatial modes of control became pressing as stations expanded. Railway companies attempted to isolate their interiors from the encroaching urban neighborhood surrounding them. They gained three distinct classes of waiting rooms, separated either by full walls or by high barriers.[75] Women were given separate train cars in first and second class, at the urging of a public health official (only third class had mixed gender cars).

Delaroy and his contemporaries sought mechanisms to control the potential dangers of massive migration and a growing urban population. Over the course of the nineteenth century, prostitutes and "vagabonds" would come to occupy the area around the station, as the railway terminals transformed the physical and social

FIGURE 4. "Une Gare," a mid-nineteenth-century caricature of a French railway station interior, by Henry Monnier. Bibliothèque Nationale de France.

environment of their urban locations.[76] These dangerous classes could not be eliminated, but had to be contained, and the station and its surrounding neighborhood—like train station districts across the world—would become the container. But as containers, they were always leaky ones.

Accounts of train station life suggest that many of the built-in attempts to separate by passenger class were also opportunities for transgression. Passengers in lower-class waiting rooms tried to sneak into the first-class rooms.[77] Even in the epoch of separate classes of waiting rooms and isolation from the surrounding city, the Gare du Nord was already a site for new forms of social mixing. Writer Benjamin Gastineau's 1861 description emphasizes that the railway station life was "society in miniature, the theater of a million scenes, a million intrigues, and a million deceptions as well." There were "multiple types of the citizens of the world, Babels of all languages, of all sentiments, packages of all kinds of merchandise, contrasts of all positions." Potential danger abounded as "thieves and deportees" could be placed among the milieu of "honest folk." Women voyagers from all the provinces of France would be subject to these spaces of "masculine flirtation" and could become the victims of "seducers."[78] The Gare du Nord still has this reputation in the twenty-first century.

Police officers could not contain this exciting and dangerous world of encounter that formed in the railway station. Although they were meant to maintain order and separations, they also participated in transgressions. Labiche's vaudeville play about the railways, performed in the Palais-Royale in 1867, included police officers acting as interminable pick-up artists, profiting from the presence of lone women travelers.[79] As we shall see, police are still ambivalent social participants—not only "forces of order"—at the Gare du Nord. The new semipublic space became a site of encounter that then led to more security interventions.

For Foucault, the dual goals of control and circulation guided governance and planning. Yet the Gare du Nord illustrated how often these goals contradicted each other, leading to new solutions. The separate waiting rooms (a control measure) created bottlenecks when it was time to board that often led to delays, thus disturbing train circulation (passengers who have taken the Eurostar train to London will recognize that this problem persists). The Gare du Nord was an embodiment of the contradictory forces that shaped nineteenth-century Paris—repressive force, utopian ideals, commercial interests, exploitation, and social engineering.

## SHIFTING BELONGING AND EXCLUSION

When the Gare du Nord was built, the government was more concerned by the arrival and mobility of rural French migrants in Paris than it was with foreigners (who were often presented as more of an interesting oddity than a danger).[80] Before national ID cards, the state imposed interior passports for rural migrants and special papers for workers so that the police could control their movement and manage how many provincials came to the capital.[81] Such measures were justified by the representations of moral degeneracy and inferiority created in a context of pseudo-scientific racial classifications and French imperialism.

The development of French colonial administration in the nineteenth century honed racial discourse, while conflicts with European neighbors (especially with Prussia) reinforced the French national project. Colonial administrations developed new means of differentiation, first between citizens and subjects (*indigènes*), and then among indigènes, who were classified according to how close or distant they were to French "civilization."[82] Spatial organization became one of the mechanisms for managing these distinctions, whether in projects confining newly classified groups ("tribes") through territorial divisions of vast rural terrain or through the establishment of new cities (*villes nouvelles*) such as in North Africa, where Haussmann-style urban districts were built next to existing cities.[83] Territorial management and urban planning were key techniques of rule in imperial France, both in the colonies and in the metropole.

The idea of a national French identity encompassing rural migrants and the urban poor emerged in the late 1800s and was connected to the expanding colonial endeavor. Before the Third Republic, the foreigner (*l'étranger*) was not a derogatory term, as Gerard Noiriel observes, and the main social cleavage was not based on nationality but on wealth.[84] By the early twentieth century, the provinces had been integrated into a nation consolidated through the policies of the Third Republic (1870–1940), including the erasure of "interior passports" and the imposition of more stringent rules about nationality. Rural migrants, workers, and the urban underclass were still treated as inferior and dangerous, but they were no longer seen as incommensurably different.[85] In the North railway company, the emerging divide between French and foreign would become codified in new kinds of separation measures. For example, by 1900, there were at least four types of train cars, each with its own hygiene regulations. The fourth type grouped "emigrants" and "animals" together and had the most stringent cleaning procedure.[86]

During World War I, more refugees (many from Belgium) arrived in France through the Gare du Nord than any other train station, leading charities to set up offices around the station. These refugees were often arrested by station police and "lumped together by the press alongside ex-convicts and vagrants."[87] In the aftermath of the war, colonial subjects including veteran soldiers, students, and workers became a visible presence in Paris, where they were surveilled by police.[88] These populations would come to occupy the position of the dangerous classes, and their otherness would help white provincials, the poor, and European immigrants to be further assimilated into the category French (though these groups would remain marginalized in many ways).[89]

The history of the once incommensurable difference of provincials and workers would be glossed over in favor of an imagined past of white homogeneity and frictionless assimilation of European immigrants into the French model, troubled only by the occasional emergence of populist xenophobia. This sanitized version has become the palatable history of French immigration; it is the one exhibited at the French national museum of immigration that was opened in 2007.[90] This version erases the struggles of integration, the fights for immigrant worker rights, and the significant presence of nonwhite people in metropolitan France, including many West Africans who helped shape Paris and its politics in the 1930s.[91]

During this period, colonial subjects came to occupy the dangerous slot that threatened the new national order. While workers and the urban poor would remain potential sources of danger and disorder from the state perspective, these groups were no longer seen as a savage race with deviant morals.[92] This assimilation was possible because colonial subjects took their place as the dangerous other, and the notion of the dangerous classes took on a reinforced racialized dimension that would be cemented over the course of the twentieth century.[93]

## SHIFTING BOUNDARIES

This history matters in understanding what Yacouba experienced and what many black people experience in French public spaces. It illustrates the centrality of racial distinctions in the creation of the French nation, and shows that racial profiling at the Gare du Nord emerged from earlier classifications and containment practices associated with efforts to repress so-called dangerous classes and ensure fluid circulation. The station has always been governed by an imperial logic. When it was constructed, the most important boundary the state and railway companies sought to enforce was not between French and foreign but rather between rural and urban, working class and bourgeois, in a system where these distinctions signified not only regional or class divides, but also cultural and moral differences that were difficult or impossible to overcome. Class divides and the division between rural and urban persist to this day. However, despite the long-standing practices of marginalizing rural populations, both groups are now incorporated into the ideology of what constitutes French identity.[94] This incorporation continues to be denied to Africans and those of African descent.

Racial profiling at the present-day Gare du Nord is also a product of postcolonial migration policy. Until the 1970s, immigration was not a problem to be solved but rather a solution that helped propel the French economy during a period of unprecedented growth in the postwar period, referred to as Thirty Glorious Years. After the Second World War, France needed more workers. In 1954, there were 1,700,000 immigrants in France according to the census; twenty years later, there were almost 3,400,000 (not including naturalized citizens). These foreign workers would become labeled as a problem in 1973 when the oil crisis and recession hit.[95] By then, almost all of the places colonized by France in Africa were independent.

New laws meant to curb migration would mean that legal workers already in France could find themselves in "illegal" status. Violent racist incidents were on the rise and being documented by activist groups. In the 1970s, xenophobic discourse was on the rise but was not yet an explicit center of public debate.[96] By the mid-1980s, however, the "immigrant problem" would be at the forefront of electoral struggles. By the end of the 1980s, Muslim North Africans, marked by religious and ethno-racial difference, would come to signify the "new dangerous class" in France.[97] During this period, as philosopher Etienne Balibar observes, racist discourse became more prevalent, and would come to be couched in cultural terms that imagined a homogenous set of French values, norms, and traditions as threatened by an influx of non-European foreigners.[98] As in the 1860s, the development of the dangerous classes would also be accompanied by infrastructural expansion. To support flexible migrant labor, the state and private companies built shaky infrastructures—including substandard housing and the RER commuter line.

The geographer René Clozier argued in 1940 that the Gare du Nord "created the *banlieues*"—making a peripheral suburban belt where there had been rolling countryside.[99] The périphérique highway would help to cement the boundary between the two spaces. When the RER—which workers like Yacouba take to and from the station each day—was inaugurated in the 1970s, it transformed the station. Today, the millions of inhabitants living in the northeast suburbs of Paris make up more than 80 percent of the station's traffic.[100] This traffic constitutes a continuous flow between center and periphery, and illustrates the impossibility of maintaining the separation between the two in a mobility hub.

## UTOPIA OR DYSTOPIA?

The development of transportation links, from the Eurostar to London to the RER to the suburbs, has created the international crossroads that makes the Gare du Nord so dear to the West African adventurers who meet there. On a cold night in 2010, Lassana sent me a message with a photo of a stone statue of an enormous head. The head was as tall as the few people passing by at that late hour. It was the largest statue that had been made for the mid-nineteenth-century station, representing Paris at an apex above the other European and provincial cities of the erstwhile Northern Railway Company (nationalized into the SNCF, the National French Railways, in 1937). Workers were taking it down as part of a renovation project, power-washing out the gray dirt that had accumulated over the last decades to reveal the cream stone underneath. He took many pictures of the statue, staying late as they lifted it from the apex and maneuvered it to the sidewalk.

Lassana and his friends always paid homage to the importance of the station's history, positing themselves as the heirs of an international vision that has existed from the station's foundation. As black men in France, they have also inherited the label of the "dangerous classes," a term that continues to have currency in French media and political speech. They stand at the crossroads of the question that has long guided the history of the station: Should the Gare du Nord be a space of progress and potential, or might it herald the undoing of society? And what role will they play in either case?

The adventurer perspective, as we shall see, suggests that both possibilities exist. Adventurers go back and forth between seeing it as a positive social space, full of potential for development (as the Saint Simonians did, though for different reasons) and a dystopian world that leads to moral deviance or deportation. As Lassana does not hesitate to say: you can just as well find your happiness there as end up in misery. Despite all the mechanisms for control and all the encounters with the police, he still finds enough at the Gare to make it worth the risk, perhaps not unlike their predecessors who flocked to the station from the French provinces in an attempt to improve their lot in life. But unlike the rural migrants who were eventually incorporated into the French fold, the discrimination and exclusion they are subject to as black, Muslim, and African exacerbates the struggle they face.[101]

In the intervening century and a half between the statue being placed to crown the new Gare du Nord and Lassana watching it being removed for cleaning, this international railway station has become more integrated with the surrounding city, eliminating physical separation and segregation. By the Gare du Nord's major expansion of 1889, separate waiting rooms had already given way to a common departure hall. In 1956, third class was eliminated from all national railway trains. In the 1970s, the platform ticket was abolished, giving everyone access to the station. As of September 2012, some regional trains eliminated first-class seating, a decision made by the regional council. Yet the destruction of concrete walls and separations may be misleading. With this inclusiveness—the so-called democratization of station space—new methods of controlling the "dangerous classes" have also developed. These methods would both build on and transform the spatial divisions and policing tactics used in nineteenth-century railway stations. When the station revolt happened during the 2007 presidential elections, participants turned the floodlights on the contradictions of the new Gare du Nord and the racialized policing of contemporary French urban space.

# 2

# The Exchange Hub

I never paid attention to the CCTV cameras at the Gare du Nord until Ibrahim Diallo, a construction worker in his late twenties who had migrated with his parents from Senegal, pointed them out to me, their bulbous heads disguising them as light fixtures. He nodded in their direction, with the warning "They're watching us." After that, I started to see them everywhere. One afternoon in late 2009, as I climbed the stairs out of the commuter rail subway area and into the station concourse, I noticed a peculiar poster standing in contrast to the hidden-in-plain-site cameras. "For your tranquility," it proclaimed, "this station is equipped with a video-surveillance system." A cartoon drawing of a wall-mounted video camera accompanied the announcement.

I paused to take a photo of the poster, an act that garnered vocal amusement from a group of Ibrahim's friends, who were chatting in the sunlight as commuters navigated around them. When Lassana saw me take the photo, he and his friend Amadou came over to say hello. We contemplated the poster, and Amadou began criticizing police harassment of him and his friends at the station. "French cameras are crap," he added, "They can't even pay for a modern system with all the colors, so they see only in black and white. Their crap system is worth nothing. They see nothing! But I see everything, so ask me if you need to know something." Lassana shook his head. Amadou's nickname was *Sécurité Sans Salaire*—Security without Salary—which he had earned for his overbearing tendency to watch over and control other men—especially other West Africans—hanging around the front square of the station.

I spotted Djibril, a soft-spoken migrant from Mali entering his eighth undocumented year in France, who came up the staircase from the metro as we were talking and joined us. He began with a series of salutations I had become familiar with—in a mix of Soninke and French to Lassana and Amadou and in what sounded like excessively polite French to me, the type he used in his job working at a bakery. He was eager to join our conversation and started complaining about being stopped by the police for what are called *contrôles d'identité* (ID checks). They are asked to show their passport or national identity card and in many cases are also patted down and searched—similar to what is called a stop-and-frisk in the United States. "It's just, one minute you're here talking to your friends and then the cop is asking for your papers, your resident permit, not really insulting you but still . . . even when they're polite, it's not okay!" he said.

"They're *not* polite," countered Lassana, "And most of these guys"—he gestures to the other West Africans around us—"don't know that because cops don't make direct insults. But they're using [the familiar pronoun] *tu* with us when they shouldn't, and we're *bledards*, so they think we don't know anything," he continued, referring to the fact that they came to France from the *bled* (an Arabic borrow word for "country" or "countryside")—in this case, rural West Africa.

Everyone nodded, murmuring their agreement.

"Remember that riot, a few years back?" asked Lassana. "It was crazy because all the journalists were coming here; they even interviewed me, but I wasn't on TV. I don't let them film me because I'm smart and I have my ways that I learned *au bled*. But I was here, and back then we used to hang out more downstairs," he said, referring to the mall area near the commuter rail. "The police arrested this guy, this African, because he was there and he was black so they figured he didn't have a ticket. He was a *bledard*, like us, but from some other place, like maybe Angola or something. Then it exploded because the *renois* were angry, they were really angry with the police. I saw the whole thing." He used the inversion slang term for black, *renois*, which for him and his friends designated the France-born children of African immigrants.

"No, no, he was from Congo. Congo *Brazzaville*," interrupted Amadou. "Those *blacks* are crazy!" Djibril and Lassana shook their heads and laughed ruefully at the mention of the Congolese to show their agreement. Although many Congolese men also hung out at the Gare du Nord—across the street in front of the McDonald's—Lassana and his friends had little contact with them. Amadou claimed that this was because the *Congolais* were not interested in meeting anyone else and came to the station only to speak their native Lingala with their friends.

"The renois are delinquents," Amadou proclaimed. "We're not delinquents like them!" he said, turning toward me. By calling black youth at the station delinquents, he aligned with the way many French government figures depict the so-called "second-generation immigrants" in France.[1] He also reinforced his own cultural authenticity as a bledard who had struggled his way out of a tough life in a poor village. Despite these distinctions, many self-identified bledards adopted the hip-hop fashion associated with the "renois," sometimes in an attempt to ward off police questioning of their legal status by trying to resemble blacks born in France. Further blurring these distinctions was the fact that the division between the two groups was not easy to maintain—Ibrahim, for example, identified with both groups, having come to France from rural eastern Senegal when he was fifteen.

Amadou, however, used the event to draw some stark lines. "The whole thing just showed what imbeciles the police *and* the renois are," he said. "That's one of the reasons we came up here," he said, referring to the front square outside of the station where we were standing. "Anyway, we meet here and then we go to a café and then we go home. Calm. But the police still bother us sometimes. Especially those black cops! They're the worst for us. They're Caribbean (*Antillais*)."

"Yeah," murmured Djibril, after he had paused to survey the groups around him, his eyes landing on a group of police officers who were making their way across the square. "Sometimes things heat up. And it smells like riot. (*Parfois ça chauffe. Et ça sent l'émeute*)."

The so-called "riot" they were talking about was the event that began when a Congolese man was stopped by metro employees (called *contrôleurs*) at the station. It had occurred in the middle of the 2007 French presidential campaign that pitted Nicolas Sarkozy against Ségolène Royal, just over a year after the 2005 "riots" in the suburbs. In both cases, the term *riot*, a highly racialized term indexing disorder and violence, was used by the press and government. Despite France's long and celebrated history of urban uprisings, *riot* is the preferred term to designate and thus delegitimize revolts in France (and elsewhere) when people of color, immigrants, and children of immigrants are perceived as being the main participants.[2]

The incident that sparked the revolt was a subway ticket verification, an interaction that happens thousands of times a day in the Paris metro. But this time was different, as Lassana remembered. The man refused to stop and pay the fine. They tried to get him to stop and he elbowed his way out; the police came and muscled him down to the ground. Several commuters passing by on their way home that afternoon pointed out that the police were violent in a way that seemed excessive for the situation. Given the location of the stop (right in one of the busiest areas of the station) and the time (the beginning of rush hour), there were enough witnesses to call attention to it. A crowd formed and what the onlookers saw were several white police officers restraining a black man on the ground. Some of the officers yelled at the crowd to keep moving. Several voices in the crowd yelled back. Someone may have thrown something at the police. The man was dragged away and taken to the police station, but the confrontations continued, pitting police against the gathered crowd and especially against the young people from the suburbs who came to the station when they heard about the excitement from their friends. Police showed up in riot gear. They dispensed tear gas, someone may have set a fire in a trashcan, and more than a few people took the opportunity to steal merchandise from the mall shops.

Although Lassana and his friends differentiate themselves from the "delinquents" who confronted the police, they also admit that they participated in important ways—such as by filming with their phones and by denouncing the violence they heard about and witnessed. As I examine in this chapter, the videos posted online (by other observers) provide an important basis for discussing the event and illustrate the disproportionate use of force. Migrants and French-African youth used the revolt to assert their right to be treated with dignity in public space, refusing the quotidian violence and subjectification of urban policing.[3]

But it was also a windfall for candidate Nicolas Sarkozy, who had been campaigning on the themes of insecurity and the dangerous suburbs. He accused his rival Ségolène Royale of being on the side of those who caused the "disorder," and two months later, Sarkozy was president. Political figures in his government would use it as a talking point even years later: Interior Minister Brice Hortefeux made his public trip to the station in 2010 a few months after I had stood discussing the event with Lassana, Djibril, and Amadou. In his speech, Hortefeux referenced the "riot" as he outlined his new security program of which the station was the flagship example.[4]

The reference to the 2007 event provided an opportunity for him to identify a latent threat of violence and disorder at the Gare du Nord and situate it within a government program that linked African immigration to insecurity in urban spaces. The speech echoed Prime Minister François Fillon's promise in 2007 to "put cameras everywhere" at the station—the same cameras that Ibrahim liked to point out to me. For many years, the 2007 "riot" was the emblematic event that proved that the Gare du Nord was a source of insecurity within Paris. In 2018, over a decade later, the event had faded from popular discourse and memory. Yet I still heard people at the station—such as Mounir, who managed a kebab shop across the street—bring it up as a defining moment that embodied the many contradictions of the Gare du Nord.

How did this event end up looming so large in the urban imaginary of the area? We can think about the revolt as what anthropologist Sally Falk Moore called a "diagnostic event"—that is, as an occurrence that revealed "ongoing contests and conflicts and competitions and the efforts to prevent, suppress, or repress them."[5] As Laurent, a French railways employee working at the station put it about the revolt, "How did we get to this point?" To answer this question, it is important to look at both the powerful ways that space has been produced (by planners, politicians, economic interests, and laws) and also the experiential, interactional, and symbolic processes that have created it.[6] To do so, we must dig into the postcolonial context of the station and its surrounding neighborhood, shedding light on how race, violence, and ideas about difference have been rebuilt into French public space in the late twentieth and early twenty-first centuries. In this history emerge competing ideas about who has a right to make claims on public spaces and who needs to be planned out of them.

By examining this event and the urban context that led to it, I illustrate one of the major paradoxes of the station's social environment: young black men who hang out at the station are excluded from the models of urban planners and architects, yet they are the people who are fulfilling urbanists' hopes to create a meaningful "exchange hub" (to use the planners' term) out of a functional space of transit. By participating in the revolt, these young men did not prove that they were unfit for French public space, as some people at the station and in the media maintained. On the contrary, they demonstrated that they had become part of that space and had adapted to what they saw as French traditions of urban contestation—a tradition itself created by migrants and the urban underclass. The reason why almost no one recognized their action as political protest was because they were seen as the new iteration of the "dangerous classes," intervening in a space where racial inequality had been built in for 150 years.

## THE BORDER ZONE NEIGHBORHOOD

Just as in the nineteenth century, the Gare du Nord still lies on the axis separating Paris's wealthy northwest from the working-class northeast. The area has maintained its character as a central landmark of immigrant Paris, in an area of the capital where more than one in three inhabitants came from abroad.[7] Its transient character was reinforced in the postwar period by the construction of workers' hostels around the station to house a portion of the millions of Algerians and other North and sub-Saharan Africans who were recruited as workers.[8] In the 1970s and 1980s, immigrant families also moved in as part of a family reunification visa program.

Yacouba, whom I accompanied on his morning commute to the station, grew up in a building overlooking the Gare's tracks. Although his parents moved to the suburbs when he was still a child, he remembers the mixed immigrant district fondly. His parents established their first home together after coming to Paris from Abidjan sometime in the late 1970s. Yacouba remembers the cracked paint on the walls and a broken toilet that led them to use their Moroccan neighbors' facilities, and a building lobby that was often dirty. The building he describes was similar to many in the neighborhood, where North African immigrant families had settled in the 1970s and 1980s, often occupying small dilapidated apartments built as workers' lodgings in the nineteenth and early twentieth centuries. He mourned the Moroccan butcher and bakery he had grown up with, now replaced by a Bangladeshi butcher—still halal, as Yacouba pointed out approvingly. In the 1990s, the area continued to grow and change as South Asian migrants settled there and opened shops, restaurants, and internet cafés in the streets surrounding the station.

Through these many transformations, one thing has remained constant: the district is still more of a border zone than a neighborhood with a defined character or identity (such as exists in nearby Montmartre, Pigalle, Belleville, and the Goutte d'Or).[9] The station is located in the north of Paris's 10th district. The official urban planning office of Paris (APUR) calls it the "Neighborhood of Two Railway Stations" because of the train tracks of the Gare du Nord and neighboring Gare de l'Est that cut through it. Station shop employees often described the area as "seedy" and most said that they did not spend any time there as it had little in the way of cultural offerings such as movie theaters. A few even called it "dead," despite the heavy foot traffic and activity throughout the day and night. The surrounding area is seen as rife with crime, prostitution, and drug use. Local residents see the two stations—especially the Gare du Nord—as being at the root of these problems, attracting what were euphemistically called "bad company" and "incivilities" that degrade the area, according to what I heard several planners, town hall officials, and inhabitants express at a meeting with the mayor of Paris's 10th district in June 2018. Despite these representations, the 10th as a whole has been gentrifying, leading to urban renewal projects that often sought in part to create barriers to "bad company" coming in on the trains.[10] The area surrounding the station is often viewed as a non-place transit area characterized by temporary housing, scam artists, and many urban ills, "an interstitial domain" separating proper Paris from the northeast banlieue.[11] Such a depiction raises the question of what makes a neighborhood and who gets to claim it as their own.

For many of the West Africans who commuted from suburbs and met at the station, the area surrounding it *was* their neighborhood—even though they did not live there. It was where Moroccan, Chinese, and French café and shop owners knew them as regulars, where they went to the post office, pharmacy, and even hospital, and often where they drank their morning coffee and had dinner in the evening, before taking the train to sleep in a shared apartment. When they had a disagreement with a friend at the station, they would wander down to the Gare de l'Est to see who they would meet there, or wander up to Barbès to see what was being bought and sold among the street sellers, sometimes going a bit farther north to the "African market" at the metro Château Rouge.

For the West African adventurers and the young African-French men who socialized there, the area around the station *was* their neighborhood. Their practices suggest that habitation—sleeping in a place—was not the only criterion for belonging to an urban area. The way they saw it, the neighborhood was not a border zone separating east from west, but rather a point of confluence bringing together the many strands of their urban lives in France, united by the station. Yet they could not make the same claims on this public space as those who resided there. White residents of these neighborhoods claimed that "African" stores, services, and people were invading or incorrectly using public spaces on which residents alone had a legitimate claim.[12] Many times I saw police officers, café owners, and station officials question the right of Lassana, Amadou, and Ibrahim to hang out in the area—inside the station and in the surrounding neighborhood.

Like the majority of the Gare's passenger traffic, Lassana and his adventurer friends commuted in each day from the city's northeastern suburbs. The Gare du Nord has been produced as an urban space through its relationship to these poorer outlying districts—areas that sociologist Trica Danielle Keaton calls "outer-cities."[13] Outer-cities are products of immigration, postwar urban planning, and de facto segregation.[14] They uphold separations between rich and poor, French and foreign, white and black.

Transportation planners would try to maintain such separations in a place that is a gateway both to European capitals like London and Amsterdam and to the outer-cities. When the commuter rail was built in the 1970s, it was almost entirely blocked off from the rest of the station, and some of that separation is still maintained today: travelers on the high-speed trains use the upper levels, while those taking the metro and commuter rail remain on the lower levels where the revolt took place. One of the employees of a station clothing shop in the commuter rail area invited my research assistant, Sorélia Kada, to observe the "social and ethnic divide" between employees and clients in the stores "above" and those in the stores "below." "Above," she explained, "there are people going to the provinces or abroad, and they are from the middle and higher classes. Below in the basement there are more often people and shop sellers who come from an immigrant background, near the commuter line going to the urban periphery."

The rebuilding of the eastern wing of the station in the early 2000s was meant to create an area that unites these different kinds of transport and populations by directing all foot traffic to a large central atrium that would make the station into the "exchange hub" (*pôle d'échanges*, translated in planning language as "multimodal hub") where users would be united and the station would become more "democratic." Without the millennial renovation that created this new central transit exchange area, it is unlikely that the 2007 revolt would have occurred on the scale that it did. The event expressed the frustration and anger of people who were discriminated against inside and outside the station, despite the fact that it had just been rebuilt as an ideal of democratic, accessible public space.

## SOCIAL PRODUCTION: HOW WAS THE STATION REBUILT? AND FOR WHOM?

Amadou—"Sécurité Sans Salaire"—used to hold court inside the new glassy entrance of the Gare du Nord, part of the station's major renovation. The big, open, light-filled arena that exists today was the product of a paradigm shift, as transportation planners and architects were rethinking how and for whom they designed

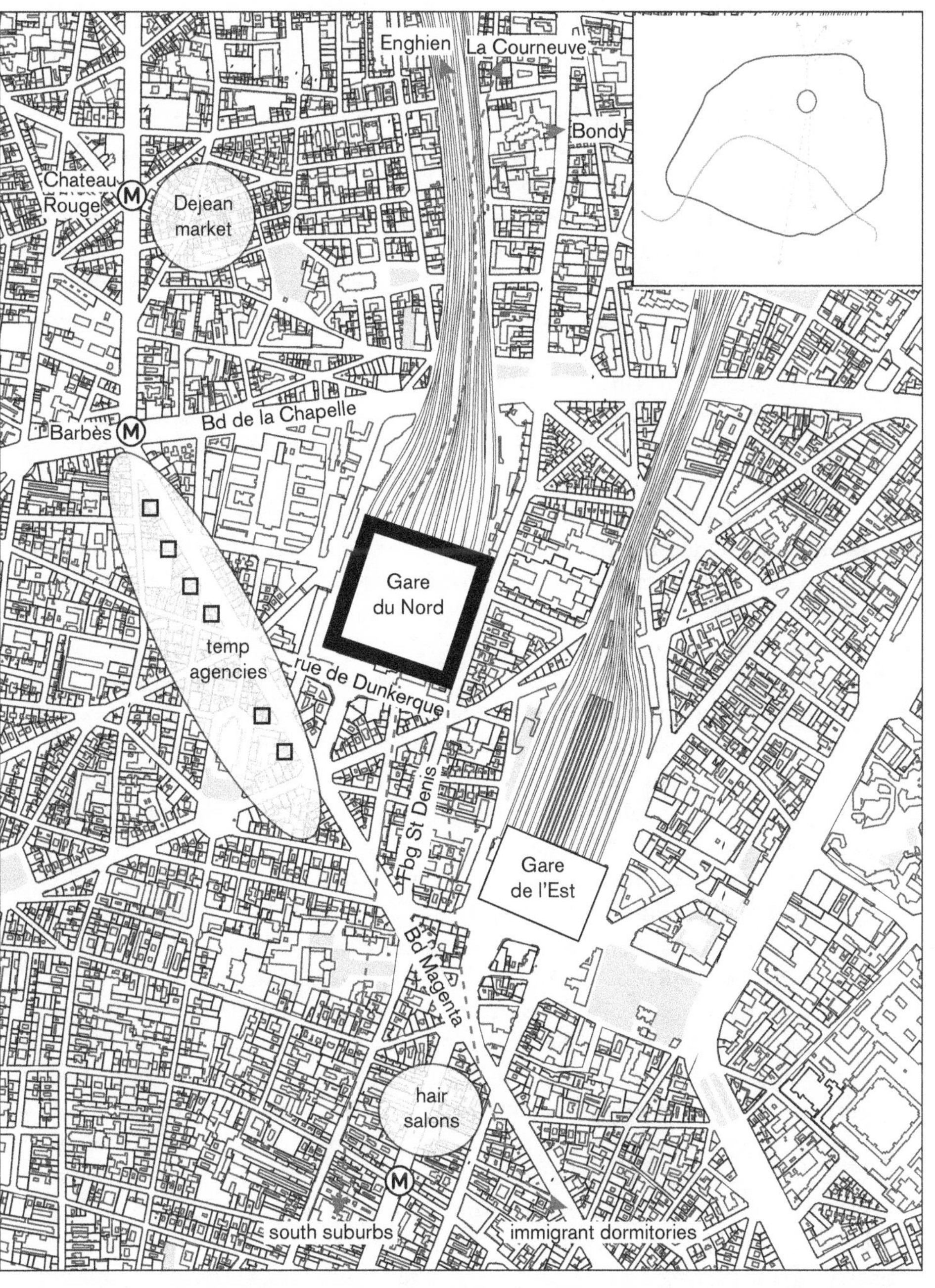


MAP 2. West African migrant landmarks in the Gare du Nord neighborhood in Paris. Thomas Massin.

infrastructure. Designers sought to shift transit from the background to the foreground of urban life, stressing the social and political importance of public transportation, and aimed to create a space that would foster what they called "social exchange." As I will explore, the social practices of migrants and others who used the station were left out of the planner's vision and dismissed as marginal. Yet it was these migrants' actions that corresponded the most to the planners' hopes that urban transport would become more than just a functional nuisance. Though it was far from what architects and planners intended, we can read the revolt of 2007 as a referendum on the success—not the failure—of their design, as users engaged with this public space, defying the idea that public transit is functional, banal, and apolitical.

In 1977, the RER was inaugurated and the Gare du Nord soon because the hub for northern and northeastern commuter lines linking suburbs to the capital. This change would dramatically increase passenger traffic and add several new train lines to the long-distance rail and metro already established at the station. RER passenger traffic would quickly surpass the TGV lines to comprise the majority of the now over seven hundred thousand passengers who use the station each day. The initial solution to deal with increasing passenger traffic in the 1970s resembled nineteenth-century planning control measures: the SNCF cordoned off the RER and its passengers from the longer-distance trains housed in the original terminus. The RER section was built below street level, and long corridors connected the two parts. On the street-level above the RER, adjoining the nineteenth-century structure, was a parking lot with no pedestrian access from the façade. These new areas created more spaces for underground economic activities, drug use, and youth prostitution, at which the 1980s renewal projects would take aim. When the international Eurostar terminal was completed in the 1990s, politicians and the SNCF pushed through an overall redesign of the station, with a focus on the commuter rail area.[15]

French transportation planners define the "exchange hub" as a transit node that facilitates interchange between different modes of transportation and links the city with its transportation network.[16] The millennium design of the station incorporates a hodgepodge of objectives—from transparency and democracy in open public space to ensuring circulation and security to promoting social mixing and providing a commercial space for shopping and leisure. These goals sit uneasily next to each other, yet together they create the framework in which the Gare du Nord was rebuilt and where the revolt of 2007 took place, enabled by this design.

"Infrastructural violence": that is how Paul, one of the lead architects behind the major renovation of the Gare du Nord referred to what the station did to users before he and his team transformed it in the 1990s. He described a world of shadows, where passengers were shuttled through long, dark corridors to transfer trains. It was also a segregated public space, where the high-speed terminal was cordoned off from the commuting masses on the RER. Only a connecting tunnel allowed for the transfer, minimizing the contact between passenger classes. It was as if there were multiple Gares du Nord, each with separate publics, and an opaque system making transfer between them difficult.[17] Paul explained that the purpose of the renovation was to create an integrated form where sections "mutually enriched each other," instead of remaining isolated.

The new design was ambitious: not only would it create a more efficient transfer system, it would also improve the social environment and promote "social mixing," creating what the architects imagined as "democratic" public space.[18] As Lucien, another main architect put it, the station should be a "place of exchange" where "social mixing" can occur, and where individuals are not "segregated" by their mode of transport. It would be a flagship example of urban "living-together" in which physical integration of the built environment stands in for the successful assimilation of diverse groups into the body politic.[19]

The goals the architects expressed—of "social mixing" (*la mixité sociale*) and "living-together" (*le vivre-ensemble*)—dodge the multicultural connotations that similar terms would imply in the US context. As anthropologist Andrew Newman points out, "*Mixité sociale* represents a highly Republican way to speak about difference by valorizing a controlled version of diversity without actually giving lip service to any specific group."[20] It emphasizes socioeconomic and sometimes generational diversity. I have heard Paris city planners invoke "social mixing" in the same breath that they discount other forms of heterogeneity that express themselves in urban space, such as racial or ethnic-based categories. As a deputy mayor in Paris's diverse 18th district explained to me in 2013, using such categories—even in the context of mixing—would be an endorsement of "communitarianism."

Station architects reflected a broader orientation in transportation planning that moved from restrictive spatial control to an open-space model meant to encourage this vision of mixing and reduce "infrastructural violence." Yet the design has led to new and expanding practices of surveillance and policing, a result that calls into question whether or not the space is now more "democratic" than it once was.[21] As they tackled the sometimes contradictory imperatives of a quasi-public space, they sought to articulate a social vision for transportation to guide their efforts.

The new station took shape in two key architecture and planning offices: the Paris Metro's concept and future planning office (the Prospective), and the architecture firm AREP (Aménagement Recherche Pôles d'Echanges, a subsidiary of the SNCF). The high concepts of new French urbanism conceived in these places had to deal with the infrastructural exigencies of transportation design and the networks and traffic that had expanded exponentially throughout the twentieth century.

The "Prospective Office" of the Parisian metro system (RATP) is a locus of metropolitan public transportation planning and design whose team leans heavily toward what they call conceptual work, or the "soft side" of transportation planning.

Their concepts have created a Parisian version of the "exchange hub" model that would also guide the architects' renovation of the Gare du Nord. Their offices are nestled high in the glassy building that houses the Paris metro headquarters overlooking the Seine river. In order to access the Prospective office, I had to obtain a badge that looks like a metro pass and then use it to get through a set of turnstiles similar to those in the subway. I then entered an elevator that took me up to the seventh floor, where a young man in thick-framed glasses and slim dark jeans invited me into his office. Glossy books on urban design dotted the minimalist shelves. I could not have felt farther removed from the Gare du Nord.

He introduced me to their work: creating Metro 2.0, a new model of urban transit that would emphasize the social and commercial exchanges of individuals, not the functional movement of undistinguished flows.[22] The Prospective was partnering with a media lab at the Massachusetts Institute of Technology (MIT) to help engage users in games and interactions that connected public transportation to virtual spaces through smartphone technology. Transportation should not only be about getting from point A to point B, but also about playful enjoyment and sociability, and their job at the Prospective is to create spaces propitious to those goals.

The office head, whom I will call Bruno, was not interested in my project. He shifted in his chair before telling me, "Train stations, they're from the nineteenth century, so the past." He explained that stations are where you are *station*ary—where you stop or park, where things are static. They had already moved beyond that model toward more mobile horizons. The older model of transit design, Bruno told me, is precisely what led to the unintelligibility of interconnections in the metro, the endless corridors and dark hallways, the stairways leading up and down and up again with which passengers in the Parisian metro are familiar. Exchange hubs would offer more usable interconnections between modes of transportation, as well as spaces for leisure, art exhibitions, and shopping.

Though it was not made explicit, the exchange hub and Metro 2.0 help create public spaces that are increasingly governed by private interests and initiatives. Over the last decades, many stations have become spaces of leisure: the nearby Gare de l'Est where trains arrive from Germany and eastern France was renovated to include a mall design inspired by German-style Christmas markets (Weihnachtsmarkt), the Gare Saint Lazare was rebuilt into a three-story mall, and London's St. Pancras station houses an upscale shop corridor, champagne bar, and hotel complex to welcome Eurostar passengers arriving from the Gare du Nord.[23] When the Gare du Nord was rebuilt, it was not only about getting rid of onerous interconnections; accompanying the rebuilding was also the construction of a new mezzanine level above the commuter line trains, with over one hundred stores and restaurants. The mall was part of the attempt to make an exchange hub out of a nineteenth-century environment, but it also corresponds to the partial re-privatization of a public good. The important thing for Bruno, though, was to invest in future-looking projects that would finally realize the true dream of the mobile exchange hub—of which, he said, the Gare du Nord, a station of the past, could not be.

The architects of the new Gare du Nord, however, were guided by exchange-hub ideals. Lucien, who had been working on the Gare du Nord since the 1990s, explained the guiding logic of his firm as we were sitting in a glass-enclosed room in the middle of the second floor of their open-space office warehouse in Paris, visible from the floors above and below. He framed their projects as guided by "openness" and "transparency," as well as by historical continuity with the nineteenth-century iron-and-glass architectural paradigm, a sentiment echoed by his colleagues working on the project.[24] They emphasized how the exchange-hub logic mimics the language of democratic values: in a separate interview, Paul also mentioned transparency, exchange, and tolerance.[25]

Lucien stressed two major principles of their renovation: first, the importance of light and clarity, and second, the idea of bringing the city street "into the station," achieved through the glass façade that faces a row of typical nineteenth-century Parisian buildings. In addition to following the line of historical design, Lucien and his colleagues sought to build a form "open to the future," within which architects and city planners yet to come would find enough room to create new spaces according to the demands of their day.

The AREP website highlights the relationship between the concept of transparency and the resulting Gare du Nord exchange hub that they built (what they refer to as the "Paris-Nord Transilien").[26] As the website puts it, the structure has "a double passenger shed [that] is completely transparent and houses the new Transilien suburban services which, structured around a central well featuring four superimposed levels with natural lighting, provides clear, safe accessways to the different transport services." Transparent goals did not always transfer well into the concrete station from the passengers' perspective: the "superimposed levels" led to overlapping staircases and escalators, creating an almost Escher-esque tableau that made it difficult for people to figure out which stairway to take to transfer from one form of transport to another. After years of research, I still sometimes got stuck on the wrong level and had to double back.

The other problem was that the project ignored many kinds of exchange and sociality, presuming a normative subject-user who resembled urbanists in social class and background (this presumption is made clear by the computerized people populating the visual models of the redesigned station).[27] Bruno, for example, was not interested in the people who used the station for social purposes, such as West African migrants or outer-city youth. "You anthropologists," he said to me when I brought up these alternative uses of a transport hub, "You're more interested in marginalized populations and minority uses [*usages minoritaires*]. Here at the

FIGURE 5. The suburban transit exchange hub of the Gare du Nord designed by AREP architects, 2007. Claude Shoshany.

Prospective, we want to understand the average user." Bruno suggests a classification of station populations and reinforces the normative "average user" as being at odds with the black men who socialize at the station. In such models, as anthropologist Ahmed Kanna puts it in his work on Dubai, "the question of 'what is built for whom' is ignored or consigned to secondary status."[28]

Bruno the poet-engineer can look out from his desk over the Seine river and conceive of a space where fluid circulation coexists with fluid and playful social interaction, much like Michel de Certeau's image of the voyeuristic planner in the high-rise, far removed from the people below.[29] West Africans who spend long afternoons in the front square and the black French teenagers who hang out in the station mall (along with other marginalized groups) stay put for too long, interfering with the types of exchange-in-movement that the Prospective model seeks. At the same time, users that Bruno dismisses as marginal are precisely those who make the space into a meaningful social environment—just not in the way that the planners imagined.

Although the station design was meant to promote openness, social mixing, and transparency, it was blind to eruptions of difference—such as those based on race and ethnicity—as they manifest in public spaces or are used by the police. Since the new design was completed, patrols have increased, using longer lines of sight that offer more opportunities for surveillance. Police targeted groups of young, black men for ID checks, whom they accused of bothering passengers and loitering—that is, staying put in a site of circulation. I saw officers hide behind strategically placed walls to catch people jumping the turnstiles without a ticket. The status of the Gare du Nord as an international border (like in airports) gave them significant legal latitude in stopping people within the station without having to provide a justification.

All of the above makes it seem like the new Gare du Nord would provide ideal fodder for cultural critic Frederic Jameson, for whom modern architecture transmits late-capitalist ideology. The station embodies the contradictions of "transparent democracy," proposing to provide tolerance while increasing surveillance and policing activities. As a space of mass transit, the Gare du Nord also embodies the contradictions of its own mission, which are magnified in an era in which urbanism is meant to be democratic and where the space must assure fluid circulation while controlling access for hundreds of thousands of passengers each day.

## RACE AND UNCIVIL ATTENTION

Like the offices where they were imagined, the guiding concepts of social exchange, democracy, and transparency appear to be distant from the texture of social life in the railway hub. Everyday life at the station contradicted the abstract language that planners and architects used, which did not acknowledge difference and categories used in practice. The exchange hub model presupposed a particular kind of subject using public transportation, a citizen-user who is undifferentiated from and equal to all other individual users. When the design became experienced space, these assumptions had to confront lived reality.

Yet the design was not a failure when it came to social exchange. It created new spaces for social gathering and led to more interactions between passengers. The underground mall became a destination in itself for young people from the outer-cities to meet and socialize. Those who had designed the space, however, did not believe that such "marginal uses"—as Bruno put it—corresponded to what they had meant by "social exchange." Perhaps this is because Lassana, Ibrahim, Amadou, and their friends, as well as others using public transportation to socialize, did not abide by the norms of what sociologist Erving Goffman calls "civil inattention," in which people both acknowledge yet refrain from interacting with strangers in public spaces.[30] In addition to going against behavioral norms, social interactions at the station foregrounded categories of race and ethnicity that French public policy and urban planning language tend to ignore.

Many scholars have argued that race is taboo in French Republican ideology, yet forever cropping up in practice and policy. Urban planning in France has developed an elaborate language for indicating race without mentioning it explicitly. According to Mostafa Dikeç, French urban policy has produced a vocabulary for expressing difference in spatial terms that stand in for culture, ethnicity, race, and religion.[31] The term *jeunes de banlieue* ("suburban youth"), for example, uses a spatial designation to index non-white immigrant-origin inhabitants of public housing. Train passengers, station employees, and police officers often used race, national origin, and ethnicity to describe and categorize people.

The revolt of March 2007 at the station may have been an exceptional event where the racialization of space erupted into the forefront, catalyzing a revolt. But there was nothing exceptional about the ticket check or the police stop; race was an everyday part of the station environment, part of social interactions and police practices. There were frequent ruptures in the veneer of civil inattention meant to ensure order and tranquility among the crowds using public transport. In these moments, race and other ideas about difference came to the fore.

Frequent police ID checks and bodily searches, preponderantly directed at those perceived as black or Arab, are examples of unjust police practices that help to legitimate differential treatment by advancing the notion that people of color are dangerous and in need of control. Many white station employees working in the mall area appreciated the patrols. In February 2010, Inès, a French-Moroccan woman working at a station clothing store pointed out the growing frequency of police stops in the station, when I asked her if she noticed any. "I see it many times a day," she said, "And for what? For being here, I guess. That's all."

Her white, French-Portuguese colleague Laura overhead our conversation and protested, "But, the police aren't going to just stop them for nothing, right? They are probably delinquents; the police know them; they already have files on them." Inès widened her eyes and looked at me as if to say, "Are you kidding me?"

"I don't know," I said cautiously, trying not to fall into a lecturing tone, "I mean, even the police chief admitted in an interview that they target young black men because they don't want them hanging out here." Laura shrugged. I continued. "Most of these guys, I know some of them, and they're really just looking to hang out with their friends just like everyone."

"But why hang out with your friends here?" she asked, gesturing at the escalators outside the store that led to the commuter rail tracks. "I mean, go to a café or to a park or somewhere; that's where we go." Inès shook her head and went to help a customer at the cash register. Her colleague used the pronoun "we" to draw a line between the young black men being stopped at the police and her own group. White workers at the station used the word "French" to contrast normative behavior to the black men situated as not-French (though many of the young men hanging out at the mall were born in France). Inès's colleague voiced what many employees and frequent users of the station also pointed out to me: that there was no good reason for anyone to hang out here, because it was for taking a train or shopping.

There was nothing unusual about young people socializing at a mall. But the presence of black men in this transit public space made them explicit targets of police attention, and the police chief did admit in an interview to doing the stops not to catch criminal behavior but to get them to leave the area because they were bothering "normal" passengers. Speaking to the writer Joy Sorman in 2011, a station employee said that he had to remove homeless people sitting on the benches; when Sorman asked why, he responded that "those benches are for real people."[32] Much like homeless folks, young black men do not benefit from the same rights to use this space as white train passengers.

Police stops attempted to exclude certain people—in particular young black men—from socializing in the station. They also bolstered the racial boundaries Inès's colleague Laura expressed, which seek to delegitimize the claim these men have on this particular space and on French public space writ large. When presented with the hard evidence of racial profiling, the two police officers who agreed to speak to me both lamented the stop and then justified them by claiming that those who are stopped are the ones who disrupt circulation and bother train users. They adopted a perspective that saw young black men socializing at the station not as "real people" or "passengers" but rather as "delinquents" or "marginal gang members" involved in criminal activity. They were matter out of place, dangerous outsiders disturbing social order by their very presence: just "for being here," as Inès put it.

Racial distinctions are part of vernacular classification schemes that reinforce the idea that certain people—in this case, Black and Arab immigrant and immigrant-origin men from the outer-city—do not belong in central French public spaces. As a Gare du Nord shop employee commented to journalist Léna Mauger in 2007, "They dance, they sing. You would think you're in their village (au bled)! They don't even say hello. They act permanently aggressive."[33] The employee appealed to a normative order that opposes "their village" and its corresponding behavior to proper public space interaction. She refers to the importance of "saying hello" in public spaces (a norm followed when service is involved, such as in a café or bakery). She contrasts this brief "bonjour" with the boisterous sociality she attributes to the youth, who "dance and sing." In a few seconds, and with a few well-chosen words, she manages to distinguish the Gare du Nord, a French public space, from this type of behavior by placing it in the African village (*le bled*). Her speech belies the proximity of former colonies and their role in metropolitan French formations: she uses the Arabic word "bled" (country) for "village," a lexical borrowing that has become common usage in France, and often refers to French villages such as one's hometown. Such borrowings illustrate the difficulty in separating the "national" present from an imperial past, much as the history of the Gare du Nord illustrates.

By describing minority youth socializing as disorderly, she opposes "their" behavior to French civilizational order. The lack of adherence to "civil inattention" in the public space of transport can lead to negative sanctions. Youth socializing at the station—staying put in a space of circulation—resists this normative order by proposing an alternative use for this transit space. The employee points to the power of their actions to transform the space, a result of boundary transgression and spatial confusion as the "bled" comes to define the metropolitan railway terminal.

Racial and ethnic designations provided a common frame to interpret station social life in the 2010s. Françoise, a woman who worked at the stand selling French sausages and cheese to tourists, complained that the station had been "blackened" over time and was now "too dirty to clean." She pointed to the graying and cracked tiles. Her husband added that the "young Arabs" who hang out in the station often steal sausages "even though they don't eat them because of their religion." They see the police as powerless to do anything other than "ineffective" stop-and-search methods. The store caters to tourists, said Françoise, and the location gives them good opportunities to profit. At the same time, they have to "put up with the delinquent youth who blacken the station . . . like those who started the riot." This Auvergnat provincial family sells "typical" French food products to tourists and identifies context as a site for both transit and exchange as tourists purchase a piece of France to bring home. Their products symbolize typical Frenchness, which, in their view, is what the station ought to represent. The darkening floor tiles she points to links the Gare de Nord's black users with dirt and pollution, the police stop is a method to control for this dirt, though she finds that is inefficient. They draw a boundary between users in racialized terms, using elements from the built environment to reinforce the racist logic that equates dirt and blackness on the one hand, and cleanliness and whiteness on the other.

The everyday exclusionary tactics based on racialized readings of this public space contradict the hopeful vision of social and commercial exchange proposed by the planners and architects. The emphasis on appropriate interaction and inappropriate sociability of certain station-goers echoes the moral valence given to norms of "civility" in diverse public spaces. Behavioral norms function as a screen for race, separating the average users from those who are marginal or matter-out-of-place.

Those norms support the consensus around civility that requires users of such spaces to engage in civil inattention or risk being accused of bothersome behavior. The behavioral norm allows for the police and other station users to parse the mass of travelers into legible populations, and thus to help maintain the boundary between periphery and center. This distinction translated into policing practices that targeted black young men who socialized in the commercial mall area of the station. These practices in turn reveal the boundaries and differentiations within this French public space, creating the conditions for the 2007 revolt.

## A BANAL TICKET STOP

On March 27, 2007, Angelo H. was heading into the metro without a ticket. Two metro officials (called "controllers") saw him and tried to stop him. According to reports, he refused to comply with them and the police were brought in to arrest him. Rush hour was just beginning, and other passengers noticed the commotion. They later described how the police wrestled H. to the ground and some people yelled at the police to stop. This drew more attention to the incident and a crowd formed, including many of the young people who had come to the station to hang out with their friends. They were on the lowest level of the new part of the station, visible to anyone on the upper levels or stairways connecting them.

Why did a "banal ticket stop"—as newspaper reports called it, it was something that happened hundreds of time a day—create all of this commotion? The perspective of an amateur video, taken in the aftermath of the ticket stop, offers a panorama of the multi-level new section of the station. The confrontation unfolded on the horizontal and vertical dimensions that this design enables, as police stood in a line on one side of the ticket barriers on the bottom floor while above them spectators gathered on staircases to watch the action alongside other teams of police making their way across the overhead walkways, some filming the action below with small video cameras. Ticket turnstiles form a long line on the lowest level of the high-ceilinged rebuilt section of the station. The central atrium provided long lines of site across three floors, with the turnstiles in full view no matter where onlookers were standing, drawing attention to the crowd that gathered around them. Media presence and the RER trains helped to rekindle the commotion: when television cameras arrived, witnesses said that participants texted their friends in the suburbs to join in by taking the commuter line into the station.

The many who commented after the event—witnesses, participants, politicians, police, security agents, station employees—had conflicting accounts of what happened and why it happened. In a conversation with Joy Sorman in 2011, a station security official attributed the incident to a policing error: "You must not keep the incident in the place where it occurred. You must immediately evacuate the individual, remove him from his group, extract him from the site. In this case he was kept [in the place he was stopped] and then it was all over." What mattered was visibility—the fact that the incident could be seen from many perspectives thanks to the new station design. The neutral language of technical policing had evolved to allow him to refer obliquely to the existence of different groups in public space.

Rudy, a railway police officer who had migrated to France from Madagascar, offered a different analysis when I spoke to him in November 2010. He was one of the first to arrive at the scene. For Rudy, the broader context of race-based policing led users to misinterpret what they saw as they entered the metro. "Passers-by suddenly start yelling 'racism' because they see a black man being arrested by white police officers," he explained. He thought they saw the whole thing through the lens of the 2005 uprisings, still fresh in their minds. New tactics of police repression, he said, further contributed to people's mistrust of the police, which in turn was what had led to the "riot."

Who participated in it? The consensus in news reports and political speeches, and among many people I spoke to, was that "suburban youth" of African descent were the "rioting demonstrators." Photographs in the major daily newspapers supported this representation. Even Lassana, Amadou, and their friends blamed the same group—the "renois"—for looting stores and destroying property, contributing to the notion that young black people at the station were potential rioters or delinquents. Rudy, however, disagreed with these accounts. He was displeased with news reports that reinforced the image that black youth were the ones looting stores during the riot.

"I stopped a white, well-dressed girl from the 16th [one of Paris's wealthiest districts] who was stealing underwear from the lingerie store!" he told me. He was convinced that the Interior minister had called in the cameras and journalists himself to ratchet up the stakes of the event. As more people arrived from the suburbs, he explained, "they stole things in solidarity with other people against the police." Rudy's account suggests that the event was not the result of a policing error, or of delinquents taking advantage of a situation. It was, rather, the broader climate of tension between the police and station users that created an "explosion."

Both the police and the participants in the revolt tried to use the station interior to their respective advantage. An amateur cell phone video posted online captures how important the built space of the new exchange hub was for both police and those who revolted against them. In it, we see several teams of police in riot gear standing on the upper staircases that overlooked the crowd below. The video lingers on two officers, themselves filming the crowds from above, then shifts to a military patrol (in the station as part of the French antiterrorism security plan *Vigipirate*) on the mezzanine level. On the bottom level, police positioned themselves on one side of the ticket turnstiles. A group of mostly young men stood opposite them, on the other side. The two groups aligned as if in battle, in a face-off across a line of turnstiles, while police and passengers mixed on the stairways above them. Within a few minutes, other police teams managed to clear most of the upper staircases and passageways, taking over the upper level observation area. As they did that, however, the group on the lowest level expanded. While this was happening, the remaining passengers observing from the stairs were yelling and whistling.

The video shows that, contrary to what many politicians portrayed as a chaotic riot, the crowd united in chanting explicit political messages. They started chanting, "Police everywhere, justice nowhere," a reference to the slogans of May 1968. After it died out, the camera cut to a new angle, filming people chanting "Sarkozy, son of a whore!" Two members of the crowd threw beverage bottles toward the police and the yelling escalated in volume. The turnstiles helped to maintain the separation between the police on one side and the protesters on the other. Suddenly, the video becomes jumpy and everyone, including the cameraman, ran backward into the underground mall area, screams echoing. We see one last glance of the standoff scene—a smoky haze obscuring shadowy figures scattering behind it. The police had thrown at least two tear gas containers.

The crowd of people could go only in one direction—into the low-ceilinged underground of the station, away from the exits. Throughout the entire moment of confrontation in the new part of the terminal, other passengers continued to file past the action, some pausing and then moving on toward their trains, while others stopped to comment or join the protestors. As the evening continued, dwindling groups started fires in garbage cans and there were a few attempts to bash in station property—one photo shows a young man taking a long stick to a plastic-encased advertisement poster. By 11 p.m., everything was calm, but "the forces of order remained vigilant all through the night, anticipating further riots."[34] They did not come, but the event would continue to reverberate in French political debates in the weeks and months that followed.

The main presidential candidates gave speeches about the event, and Nicolas Sarkozy passed through the station to comment on it. He praised the police and condemned the Gare du Nord as an unlawful public space, saying a democracy demanded "a minimum of order, of respect, of authority, of tranquility." In a frequently quoted sound bite from the most popular nightly news show in France, the far-right-wing candidate Philippe de Villiers called the riot the work of "ethnic gangs" and "barbarians" who "think that this is *their* territory." Sarkozy called them "hoodlums," "swindlers," and "cheats." His opponent, Ségolène Royal, interpreted the event diagnostically, as Rudy did. For her, the event "illustrates a climate of tension" and the violent relationship between "the police" and "the population."[35]

"That's all too complicated," complained Soumi, a black teenager who hung out by the Footlocker, when I asked him in 2008 what he thought about the various representations of the event. "The media and everything, the riot, we've had enough of that. We don't want to talk about it anymore. I'm not *caille-ra*," he added, using the inversion slang term for "scum." "We're here to see our friends, maybe meet some girls. It wasn't what you all think. Everyone who saw it was mad. You know, they just saw a guy getting taken down by the police and they said, what is that? I wasn't there but it was too much. We heard some yelling so we went to see what was going on, maybe we could have some fun. But when we saw what was happening, we thought, OK, let's do this. Our friends were there and they saw it, and they said, we're annoyed with this. Every day we get stopped [by the police]. They just said, enough. Enough. At some point, you can't any more. The cops can't just do whatever."

Soumi and his friends came to the Gare du Nord to meet up with friends who did not live in the same suburbs as they did. It was a useful network nodal point where they could see those friends and spend time with them outside of the watchful eyes of parents and older siblings in the neighborhoods where they lived. It had also been made into a mall, with lots of stores that targeted young people. The main discussions around the event and its participants—including from West Africans at the station—reinforced the idea that young black men were the main instigators and participants. The color of their skin and the fact that they spent time at a railway station were cited as reasons for believing that they must be delinquents at odds with the police. They were also young folks hanging out at the mall, a practice that teenagers of many backgrounds engage in across the world.[36] The difference was that they often experienced belittling interactions with the police, which helped spark their reaction to what happened on the afternoon of March 27, 2007. "We've had enough," as Soumi put it.

Whatever the various interpretations or reasons for participating, the evening-long revolt challenged the veneer of tolerance, democracy, and exchange that had guided the station's renovation. In the riot, the contradictions of the exchange hub came to the forefront: it was built as a space that promotes social mixing and democracy while policing and surveilling populations through racial classification. Participants made the architect and planners' principles of exchange come alive by making the station into a meaningful space for a political action of protest that united the many types of people brought together by public transportation. By using the leftist slogan "police everywhere, justice nowhere," the crowd used a political message that connected them to the French student activists of 1968. They refused the normative and legal contexts of the space of public transit, the backdrop of a script that casts station actors either as "real people"—that is, inattentive clients of public transportation, or as hoodlums and scum. Enlivening fears of disorder, the muscled intervention of the police highlighted for many onlookers the discrimination faced by black people using public space. Two years after the *banlieue* uprisings, the police were still using force to reinforce a boundary. The reaction was a collective action that transgressed the boundaries represented physically by the ticket barriers, legally by the police stop, and conceptually by the racial categories embodied in the spatial term *suburban youth*.

Police justified targeting black youth in the station by appealing to their mandate to uphold public order and maintain fluid circulation. According to one police officer quoted in the left-leaning French weekly magazine *Marianne*, "suburban youth" congregated in groups, blocking circulation and bothering station users. Police officers, he said, targeted them for identity checks not to discover whether any laws were being broken but in order to dissuade them from loitering, from staying put in a site meant for circulation.[37] In other parts of the capital, people defended the right for young people to gather and even protest. But not at the Gare du Nord, where such actions were construed as out of place.

The riot was a struggle over what this space meant, who it was for, and how people ought to act within it. It was a struggle over who has a real right to the city, and who is included in the ideals of social mixing.[38] The sudden action of hundreds of station users transformed the normal activities at the heart of the Gare du Nord. They brought the exchange hub to life—although not as its planners intended—and proposed a socially and politically meaningful vision for a transit hub. In its aftermath, the event's signification would go beyond the confines of public transportation and a Parisian railway station.

When Djibril, Amadou, and Lassana discussed the riot with me in 2010 in the context of their own experiences of being stopped by the police, they used its retelling to offer their own perspective on the station's populations, which superficially aligned with the police vision of black youth "delinquents" but also criticized the police's lack of ability to analyze the differences between the many groups who used the station. In a similar vein, a French-African rapper from the suburb Noisy-Le-Sec told a journalist: "Be careful; here we only accept the *entiers* [wholes] while the *Antillais* [people from the Caribbean] have other territories, such as Les Halles or La Defense." By "entiers," he meant Africans and people whose parents had come from Africa, which he opposed to Caribbean French folks who are often assumed to have lighter skin and mixed ancestry.[39] Citing other RER commuter rail hubs in the Paris region, he enforced a boundary unimagined by the police, which emphasized different histories of colonization and migration to France—one from Africa and one from the Caribbean.

In reality, "entiers" and "Antillais" moved in between all three sites, and several West Africans refused this exclusionary logic. "That's a renois perspective," observed Lassana when I showed him the quote. He replaced one distinction with another, "Everyone can come to the Gare du Nord." Using this moment of conflict as a foundation, they did not diminish the existence of difference in public space or claim "We are all French" (or black, or African), but rather proposed that it was an inclusive space where affiliations could shift and different groups coexisted. You can't see anything if you see it in black and white, as Amadou said about the French camera surveillance system.[40]

The revolt itself was a case where the ideals of equality in public space confronted unequal treatment through racial profiling.[41] The station renovation was intended to integrate the Gare du Nord into the urban life of the street, to democratize this semi-public, semi-private space, to increase transparency, and to foster social and commercial exchange. The built form that resulted from this design, however, led to increasing surveillance and policing based on racial categories.

When users revolted in 2007, they reacted to the paradoxes embodied by the exchange hub and they also brought it to life through collective action. They used and transformed the imperatives planners and designers imposed. Participants refused the differentiations that saw them as "matter out of place." But they did not dismiss the relevance of social boundary-making and even cultural difference in the social world of the station. Rejecting a discourse of sameness, they sought justice. They redrew boundaries that circumscribed them in space. They were not marginal to the center, not only blacks to white, but also renois, bledards, entiers and Antillais, carving out a space for their encounters. The revolt attempted to actualize the exchange hub dream of an open public space: one that did not gloss over difference and discrimination, but recognized it and addressed it head on.

It turned out that the answer to segregation and "infrastructural violence" was not the technical expertise of planners and architects, but rather collective action of those excluded from their models. From the French planners' perspective, the station is a "social space of democracy and transparency" for "average users." When a Congolese man was muscled to the ground by two policemen on March 27, 2007, the contradictions built into the station erupted into a revolt. Colliding forms of control and inequality were suddenly visible all at once, at the beginning of rush hour, in the middle of Europe's busiest transport hub.

## CODA

I must admit that most of the people who worked in the station's commuter rail mall rolled their eyes at me in 2009 when I asked about the "riot." They were suspicious of someone dredging up this event and resented that it had become an emblem of the Gare du Nord. Most employees highlighted other aspects of their work, such as their store's high profit margins, to offer a more positive image of their place of work. They indulged my questions because I was there so often, said Nicole, who worked at the Footlocker, and because I was a student from the United States, not a journalist. One person refused to discuss the revolt at all: Yann, a shop employee from Martinique who had been working at a station newsstand near where the confrontations with the police took place. He was a thoughtful and astute social observer, and I was sure he would have some insights about it. Yet he refused to recount what he remembered from that March evening. When I insisted, hoping that he would correct some of my own misperceptions, he replied with an account of a horrific event he had witnessed around the same time.

"Enough! Enough!" he exclaimed. "Everyone makes a big deal about the riot. But that was just for the television, the elections, all that. I was here but nothing was different, we just closed early. There are more important things, but no one talks about them. Like I was working one day and the police shot a man right here, an Algerian man, right here in front of the store. They said he had a gun, but he didn't have a gun and they shot him and he died—right there! And they just came so quickly; that was what surprised me, how quickly they came and cleaned up and took his body away. Ten minutes later, it was like nothing had ever happened here. No one did anything, just kept on walking toward their train, because that's what you do. But I saw it! Write about that!"

Yann challenged me to consider the blind spots that the focus on this event also created, as the "riot" story became so emblematic that it covered up other events, even the police killing of an unarmed man. My own inquiry, he suggested, was contributing to the process of what Michel-Rolph Trouillot has called "silencing the past," whereby events that challenge the official version and social order are suppressed and replaced with a more amenable story.[42] The police killing of this man and its quick cleaning up were, Yann argued, more revealing about how the French state controls marginalized populations, but these events did not fit into official narratives about who perpetrates violence and threatens public order.

By offering his account of the Algerian man who was shot and killed by station police officers, Yann points to the presence of state violence in public space. He blames the norm characterized as so-called "civil inattention" for creating a place where a man being shot could be ignored by commuters rushing to their train. Police claimed that they thought the older Algerian man was brandishing a gun (he was not) and so they shot him. It made the *fait divers* (miscellaneous news items) column of newspapers, but never became a media event with a political charge. Yann countered this silencing by narrating the shooting, this injustice that had sparked no uproar. By telling the story and refusing to discuss the revolt, he offers an alternative to the media, police, and even my ethnographic framing of the Gare du Nord.

Yann's story also illustrates how the violence that sparked the revolt is not exceptional or remarkable: it is an everyday part of a station redesigned to be democratic and transparent. As the physical boundaries that divided the nineteenth century station were removed throughout the twentieth century to favor smoother circulation, policing and surveillance adjusted to maintain the separations of French from foreign, outsider from native, average use from marginal, civil inattention from social engagement. But as a mobility hub with sometimes one million people going in and out of the station in a single day, maintaining such separations has proved impossible.

It is on this stage, set over almost two centuries of urban change and migration, that West African adventurers have encountered the Gare du Nord. Like several waves of migrants before them, they have refused the position that the station occupies in the French urban imaginary. To confront their marginalization and precarious legal and economic positions, they apply techniques learned on the road in cities from Abidjan to Douala to eke out a living in Paris. In doing so, they confront the police, hack French transit infrastructures, and connect the station to their transnational circuits of exchange and social ties.

Working across the many dividing lines crosscutting the station and cemented over 150 years, West Africans used the mobility hub to create an alternative moral community premised neither on the French state's nor on their elders' expectations, but rather on their quest to build ties outside of their immediate networks. Adventurers, faced with racial discrimination, uncertain legal status, and economic marginalization, tried to rewire the station's circuitry. Their goal was to build meaningful relationships, make money, and "become somebody" in this urban wilderness. This was what they called "the Gare du Nord method," and it is to this method and its consequences for understanding migration and French public space that I now turn.

3

# The Gare du Nord Method

## HOW TO DEAL WITH POLICING AND SURVEILLANCE

On a chilly afternoon in 2010, I was standing with Lassana, Amadou, Ibrahim, and a few of their friends at their usual after-work meeting spot in front of the Gare du Nord. As we were chatting, a young man approached the group to say hello. The others broke down laughing, doubling over as they shook the young man's hand in turn, placing their hands to their hearts. Amid a series of "No way!" and "It's been a while," they exchanged a long series of greetings in Soninke with the newcomer, interrogating him about where he had been and clapping him on the back, and then breaking out in laughter as he explained in Soninke what he had been up to. As the laughter died down, I asked what the fuss was all about.

"See this guy?" Lassana replied, indicating the newcomer. "We haven't seen him for a while. He hasn't been around. . . . He has been with the *sans papiers* [the undocumented workers' political movement]. He said he did that for a year and didn't get anywhere. He didn't find his happiness with the *sans papiers*, so now he's trying a different method. The Gare du Nord method."

Everyone broke into laughter when he said "the Gare du Nord method," the newcomer laughing the most heartily.

"They all come here eventually!" added Amadou. "What can the sans-papiers give us? Will they find us a job? A house? A woman? No, we can't get anything from them."

"You see, Julie," said Lassana, "We're all looking for happiness, and some find it at the Gare du Nord, and some haven't found it yet. But it's an *international* station here! There's room for everything."

"What's the Gare du Nord method?" asked Doulaye, who had recently arrived from Mauritania.

Lassana just shook his head, as if it was too much to explain. Amadou jumped in: "Look, new guy, the Gare du Nord method—"and here he paused, making sure everyone was paying attention—"It's something you have to learn from us. You have to learn it here. You learn from your elders. We'll teach you, if you're lucky."

"You, you're a *bledard*—you're an adventurer, or what?" Lassana asked Doulaye, who nodded. "You know struggle. You'll struggle for a while and you'll learn."

"First," Amadou told Doulaye, "There's the police." He nodded to the group of gendarmes walking around just inside the station. "You have to learn how to avoid them, but also how to work with them."

At this, Ibrahim gaped. "Ah, no, we don't work with the police here!" he proclaimed loudly, giving me a pointed look.

Amadou, shaking his head, cleared up this misunderstanding: "I mean, that you need to work with them, you have to work even if the police are here, you have to learn their methods," he said.

"The adventure is a lot of work," agreed Lassana. "And those gendarmes can be dangerous."

To explore the Gare du Nord method from the perspective of adventure, it is important to understand how those who practice it distinguish themselves from other groups at the station and from other West African migrants. As any observer would notice, they are not the only group of migrants who congregate there. There are many North African, Central African, and Eastern European men who also meet and socialize at the station. Lassana and Amadou highlighted the importance of encounter as the distinguishing characteristic of this method, claiming that these other groups "stayed among themselves" instead of seeking to meet new people at the station. (Based on my observations, they overstated this distinction.) "They only speak one language," Lassana claimed, not counting French. Lassana added that they did not come from a long line of adventurers as he did, and so they could not have inherited the same techniques. (When I asked how he could know this was true, he claimed that he had spent a long time at the station and knew everyone who was a regular there.)

As much as they used a West African cultural repertoire to differentiate themselves from other migrants who came to the station, they also distinguished themselves from fellow West Africans living in immigrant dormitories who, Lassana said, "stayed on the sidelines." They elevated their adventurer status by claiming they were living out a more authentic version of adventure by leaving the confines of their kin group and entering into an unknown and dangerous urban arena where a true initiatory journey could unfold.

Along with Doulaye, I began to learn more about what they meant by the Gare du Nord method, a set of strategies for overcoming risk and finding success on their voyages abroad that used this "international station" to make networks outside of their kin and village communities in France. Unlike the "sans-papiers method" that their comrade had tried, they did not seek the rights of citizenship, but rather sought to meet new people—including European women and potential patrons or employers. Such social relationships, they hoped, could help them find their own happiness and success abroad, and help them to move on from France. But before they could begin, as Amadou put it, the first thing to learn was how to work with the enormous police and security presence at the station, who could cut short their voyages before they had had a chance to succeed. To learn how to deal with the police, they had to either avoid them or figure out how to respond when subjected to the ID checks that police officers used with young black men at the station. The migrants I got to know at the Gare du Nord always emphasized their ability to confound policing strategies and I observed many inventive ways that they dealt with the police presence. But as innovative and ethnographically interesting as those strategies may be, it is important not to lose site of the fact that certain populations—especially Muslims, migrant workers, and people of color (of which they were all three)—are subject to police violence and abuse that goes underreported.[1] The stakes can be very high.

As many scholars and activists have argued, violent police encounters are not the result of a few bad police officers or poor police training. They are part of entrenched social inequalities and the economic, racial, and spatial segregation that was built into French cities.[2] Police practices, as Didier Fassin argues, seek to enforce not only public order but also the inequality of French "social order," in which immigrants and their children occupy a subordinate position.[3]

Keeping the larger structural framework of French urban policing in mind, this chapter examines how the fraught, difficult, and even dangerous interactions between West African migrants and the police produce new survival strategies, as adventurers try to transform the stops—meant to reinforce their inferior status—into moments where they can assert prestige and dignity. These unavoidable interactions have become a central part of their Gare du Nord method. By retelling their experiences of identity checks, they parlayed them into symbolic capital. Far from being a moment of pure control and subjugation, encounters with police also became important moments for enacting their adventurer personhood. As they did so, they remade the cultural framework of adventure to fit their circumstances in contemporary France.

By showing an ability to cope with the risks that came with migration, adventurers gained the respect of their peers, upholding dignity when it seemed that every representative of the French state was trying to undercut their goals for onward mobility. Some of the West Africans at the station who had legal status attracted police attention to confront or criticize the officers patrolling the Gare du Nord. They were not only socializing or hanging out with friends, but also doing the hard work that could help them get out of the suffering they faced as underemployed and often undocumented migrants. The encounter with the police could pose a real threat to their well-being, especially for those who were undocumented. But the successful negotiation of the identity checks became a key marker of the true adventurer, conferring social prestige in a situation of overall marginalization. By proving their resilience in this context, they also challenged the idea that the only legitimate places for Africans in France were as obedient hard workers or as subordinate victims deserving of care and pity.[4]

## POLICE CONTROLS

There was a reason why the Open Society Justice initiative used the Gare du Nord as one of its two main sites for their 2009 study of racial profiling and bias in French policing. It was because there were more visible police stops there than anywhere else inside the capital. The study proved what most people at the station already knew: men perceived to be black were eleven times more likely to be stopped and questioned by the police than men perceived to be white. A single day in the commuting life of Mamadou, a Malian man in his twenties, offers a sense of how pervasive these stops were at the time.

On April 5, 2010, he took the train from a suburban station near his apartment, where railway workers (called "controllers") stopped him and asked him to show a valid train ticket. When he arrived at Gare du Nord twenty minutes later, he was stopped again by rail ticket controllers. He said that there were too many people to stop everyone, so they seemed to single out "the other young black and Arab" men. He took another train to work; on his way back in the evening, he was stopped by three police officers at the Gare du Nord. They asked for his papers and searched him. After he was patted down, he watched other young black men being searched. One of them refused to show his ID and was taken into the police commissariat.

From the station, Mamadou went to buy something at the Barbès street market, a short walk from the Gare. As he descended into the Barbès metro with his shopping bag, he was stopped by a group of uniformed police officers and asked to show his ID. They asked for his name, birthday, and address and where he was going, and he answered as plainly as he could. Mamadou noticed that the officers were stopping "all the black men" exiting or entering the subway station—as they often did at that time at the Barbès metro. Once they verified his ID, he went back to the station to see some friends before heading home, where he was again asked by SNCF employees to show that he had a valid train ticket card. Mamadou admitted that this was not a typical day—"I'm only stopped once or twice, max"—but he wasn't surprised by it. "We are all used to it now," he said. Many of his friends at the station adopted this blasé attitude. But for those who were undocumented or had any police record or said the wrong thing or reacted in any way, the stakes were high. They all knew people who had been stopped and hurt by the police, or deported.[5]

Mamadou, like many of his friends, was stopped most often by the national police officers for identity checks, but he also knew the other patrols at the station. Adventurers put station security forces in a hierarchy: the gendarmes were the smartest and knew the station almost as well as they did; the RATP metro police were the strongest, the military personnel with their automatic weapons did not know much but were well trained. The officers they saw most often—the national police and the railway police—were at the bottom. "The SNCF police know more but they can't do anything, they don't even have guns. The police officers don't know anything," Lassana said of the national force. Most of his friends testified that at least once, those officers had used insults to provoke them.

They are not alone—the national police have been documented using racist and homophobic insults when stopping black men, and they have defended their use of such insults, for example, saying the racist term *bamboula* is "more or less appropriate" for police to use.[6] The term (a transformation of the word for "drum" in the Sarar and Bola languages spoken in Guinea) emerged as an insult during French colonial rule in West Africa.[7] It evoked the racist notion, popularized in the colonial encounter, that African men were both childlike and violent, and in need of civilization in order to tame an overflowing sexuality.[8] Three men stopped by the police at the Gare du Nord told me that officers called them derogatory terms for women—such as "slut" (*salope*). The police who use this language make the routine event of stopping someone into a display of sexualized domination. Many of the West African men who frequented the Gare du Nord had to deal with such degrading interactions on a daily or weekly basis.

In French, these routine stops are called *contrôles d'identité,* which I have translated as "identity (or ID) check"—in the sense of verifying a government-defined identity through official documents, such as a passport, resident permit, or national ID card. By law, everyone must carry at least one such document with them at all times. The check often includes a bodily search. Police need to provide probable cause for these stops, but in practice the police had a wide latitude to stop almost anyone they wanted almost anywhere they wished.[9] At the Gare du Nord, even this light constraint has been scrapped. Since transit hubs are considered to be high-priority security sites within the European Union, the police do not need to give a reason for stopping someone. The state of emergency declared after the November 2015 terrorist attacks in Paris have provided justification for intensifying patrols and police stops overall, and especially within hubs like the Gare du Nord. Legally, the station is like an airport, where anyone can be stopped and searched at any time.

*Contrôles* at the station are not arbitrary and ID verification is rarely their main objective. They target particular populations and are part of broader attempts to police immigrant and minority communities to control public spaces and "define what is in or out of place."[10] They are an example of what Simone Browne calls "racializing surveillance," which aims to "reify boundaries, borders, and bodies along racial lines."[11] According to a study by sociologist Florent Castagnino in 2015, the railway police team at the Gare du Nord used categories based on skin color and nationality to determine risk and differentiate among the station population.[12] Officers employ different forms of surveillance and policing according to the area of the station and their perceptions of populations who use it. The commuter rail level needs more direct policing and identity checks because, according to Castagnino's police interlocutors, there are many "blacks" and "Pakistanis" down there.

Police reinforce these racial boundaries and exclusion by deploying humiliation and disrespect strategically, such as when they use the informal pronoun *tu* with the West African men (and other men of color) whom they stop. Their practices are aimed at delegitimizing the right of those stopped to occupy public spaces. Riad, a French-Algerian employee at the Gare du Nord florist said in 2010 that he was stopped on his way to or from work once inside the station. "It's humiliating," he said. "They abuse their authority; they use *tu* when they ask for your papers. . . . Once, a police officer looked at my ID and then asked, 'You, do you work?' so I said, 'Why, are you hiring?' and he threatened to charge me with insulting an officer, so I let it go."[13] The station is a microcosm of French public space writ large, where police stop people of color without the pretext of legal protections.[14] Let us now look at how West Africans at the station reassert their place in French public space, drawing on and cultivating adventurer know-how to do so.

## PRECARITY AND POSSIBILITY: CONFRONTING RISK

The spaces of public transportation are infamous among immigrant populations for their heavy police presence, and the Gare du Nord is the example par excellence. "When I got to France," said Dembele, a Malian immigrant without papers who arrived in 2004, "everyone at the *foyer* (immigrant dormitory) told me, 'Avoid public transportation, and if you take it always buy your ticket.'" This advice is given enough that it has become a cliché, even reproduced in the 2014 French film *Samba*, about an undocumented West African migrant in Paris. Yet most migrants cannot avoid public transit because they rely on it to find work, get to work, and maintain the networks that will allow them to survive in the capital. To reduce the risk of being stopped, Dembele says he has memorized where the police go at certain times of day in order to avoid them. He always keeps an eye on entrances, exits, and escalators, ready to make a calm departure in case the police show up.

"It's the first thing you have to learn when you get here," explained Seydou, who had arrived in France the previous year after spending two years working on a farm in Spain. "The police are everywhere we go. At the station when we leave for work, and at our metro entrance when we go back home. What can we do? We don't want to go back. So you have to learn, be careful (*Tu dois apprendre, faire attention.*)." At the time, police teams were carrying out a method of ID verification where units of the police, under special order of the *procureur générale* (similar to the attorney general) would position themselves at key locations, such as metro exits where undocumented people would tend to congregate, and then stop hundreds and demand to see their papers. Undocumented migrants had to anticipate these police stops and avoid them. Dembele said he relied on his own careful observations. Lassana performed a simple but secret ritual of protection each morning that he had learned from his grandparents in Mali, which he said protected him from many threats, including the threat of deportation. Seydou and Doulaye learned what they could from the "old-timers" (*les anciens*)—the West Africans who had been coming to the Gare du Nord for decades.

Undocumented migrants were not the only ones threatened by these police stops. Police patrols would also perform targeted stop-and-search operations where they would verify IDs and railway tickets.[15] As we have already seen, the police claimed that they were not profiling or harassing these young men because, according to the police, they bother train passengers by congregating in large groups and making it difficult for others to pass. In other words, they were preventing fluid circulation. The police thus adopted the public identity check not to ferret out criminal activity but as a strategy to dissuade young black men from hanging out there.[16] After the renovation in the early 2000s, the police began to perform more identity checks, just as more CCTV cameras were installed and surveillance expanded.[17]

The 2007 revolt may have been exceptional in its scope and effect, but the racial profiling and police violence that provoked it are something that black residents taking public transportation confront every day. Undocumented residents in particular find themselves in a double bind: they must use public transit to make a living, but it increases their chances of being stopped and deported. While I was doing research, several young men disappeared and were rumored to have been sent to migrant detention centers.

Dembele was often worried, talking about how he still did not have a secure job and did not know how long he would have before his time came and he would be arrested and deported. If he was fired, he would have little or no legal recourse, and he knew people like him who had been kicked out of their apartment and unable to find another one. His life, like many of his peers, has many of the hallmarks of what scholars call "precarity"—that economic and existential condition of radical uncertainty that is the lot of more and more people across the world, when presumed life progressions and future expectations are shattered by changing wage-labor economies and, in this case, increasing restrictions on migrant livelihoods.[18] But dealing with such uncertainty was part of life for these men, who mostly came from the Senegal River Valley, an area that had seen several droughts since the 1970s. The Gare du Nord was another method growing out of the toolkit they had been learning to build since they were young.

Relying on public transportation may have introduced greater uncertainty and risk because the police seemed always to be lurking just around the corner. Yet the station provided the social relations that these men used to lessen their precarity in France. For Dembele and his peers, these two seemingly contradictory aspects of station life were in fact complementary—that is, the risk was integral to their self-fashioning as adventurers. They did not simply avoid or resist police control; rather, they incorporated the police into their social relationships at the station.

Their interactions with the police provided a method for becoming what they called a true adventurer, the opportunity to assert their dignity in a context where they were otherwise being denied it. They sought to establish a good reputation among their peers by out-policing the police: they adopted the policing tactics of vigilance and spatial mastery as marks of what it meant to be a good adventurer at the station. The police also provided a referent and audience for the varied styles that accompanied the Gare du Nord method. For example, migrants used specific forms of speech and dress to do several kinds of work: a hairstyle could be part of a survival strategy to ward off police attention; it could also signify social status among adventurers in ways that ignored typical status distinctions (such as undocumented versus documented) and that were unintelligible to the police.

West Africans used the mall and the station's front square as social meeting places and these areas became targeted for police patrol and surveillance. The Gare du Nord method these men developed to confront their precarious position, then, had to incorporate policing in order to deal with it—they had to "work with" the police, as Amadou put it. In interactions with officers, they performed their own forms of masculinity to gain prestige, fashioning themselves as adventurers out to conquer the complex social world of the station.

## KEEPING WATCH

In 2007, the French prime minister promised to "put cameras everywhere" at the Gare du Nord, in an attempt to make it a "place of security." Today, there are hundreds of CCTV cameras throughout the station. The station renovation provided long lines of sight to render visible actions that might have once taken place in dark corridors. At first glance, these renovations have made the station into a primary example of the way technology, architecture, and design enable surveillance used to discipline those subjected to it—the cameras and spatial layout of the station try to get people to conform to normative ways of acting and using the station.[19] These expanding technologies and spatial control measures are not just examples of an oppressive, all-seeing eye of the state. The technologies of surveillance that thrive in the redesigned station environment take on new meanings within West Africans' station practices. They make a claim on this space and reorient its design and forms of surveillance for their own ends, refusing to abide by the norms imposed on them.[20]

The camera that provides a video feed of the new front square of the station embodies the way that surveillance technology can take on new meanings among those it targets. In the far corner of the square stood a high, visible camera that surveys all the comings and goings. A few participants in small-scale drug dealing hung out near the camera, but as many observed, they would never catch anyone red-handed, considering its conspicuousness. Lassana explained that, instead, the police use it to recognize the Africans who spend "too much time" here, whom they will then target for identity checks. Although the police officers did not admit this purpose, it corresponds to the official reasoning the Paris police chief used to explain why black youths are targeted for stops in general at the Gare du Nord: because they bother the real train passengers by staying put in a mobility hub and by failing to respect the norm of civil inattention.

The camera is part of the larger performance of state authority and spatial domination in which police patrols and identity checks also play a role. According to Sans Souci, a young Senegalese man who had frequent run-ins with the police at the station, the theater around the installation of one particular camera was so exaggerated that it became absurd. The police came several times before they installed a camera in the front square, he explained, warning everyone that a camera would be installed. They chose the early evening of a weekday to install it, which Sans Souci speculated was because they were hoping for the maximum number of spectators. He said that the police forced them to leave what they were doing inside the station and come outside as the technicians installed the camera. "We're watching you," the police said to the men who had gathered, "Now we'll see how long you are going to stay here."

"Great," Sans Souci said to the officers, "Now we'll be on television again!" and everyone laughed. "See you guys soon," he called to the police, laughing as they walked back inside the station.

He told me this story as we were standing below the same camera. "We don't give a fuck about the camera," Sans Souci said, turning toward it and addressing the camera. "We know those cops. They know us. They are out here every day. We are out here every day. Do they think we don't know there are cameras all over this place? They think we don't know them."

By retelling his version of the camera's installation (which one police officer said did not occur this way), Sans Souci demagnetized its potential as an impersonal device of discipline set up by an all-seeing abstract entity. He situated it instead within the ongoing social relationships between the young black men and the police who interacted at the station. This narrative recasts the police performance of authority as a communicative misfire: instead of imbuing the camera with importance, the police made it an object of ridicule.

The officers in the story hoped the surveillance camera would reduce loitering at the station entrance. "Go home!" ("Rentrez chez vous!") the police often told young men hanging out late at night. The order as it was understood meant to leave the station and go back to their house in the suburbs, but the same language was used to tell immigrants to return to their countries of origin. Sans Souci recognized that their intention with the camera was to change how he and his peers occupied this space and to convince them to go elsewhere. But it had no such effect. Neither did it become a focus of protest or resistance. Instead, it was incorporated into the social scene unfolding in the square each afternoon, becoming a reference point for people like Sans Souci and Ibrahim, who used their knowledge of less conspicuous camera locations to display their expertise about the station's policing and surveillance mechanisms.

The police also used the architecture of the new part of the station to see without being seen, hiding behind walls to surprise people trying to get into the metro without a ticket or patrolling all three levels from a bridge passageway on the highest level. Such positioning was not the exclusive domain of the police. As I stood with Dembele in a corner that he used to meet with friends while keeping an eye on the comings and goings of police teams, I could see Ibrahim's afro and bright green track suit on the other side of the glass doors. He too was standing in an advantageous location in the corner of the front square, in the shade, from where he can see everyone who arrives and departs the station but not be noticed by them. We could also see Amadou standing near the center of the front square, in the sunlight, and making grand gestures as he talked to a small audience gathered around him.

Dembele, on the other hand, standing in a corner, used small movements and spoke in a low, measured voice. From this position, he kept watch over two floors below and could see almost every stairway and escalator that leads to the street level of the station. Later, as we were talking, I saw Dembele glance sideways and then take an almost imperceptible step back so that his back was against the wall. He had noticed something. Before I could turn around, Ibrahim walked up to us, smiling broadly, and shook Dembele's hand, placing his own hand to his heart. As they exchanged greetings, Dembele kept his head down, his eyes shrouded by his baseball cap. As he talked to Ibrahim, I saw him glance down the stairs toward the entryway. He was keeping watch. Dembele maintained his vigil even as he spoke to his friends, and around them several other small groups of West Africans were also positioned to keep watch as they socialized. Their scanning eyes sometimes paused, hovering, as they spotted me, and sometimes I noticed they would stop talking mid-sentence, as if to take a mental note of my presence to inquire about later, before returning to their conversation. Any unexpected presence could signal potential danger. Lassana explained that a big part of the Gare du Nord method was learning how to watch, how to read body language, and how to gain a sense of the totality of this expansive and complex space.

As Dembele kept watch, removed from the passenger crowds below us, I was again reminded of Michel de Certeau's metaphor for urban planners who occupy the view from above, looking down at the city from afar, and thus removed from everyday urban life.[21] Unlike the planners, whose location high above the crowd signifies a position of power, Dembele watched because of his subordinate status as an undocumented immigrant. Furthermore, unlike de Certeau's image of the planner as a distant "voyeur," Dembele's position enabled him to look down across three levels of the station while interacting with his friends.

He and his peers' engagement with space frustrates de Certeau's divide between the practiced and walked city, on one hand, and the systematic planned city, on the other. Dembele and his peers both watch and are watched, and through their engagement with the space and with each other they propose alternative systems of control and surveillance. Social status and survival in the world of the station depended on mastering the station space—that is, knowing the ins and outs of who could be seen from a given point, who uses which spaces when, and which overlapping staircase or escalator leads where.

Each of these men mobilized practices similar to what Andrew Newman calls "vigilance," which he contrasts with state surveillance: "In contrast to formal surveillance, people remain vigilant for themselves, their friends, and their interests, in pursuit of goals that don't simply further the interests of dominant regimes or diametrically oppose it either."[22] Confronted with the legacy of state surveillance focused on immigrant and minority populations, monitored groups employ vigilance to protect themselves. By paying attention to vigilance, Newman sheds light on how keeping watch is used also by those subject to state surveillance. As he puts it, "Watching takes place not only from the top down but from side to side, and from the bottom up. . . . Residents also survey their surveyors."[23]

Vigilance, in this sense, requires skill and savvy to be deployed successfully. Depending on their social and legal position, West Africans at the station used different tactics to engage vigilance and surveillance. Dembele could not afford to be noticed by the police; his very survival in France depended on avoiding identity checks. On the other hand, Ibrahim, who had residence papers, could put himself on display while monitoring the social scene in his own way. Like the police, Dembele and his peers kept watch, seeking to master the physical and social form of the railway hub in order to exploit its potentiality for helping them succeed on their adventure. They used everyday forms of keeping watch that appropriate the surveillance that police and security guards practice.

## MANEUVERING

As Lassana points out, keeping vigilant and staying out of trouble at the station require hard work and a skill set built during years on the road in African (and in some cases, European) cities before arriving in Paris. Migrants often must find substitutions for the wage labor that they can no longer depend on for their survival abroad.[24] In precarious contexts, they must adopt ways of tactical movement or, in other words, of maneuvering—in both the sense of "moving with skill and care" and the original meaning of performing manual labor.

Maneuvering is an example of what Stuesse and Coleman call "altermobilities," or tactics of survival and resistance migrants use to cope with the intensified policing of their communities.[25] Altermobilities are not only the ways that people mobilize together to protest unjust policing practices but also the tactics of avoiding police stops altogether. In this line of thinking, Dembele's vigilance is altersurveillance, a strategy used to enable survival—since he needs to use public transportation to get to work but must avoid police stops. Policed communities often produce inventive maneuvers like Dembele's because they are targeted for harassment, detention, and deportation.

These maneuvers have adapted to a changing landscape of French public space, transformed by legal reforms that have expanded the reach of policing and surveillance, such as teams from a special unit of the French police sent to check IDs in order to discover undocumented migrants. These changes have created new ways for the state, in the name of security, to control who has access to public spaces. They are also further evidence of a racial common sense that has been fundamental to urban space governance. Although it may seem shocking in a country whose "color-blind" Republican ideology does not even allow race-based categories in statistical research, race has nonetheless been used as an explicit criterion of exclusion, such as when the Israeli president came to France in 2013 and "Black and North African railway workers" were banned from the Gare du Nord when he passed through the station.[26] Antiterror measures, immigration control, and race-based policing create an environment that leads to significant risks for West African adventurers. Precarious maneuvers, including everyday vigilance, take on these risks to reconfigure police control.

By examining the railway station as a common sphere where both police and policed use vigilance and control—though in very different ways—it is possible to avoid reproducing the idea that the state, embodied in the police, occupies a position of all-seeing control "from above" while the targets of control are subjected to it "from below," with no view of the system.[27] Of course, a French national police officer has far more resources and power and much less at stake than an undocumented West African migrant. Vigilance is a necessary survival strategy for someone like Dembele, while it is a technique of control for the police, who have an ever-increasing legal latitude for arresting and detaining people. Yet the police do not get to dictate the meaning of the stops, which are also moments of social interaction and theatrics that take place in public and with an audience. They often involve stakes that escape the police's purview and understanding.[28]

## OMAR'S BLUFF

On a bright fall evening in 2010, I stood with Lassana and Amadou watching the crowds of the evening rush hour in front of the station's glassy entrance. From the Autogrill café, across the front square, to the bicycle racks, small groups of young West African men were exchanging greetings, chatting, and surveying the passengers streaming in and out of the glass doors. Six hefty policemen were standing near the entrance, also watching. "It has been heating up around here," said Lassana, gesturing toward the men in uniform.

As if to prove his point, the police soon approached Lassana's compatriot, a young, talkative Malian named Omar, a few yards from where we were standing. He had been spending the afternoon skipping back and forth across the square, stopping to strike up conversations with young women who crossed his path on their way in or out of the station, who attempted to navigate around him. The police split in two groups and managed to block Omar from continuing his back-and-forth jaunts. "What is it this time?" he asked them, loudly enough for all of us to hear. The police spoke in hushed tones, their stern faces turned in on him, their hands moving to rest on their belts. They had stopped Omar before and did not ask him for his papers (passport or otherwise).[29] Still, Omar took out his wallet and removed his *carte de séjour* (resident and work permit), flashing it in their faces. The police appeared uninterested, shrugging their shoulders and exchanging looks, shaking their heads. "Oh, that's not what you want? What is it, then?" Omar asked, as he took out what looked like a French driver's license—a rare commodity among his peers—and waved it in front of them. He then started taking other cards and papers out of his wallet, including his green health insurance card and his bankcard. The police did not seem impressed, their expressions impassive. A few people exiting the station slowed their gait as they approached the scene, looking over their shoulder at Omar as they walked by. One officer motioned with his thumb to ward them away: keep going, nothing to see here, said the gesture. Other commuters, with downcast gazes, stepped gingerly and efficiently around the group, as if doing all they could to avoid the scene.

"The police have been stopping a lot of people," Lassana told me as we watched the interaction unfold. "Just the other day, this one"—he indicated Omar—"was being aggressive with the people leaving the station. The police took him in and then the rest of them started stopping everyone else who was there. When people tried to get into the station, the police said, "You can't go in unless you have a ticket."

"So they were checking your tickets to let you into the station?" I asked, surprised.

"They were saying that if you don't have a ticket, you can't come in," responded Lassana, which meant that the police had activated an entrance requirement that had been abolished decades before.

Lassana's friend Sans Souci, whose many tattoos and piercings made him a frequent target of police controls, was talking about what a nuisance Omar had become, saying that he was starting trouble for no reason, talking too much and acting like a braggart. Some of the other young men had begun backing away, trying to melt into the crowd before heading into the shelter of a café across the street. Lassana explained that some were undocumented and worried that Omar's demonstration would annoy the police and lead them to ask everyone present for their resident permits. Omar had long been undocumented himself, but then had had a child in France with a French woman, and through that obtained a coveted ten-year resident permit. Lassana, however, kept his distance from the police. Before he had received his papers, he had been subject to several stop-and-search operations and twice was taken into custody for having a fake resident permit. He was not deported in either case, thanks, he said, to knowing how to protect himself from the police and anyone else who might wish him ill. He said he had learned these techniques in part through his experience on the road, in part from his father and grandparents before he left Mali. Although his family had no experience with the French police, they had passed down the "secret" keys of getting out of tough situations.

Lassana marveled at how someone like Omar had been able to get this far in France: "He's Khassonke," he said, referring to Omar's ethnolinguistic group, a minority in the Kayes region of the Senegal River in Mali. Khassonke have long been in close contact with Soninke like Lassana, who comprise the majority in that region and in France among West African migrants. "And they like partying too much (*ils aiment trop l'ambiance*)." Omar was one of the most gregarious young men at the station, and was prone to giving long speeches about subjects ranging from police racism to Parisian nightclubs.

As Lassana and his friends were commenting on Omar's failed attempt to get attention, the police moved out of his way and started walking toward the entrance. Omar walked backward away from them, backing into a group of his friends and interrupting their conversations with, "Did you see that? Fucking police!" Most of his peers did not respond, but in addition to showing off his papers, this framing suggested that he was drawing public attention and gaze to police harassment.

Days later, Omar was still talking about the incident to anyone who would listen, explaining that it was another example of racist police. His friends dismissed these long speeches, interrupting Omar to poke fun at him. Sans Souci told Omar he asked for it. "I get stopped by the police seven times per day, for doing nothing. You saw the police and you did your *show*," he said.

He used the expression "*faire le show*" (to bluff or fake something), a popular term in the poetic urban French hybrid language spoken in Abidjan, the capital of Côte d'Ivoire, where many of these men lived before coming to France. Anthro-

FIGURE 6. The front square of the Gare du Nord on a Friday evening in June 2018. Rachel Fish.

pologist Sasha Newell illustrated how successful "shows" or bluffing in Abidjan call for "a display of the cultural mastery of the symbols of urban identity" such as Western brand names and consumer goods.[30] Seeing his "show" in this context, Sans Souci is suggesting that Omar bluffed unsuccessfully when he used his various *real* ID cards in front of the police. His peers at the Gare du Nord were more impressed by good fakes that took work and skill than by "authentic" French papers. Adventurers liked to recount well-worn stories of comrades who had outsmarted the police, getting out of detentions and deportation by bluffing and faking other identities. The high value placed on good imitation inverted the typical hierarchy—presumed by the police—in which the undocumented migrant from rural West Africa occupied the bottom rung. They saw it as a bledard skill honed through their migration routes in metropolises like Abidjan and then further developed at the Gare du Nord. This skill, when mastered, was a major source of pride.

Omar's use of this social scene and his interaction with the police show that "identity checks" were about police control but also about social relationships and status distinctions among West Africans. The police embody domination through gesture, stance, and language when they patrol the station and do the identity checks, but the effects of their policing escape their control. Far from being a pure moment of state domination over a marginalized group, West Africans use the identity check to display their own skills and savvy, gain prestige, and enforce alternative boundaries and hierarchies. Omar's interaction with the police in front of the station that day became part of a narrative that was retold at the station, transforming into a cautionary tale for newcomers who were warned against being too flashy. At the same time, it was an opportunity for these young men to comment on and reframe the meaning of the identity check.

By complying with the premise of ID verification, Omar satisfied the police officers' quest for official papers and tried to use the possession of state documents as a status symbol. Sans Souci and his peers' reaction, however, suggested that he had missed the point: those documents might signal status and rights for the French state, but they had little purchase in the community of adventurers at the station, who believed that real status was to be found elsewhere. Getting status in the Gare du Nord depended on other achievements and characteristics, such as charisma, a reputation for hard work and generosity, and the ability to make money (that could then be redistributed). This redefinition of what confers status provides a form of social commentary. They were saying they knew that even though it could keep them from getting deported, a resident permit would not get them a job, confer rights, or save them from police violence and domination.

Much of the formidable activism and writing against racial profiling and police abuse in France and elsewhere has focused on denouncing these forms of humiliation and state-sponsored racism.[31] Omar's own reaction to the police invoked such denunciations. When I first met him at the station, he discussed police abuses and gave examples of racism that he had witnessed. I recorded what he told me in my field notebook, noting that it corresponded to the injustices I had read about. I was surprised to find how dismissive Omar's peers were of his viewpoints. For many of the other men, who were also frequently stopped by the police, such denunciations were self-serving, banal, and even pointless. *Of course, the French police are racist,* Lassana said dismissively when the topic came up. *And so what? They also don't understand anything about anything.*

But it would be a mistake to interpret Lassana and Sans Souci's reactions as apathy to everyday racism exhibited in these interactions with the police. Their point, rather, was that the police do not have the final say on the meaning of the identity checks. From this perspective, what the police say and do provides a backdrop or fodder for other displays of masculine prowess or social mastery that end up undermining the police's claim to ultimately control the station. The police did not have the power to define even the meaning of their identity checks. Rather, as we shall see, their signification arose as those interactions were commented upon, retold, dismissed, ridiculed, denounced, and used as evidence for trustworthiness and inclusion.

## MASCULINE DOMINATION AND COMPETITION

As Lassana, Ibrahim, Amadou, and almost all of the other West Africans I met hanging out at the station told me, they were there to meet women.[32] In this endeavor, they did not see the police as potential obstacles, but rather as their main rivals. In my experience as a woman at the station, they were right: several times, police officers asked me for my mobile number or to have a drink after work, though they otherwise refused to speak with me about my research. The terrain of seduction and the display of masculine domination was a place where police and adventurers met, and West Africans attempted to display superior abilities. They used displays of masculine prowess to challenge the submissiveness imposed on them by the ID checks.

The police often acted incredulous when adventurers told them that they were there to meet women. On a warm afternoon in early spring of 2010, Lassana recounted the following run-in with the national police to his friend Adama and me:

> The police came up to me; in the middle of everyone else, they chose me and asked for my papers. I gave them my resident permit. Then they searched me and found my lighter, but that's all I have—you know I don't do drugs or drink alcohol or anything—and then, they say, "Tell us, why do you spend so much time every single day here at the big entrance? Don't you have somewhere to go?" I said of course, I have somewhere to go, I have an apartment and everything in La Courneuve [a nearby suburb]. And they said, "So what are you doing here?" I said, just like that, "I'm hitting on women." Just like that! And can you imagine, the policeman, he didn't know what to say! He called his partner over and asked me to repeat what I said, so I did. He called his friend over and asked me again, so I said, okay that's enough, I told you what I'm doing, there's nothing wrong with that. The third guy asked, "But why do you do that here? Why don't you go to the clubs or something?" And I said, "Well I have my way and you have yours, and that's it." You know, I don't go to the clubs because the girls there are drinking alcohol and I will find my happiness here at the Gare du Nord. It's an international station. But those police were laughing and laughing, they couldn't get over what I said! They couldn't believe it! One was just like you, Julie, he asked me "But does that work?" And told me that it couldn't possibly work. "We'll see," I told him. When they left, he said—something—like, "it's a miracle!" He meant it's a miracle I can meet girls and he can't. Because you know the police, they are the worst seducers of all, they never do any work, they just hit on women and bother us! Much more than we do.

When he retold the story, he glossed over the way that the police officers were laughing at his expense, making fun of what they saw as his misguided attempts to meet women. It is likely that the officer said something to him about the station being a *cour de miracles,* a derogatory term that French railway police used to describe the groups who spend time around the station. It is an ancien regime designation dating back to the first waves of immigration to Paris, and was used to refer to areas where marginalized groups lived in squalor. He transformed this insult into a confirmation of his masculine prowess, which surpassed the cops' abilities in seduction. Many of his peers did the same when retelling insulting interactions with the police. They often sped through what the police said and offered new interpretations and sometimes lengthy commentary. These retellings provided a way for them to make sense of hurtful exchanges, to come to terms with perceived aggressiveness, unwelcome curiosity, and, often, racism. West Africans who were the targets of police control reframed what happened to cast themselves in the dominant position and lessen the humiliation. Many would brush past their compliance with identity checks, which implied submission to the police. They replaced the moment of compliance with a value judgment (such as "Police don't know how to hit on women") that asserted their owns skills and highlighted the police officer's cluelessness.

The police, as it turned out, were but minor players in these stories, which were also used to communicate among adventurers, reinforcing social boundaries that were invisible to the police. Two weeks later, Lassana retold the same story about the police stop to Ibrahim, at a time when Ibrahim had been spreading rumors that both Lassana and I were working with the police. Lassana prefaced the tale by commenting on Ibrahim's ethnicity (Fula/Peul), which he knew was a big source of pride for Ibrahim. He said, "You, you are going to understand this because you're a hundred percent Peul and I know that Peuls are very, very dangerous—" in other words, very adept at hitting on women.[33] Ibrahim nodded and Lassana launched into the story. He added a new part: "When they said it couldn't work [to hit on women at the station], I said I could teach them how to hit on women, and they said, 'Oh really?' and I laughed and said, 'No. You don't talk to me, and I don't talk to you, and it's good for everyone like that.'"

In addition to his clear message of "I don't talk to the police" for Ibrahim's benefit, Lassana highlighted the officers' desperateness and gullibility when he offered help, and his ultimate control over the situation as he embarrassed them by dashing any hopes they might have of building rapport with him and learning his secrets. He left out their shaming laughter and "miracle" comment. Ibrahim nodded and picked up on Lassana's entreaties, responding, "That, that is Peul! Sometimes I think you're not a real Soninke." Lassana clasped Ibrahim's hand and said, "You know I'm Soninke one hundred percent and you're Peul and that's true." The initial exchange with the police helped to rebuild trust and relationality between the two men. What was inflected at first by the display of masculinity ("I'm here to hit on women") became, through the retelling of the interaction, an opportunity to emphasize a shared repertoire of ethnic referents that were opaque to the police.

Like the surveillance spectacle, a large part of the efficacy of the identity controls or stop-and-search practices are found in their performance, not in whether the action "uncovers" delinquents or undocumented migrants. Both the controllers and the controlled are often aware that they are "playing out a mutually convenient drama;" in the case of the station, the drama was over control of the space: who dictates the social norms and defines the type of action and relationships that can take place there.[34] The police act as a foil for these young men and vice versa; their interactions offer opportunities for both sides to perform authority, know-how, and masculine prowess. The strategies employed in the Gare du Nord method are evident in these encounters between police and the young men and include modes of dress, speech, and performance. To be successful adventurers, these men need to know how to work this social scene, and that work involves stylistic choices that are attentive to their peers and to the police presence.

## "LE BRONX" VERSUS THE SUIT-AND-TIE

What do adventurers wear? This simple question has many implications for the kind of police interactions they might have at the Gare du Nord. Ibrahim curated his image in person and on social media. He often posted selfies at the station, in which he would sometimes be pointing to plainclothes police standing near him in a display of his skills at identifying them. He sought to set himself apart from those who had "no style"—for him, the bledards who were "carbon copies" (*des copies conformes*). He wore matching neon clothes and shoes, his hair either in a distinctive afro or in careful braids, a hip-hop inspired style he said matched his love for US rap music that he had picked up in Dakar as a teenager. He acknowledged that this style made the mostly white police force able to pick him out from a crowd, even at a distance, whereas they had some trouble distinguishing between the close-shaven African men.[35] Similarly, Sans Souci's tattoos, piercings, and bleached hair were part of why he was stopped more than his peers; such styles were associated with a group of young men whom the police considered to be a gang.

Sartorial styles illustrated the multiple strategies they used to get by in France. Some, like Ibrahim, drew on what they called "Le Bronx" style associated with those they called *renois* (French-African youth) and inspired by American hip-hop, while others went with a three-piece suit, the "*costume-cravate*" look.[36] An *aventurier* might change styles several times over the course of his station career. The Gare du Nord method was not characterized by a particular style, then, but rather by the flexibility and adaptability that being an adventurer required. If ID checks sought to perform authority and uncover "identity," these young men's styles frustrated attempts at connecting particular styles with a sub-group identity. Instead, their styles played with many of the assumptions that the police and other users projected onto black people in France.

Omar, Sans Souci, and Ibrahim adopted style strategies that offered them a respite from urban anonymity. Their style displayed social position and their ability to remix international trends. Clothing choices and other accoutrements (such as having several mobile phones) could demand respect by signaling an important role in "*le bizness*" (small-time illegal activities) that differentiated one from marginalized African migrant laborers. Being known by the police became, for Ibrahim, a source of pride. He also believed it protected him from stop-and-searches that were always done in full view and could be humiliating. "They never stop me anymore," he told me, "They know me, they know I won't be carrying anything."

European signifiers of class distinction were not always effective in the station. The "suit-and-tie" style could signify status, though an ill-fitting suit without the right accessories, gestures, language, and largesse could communicate a lack of status and know-how. An Ivoirian man, who used to be a major player in the informal commerce of stolen cell phones at the Gare, liked to show off his success by returning in three-piece suits and expensive-looking Swiss watches. When he stopped by his old stomping ground, younger men would crowd around him to listen to his stories and advice about getting by at the station, which he offered with an exaggerated Parisian French accent, and which was often interrupted as he took important telephone calls. It was never clear what business he was in, but he had mastered a form of the "bluff," creatively imitating European clothing styles to display or gain status.[37]

Style differences and flexibility illustrate that adventurers do not adopt a single stylistic code that would reveal a shared African culture or a common subculture of resistance, but rather create an individual appearance through their encounters with police and peers. Young men at the station adopt a range of "cultural styles" that index their social and economic position, their immigration status (undocumented or not), their belonging to station subgroups, and their ability to get by using the Gare du Nord method.[38] Choosing to wear neon-green Nike sneakers and a matching hoodie is not anodyne; it conveys a wealth of semiotic information and mobilizes a particular strategy for survival in a marginal urban world.[39]

Undocumented migrants who had recently arrived maintained what the others called "bledard" style: a uniform of corduroys, sweaters, a clean-shaven face and close-cropped hair. They still drew on the networks of the Gare du Nord in attempts to find work and housing but adopted a much more understated look and avoided confrontations with the police. Their power was their discretion, standing above the fray, but they also were susceptible to identity checks based on racial profiling. These adventurers were more likely to speak in their native Soninke, Pulaar, or Bamanakan (and variants, spoken in Mali, Guinea, Côte d'Ivoire, Senegal, Burkina Faso, and Gambia), even if they knew some French. But "bledard" style did not necessarily signify undocumented status. Dico, a thirty-something Malian who had obtained papers through marriage, continued to wear this unassuming garb after over a decade in France.

FIGURE 7. Lassana and his friend sitting in a café inside the station in 2010. Author.

Changing cultural styles also indexed social and legal positions at the station and in France. Lassana arrived in France in the bledard uniform, but once he began hanging out at the Gare du Nord, he adopted a hip-hop-inspired style. Wearing a backwards Yankees hat, a jersey emblazoned with "The Bronx," low-slung jeans, and braided hair, he thought, would differentiate him from the undocumented bledards and help him to fit in better with the other men there. He saw this style as a kind of strategic mask that would dissuade police attention: he was dressing like a "renoi"—born in France—instead of like a bledard. This strategy appealed to his knowledge about how the police categorized populations and singled out undocumented migrants to be stopped. After he received papers, he shed the defining characteristics of this style—first getting rid of the braids, then the low-riders, and finally trading in the Bronx jersey for a navy V-neck sweater. He could go back to looking like a bledard because, he thought, he did not have to worry about deportation. He also grew a longer beard that displayed his Muslim faith and more senior status. His friend Dico started wearing a keffiyeh scarf after he got legal status, as he was no longer worried about attracting even more police attention as a Muslim.

The Gare du Nord method meant experimenting with the different possibilities for getting by in France. Adventurers had to change their style as they moved between multiple economies—from participation in informal "gangs" and the petty drug trade to trying to find a job in retail or construction. When I first met Fodjé, a Guinean man in his twenties, he wore his jeans low with an oversized black Wu-Tang sweatshirt. He was known as "Thuglife" to his friends at the Gare. In early 2010, he disappeared from the station, leading to speculation that he was in prison, from where he would receive the "double penalty" of deportation once his sentence was served.[40] Several months later, a man in a conservative striped polo shirt and khaki pants said hello to me outside the station. I had to do a literal double take to realize it was "Thuglife," who smiled widely.

"I used to do a lot with the broom!" he said, mimicking a sweeping movement.

I gave him a quizzical look. "Oh really?" I said. I had no idea what he meant.

He shook his head and laughed before elaborating. "I mean," he said, "I was sweeping, you know, I was undocumented, I survived doing stuff that's not totally legit. I didn't know much about what was going on, but I made a little money that way." I nodded: "sweeping" indicated peripheral involvement in illegal activities in order to eke out a basic living.

"But now," he continued, "I work at the big Carrefour supermarket out in the suburbs." His new clothes accompanied his new job and his newly acquired ten-year resident permit, obtained through an asylum request, which he handed over to me for inspection. "It's me, it's Fodjé!" he said. "Even though you didn't recognize me, see, *c'est moi*! I'm finished with sweeping now, I work at Carrefour!" The nickname "Thuglife" was gone, abandoned for a job and a new look.

Contrary to the shared forms of habitus and cultural capital that become a mark of subcultural belonging, the Gare du Nord method does not require a particular style (bledard or renoi, costume-cravate or hip-hop) but rather demands the flexibility and know-how to deploy a variety of styles, depending on the situation. The adventure was a period of flux and change; cultural styles in the Gare du Nord corresponded to changing social categories. They were an important way that migrants embodied a flexible adventurer persona with the know-how to intuit how others—especially the police—would see and interpret their appearance.

## SECURITY WITHOUT SALARY

Amadou, the self-declared "President of the Gare du Nord," had also once been involved in "sweeping" but by the time I met him he was hoping to follow in the path of someone like Omar, who had met a white woman at the station and now had a resident permit and a French family. He had grown up in a village in the Kayes region of Mali and was known as an excellent pick-up artist (*dragueur*), which his Soninke friends often jokingly attributed to his Khassonke ethnicity. Most of the time, Amadou was not hitting on women but interacting with his friends at the station, often in ways that displayed his own dominance.

On three occasions, I saw him approach a group of people he knew and demand that they show him their "Gare du Nord passport." He would mimic the police in stance, tone, and language, shaking his head and feigning anger when they took out their national passports. Each man in turn would try to satisfy his request with their metro cards, drivers licenses, and other documents, but each time he would say, "No, not that! The passport of the Gare du Nord! Show me your papers!" After a few rounds, someone who knew the game would eventually take out a pack of cigarettes and offer him one. "*Voilà!*" he would say, "That's it, that's the passport of the Gare du Nord." While the police ask these men to justify their presence by showing their state IDs, "Sécurité Sans Salaire" instead asked his peers to justify their presence in this social setting by offering a symbol of sociability—a cigarette—that is the property of the group. These kinds of performances also earned him his nickname: like the police, he attempted to control many of the social interactions that took place at the station. Unlike the paid security guard, he lacked a salary, but he also had more respect from his peers than the guards working in poor conditions.

The nickname also suggests that hanging out at the station and socializing there was a form of work. Amadou built social capital and displayed his status by showing he could control one of the main (perceived) sources of value: relationships with white women. When Doulaye had just arrived, for example, his shy smile had gotten him some attention from women in his first few weeks, though he had not succeeded in getting their phone numbers or taking them out for coffee or dinner across the street. One evening, he approached a young white woman who had just arrived at the station, asking her for a cigarette, even though he did not smoke, and then asking where she was coming from. "Anything to start conversation," he told me later. They had been talking for three minutes when Amadou pushed his way between them.

"Hey, you, who are you?" Amadou asked Doulaye.

Doulaye, noticing the aggressive tone, turned toward Amadou and said amiably, "Ah, how are you?"

Amadou ignored the question and turned to the woman. "Is he bothering you, miss?" he asked.

"No, it's okay, thank you," she replied, looking from Amadou to Doulaye.

Amadou nodded and then turned back to Doulaye. Looking out at Lassana and me and a few others who were standing around watching, he said, "We're going to take a little walk, okay new guy?" He put his arm around Doulaye's shoulders and steered him toward the door, entering the station, leaving the woman to shake her head and walk in through another entrance, amid our chuckles.

I witnessed Amadou do similar things when his friends were talking to women in the front square. He was charismatic, and he asserted his authority by questioning the identity of more recent arrivals ("Hey you, who are you?"). He mimicked police identity checks to reinforce his authority, but also to mock the police and their self-importance. He also communicated important messages about what Doulaye must do to become a true adventurer: he must be able to observe, read, interpret, and act upon the social scene around him, to learn the hierarchies that existed at the Gare du Nord. Only then would he be able to succeed. The station offers an alternative realm for exploring new venues to create value, which engage with the French policing terrains of ID verification, masculinity, and vigilance.

## THE POLICE NEED US

"What would they do without us?" Ibrahim joked one day, gesturing at the officers patrolling the front square. In a parallel way, it is hard to imagine what the West Africans' Gare du Nord method would look like without the display of police control, the heavy security, and the confusing open-space architecture made by the exchange hub design. The police are at once a potentially destructive nuisance and a key part of their social scene. One of their favorite pastimes was recounting the stories of identity checks and other encounters with officers, which showcased their own prowess in front of their peers. They resisted the categories and boundaries proposed by policing and urban planning. Unlike in subcultures created through resistance, here there is no uniform cultural code but rather a bricolage of opposing styles that highlight a multitude of border-crossing, flexible strategies that define the adventurer.

The strategies that make up the Gare du Nord method help adventurers cultivate respect in an urban environment where they are the objects of police attention. Their styles, interactions, and narratives are not only interesting fodder for the ethnographer or tourist gaze, but also survival strategies in their marginalized positions. I have highlighted how their method relies on tactics of control often associated with the police. But their mobilization of these tactics does not mitigate their precarious position. They sometimes help to avoid being arrested and to assert dignity, but they do not spare them from the dangers of deportation, humiliation, and bodily harm that interactions with the police may bring. Nor do such tactics combat the effects of economic crisis and labor market contraction, which affect their ability to provide for their families at home who depend on them. To be seen as successful adventurers, they also need to be able to secure livelihoods and redistribute wealth—in the form of social, economic, and symbolic capital. Next, we shall see how their adventurer's repertoire is put to work producing economic value through the material and social channels that converge at the station.

# 4

# Hacking Infrastructures

## *An Adventurer's Guide to the Gare du Nord*

Could a railway station help West African migrants in Paris build their livelihoods and plan for the future? Those who raised their doubts about the Gare du Nord's potential were told the story of Hafidou, a young man who had come to France from rural Mali. Hafidou—so the story went—had spent many difficult years on the margins of urban life, struggling to get by undocumented and underemployed. When he first arrived, cousins helped him find temporary work on night shifts throughout the city—cleaning, making pastries, and working security. He slept a few hours each day in a crowded room in an immigrant workers' dormitory outside of Paris, before having to give up his bedroll to a senior inhabitant. Deprived of a warm bed, he would wander the streets around the periphery of the city during the day before heading back to work in the evening. It was a long commute. He switched lines each day at the Gare du Nord. His coworker from a short stint in a bakery, a Senegalese man with whom he shared a maternal language, introduced him to some other West Africans who met there every day.

After several years of living in undocumented *galère* (struggle, difficult times), Hafidou was still looking for his "*bonheur*" (success and happiness) in France. His cousin found him some odd jobs to do, but the work was unreliable. He had to borrow money from friends and had to put up with the insults of his family in Mali who berated him for not sending enough home to support them. He sought help from his uncles at the immigrant dormitory, but they scoffed at his inability to find work given his youth and good health. Instead of offering support, they insisted that he either start paying for his bedroll or find another place to sleep. During periods in which he was out of work, Hafidou started taking the commuter rail to the Gare du Nord at midday to spend the afternoons and evenings with other adventurers.

After a few months, Hafidou met an older French man—called the "old Jew" in the story—who was passing through the station and they started talking. He told the man about his suffering, the difficulty of finding a stable job and living under the constant threat of being sent back to Mali. The "old Jew" was sympathetic and offered Hafidou pocket money and lodging in an empty studio apartment he owned in Paris. He told him not to have guests over in the apartment. One evening, Hafidou's cousin needed a place to stay for the night. His cousin left the next morning, but later that day, the old Jew summoned Hafidou to his home and when he arrived the old Jew was very angry with him. He told him that if he ever had anyone over again, he would kick him out of the apartment and stop giving him money. Hafidou returned to the station a few times after that to take his friends out for coffee and demonstrate his largesse by lending them money.

I heard other versions of this story from West Africans at the station, who invoked Hafidou at newcomers' skepticism or when offering encouragement to those ready to give up on their adventures or on the Gare du Nord method. I never met Hafidou, but his story served both as cautionary and inspirational tale on how to be a good guest and client for potential patrons at the station. Hafidou's encounter with the classic figure of the outsider allowed him to get out of his *galère* by getting a house and an income. He did so by forging a particular type of relationship across perceived difference and hierarchy, by becoming the client of a patron, toward whom his responsibilities were unclear. The tale was cautionary because despite the success of such an encounter, Amadou and Lassana warned against following the "Old Jew's" rule limiting Hafidou's interactions by not allowing him to have people at his apartment. It was important, they said, to refuse such limits. Otherwise, you might not meet the people who could enable your onward movement.

This story captures a central tenet of the Gare du Nord method. Adventurers seek to create social ties with strangers and bring them into their social networks, a practice akin to what Robert Putnam and others have called "bridging social capital" (as opposed to "bonding social capital," which is focused on kin and community networks).[1] For adventurers, the station harbors the possibility of finding happiness abroad because it is suffused with movement, a coming together of many pathways. In order to harness this potential, the struggling migrant must know how to reconfigure himself—as Hafidou did—into a heroic adventurer and cultural translator with the interactional know-how to create relationships. This set of incorporated knowledge and practices emphasizing the potential of encounters across difference encapsulates how Lassana, Amadou, and their peers understand what they are doing at the Gare du Nord.

Successful adventurers in this context are those who can understand and work the social and economic world of a transportation hub. Hafidou's story follows the forward-moving trajectory that they hope for, taking him from "struggle" to "happiness," while highlighting the potential pitfalls and ambivalent outcomes that migrants encounter along the way. Acting with generosity and reciprocity is another moral of the story: Hafidou came back and helped out his comrades at the station, just as he had received their help when he was struggling. The story emphasizes the importance of hard work and perseverance in difficult circumstances. It suggests that leaving the immigrant dormitory behind was a condition for finding happiness. It also suggests that their precarious day jobs—in cleaning, construction, and food service—are insufficient. Adventurers have to work a double shift: during the day to make a wage, often building buildings, and in the evening at the station, building their networks.[2] I never met Hafidou, and if he did exist, I doubt that a story retold for years provides an accurate account of what he experienced. Over time, it had become more of a fable; adventurers used the story to provide a moral script for how to act in this improvised community.

This chapter examines the work migrants put into the Gare du Nord and what they get out of it. Rare were the men who got big material returns (housing, papers, or long-term employment) directly from the Gare du Nord method, but many did find a temporary fix there to complement other income or to avoid becoming destitute. It puzzled me at first why they invested so much in the Gare du Nord even when it was not very lucrative—but then, economic activity is never only about monetary gain.[3] In addition to the techniques they developed in order to accumulate wealth, they also built a more intangible kind of capital that they then hoped to translate into prestige and wealth elsewhere. Not only did they generate social capital at the Gare du Nord, but they also saw a chance to cultivate the courage and cunning of the adventurer. These skills were like a shield against the demoralizing experiences they had with police and as workers in France.

Beyond the exigencies of migrant life, beyond its convenient location between home and work, beyond instrumental strategies, the aesthetic experience of mobility that defined the rail hub was part of why these men spent so much time and effort at the Gare. As they struggled to get by, to get papers, and to find stable employment, the enclaves did not seem to help. They departed from them, venturing into the railway station where, they had heard, they could find new opportunities. Many West Africans at the station told me that their reason for being there was not only to find work and meet women or potential patrons like the "old Jew," but also to learn how to be a successful adventurer by listening to the cautionary tales and advice of others at the station. Most were still looking for happiness, and the Gare du Nord seemed like a good place to find it.

They used the space of a railway station to construct alternative pathways that they hoped would enable their social becoming and economic flourishing. These new paths may have ambivalent outcomes for individual migrants' success, but they nonetheless have created a durable social infrastructure that alters the station's social environment. Their activity at the station is an alternative form of integration and value creation when traditional pathways of socioeconomic integration—such as the labor market—come up short.

## HARD WORK IN THE INTÉRIM

Hafidou begins where many of the men I interviewed began: living in a crowded immigrant dormitory and working temporary low-wage jobs. "We are here to work," I heard, over and over again, from Lassana, Amadou, Ibrahim, and their comrades. They meant, first, that they were in France to be wage laborers, to make money, and to send money back home. Like people in many places across the world, they derived meaning from their work and careers. They had grown up in places that attached great importance to hard work, seeing it as something that dignified a person. Not all work was dignified: West African migrants in France often work in sectors (such as in cleaning, construction, or street selling) that would be considered shameful were they to do that kind of work in their home villages.[4] By working in these sectors, they demonstrated they had what in Soninke is called *len siren*—courage (literally, being a good child)—which implied being raised well by one's parents, an attribute seen as key to success abroad. "The adventure is hard work!" as Lassana would say.

When they first arrived in France, many West Africans at the station told me that they found work through a family connection, using a fake resident permit or someone else's documents to be hired. Amadou's first job in France was doing manual labor on a construction site. Lassana's first job was cleaning SNCF trains for a subcontracted cleaning company. Many of the men at the Gare du Nord tried to enter the construction industry, where they saw the possibility for moving up the ladder from general laborer ("*manoeuvre*") to specialized positions such as frame-setters (*coffreurs/boiseurs*), roofers (*étancheurs*), and reinforcing-iron specialists (*ferrailleurs*), and even becoming masons. They began working undeclared for small-scale contractors (*artisans*) who were often immigrants themselves. They then moved up to day laborer work through temporary work agencies, where they tried to gain skills on the job or through training programs. Most of the men I knew had never received a longer-term contract, spending more than a decade in day laborer positions.

Temp agencies were part of a system known as the *intérim*, or temporary work sector. Their growth was the outcome of labor flexibilization in the twentieth century. The intérim offers precarious employment, with workers sometimes not knowing whether their contract would be renewed for the following day until they left in the evening. The intérim sector was created by a conjuncture of legal and economic changes in the 1960s and 1970s that rocked the construction industry at the end of the euphoric period of postwar growth in France. Already in 1962 and 1963, construction companies recruited foreign workers to protect their profit margins from the high salaries required by French workers.[5] A 1972 law led to the growth of temporary work agencies (*agences d'intérim*) by giving them the exclusive right to provide workers to other companies (which was otherwise forbidden by laws that made subcontracting of labor illegal).[6]

The presence of these agencies on the streets around the Gare du Nord was one of the many reasons West Africans were drawn to the station. They got to know the neighborhood because they could spend a day going from agency to agency to look for work, just to be turned down. It was a difficult and sometimes humiliating experience in which they were often subjected to racist insults; at the end of the day, they would return to the station to share their experiences with their friends.[7] When they did find work, it was often grueling and heavily surveilled, especially for workers hired at the so-called unskilled level. They had to be constantly moving, or appear to be doing so—just a moment of rest while waiting to be able to complete a task could merit a sanction. As in their interactions with the police, West Africans endured insults at agencies and worksites meant to remind them of their inferior place in the social hierarchy, and they had difficulty obtaining specialized posts—even after they had acquired the necessary skills. In construction, an African worker is often referred to as a "Mamadou," after a common first name. They were excluded from positions of authority; as a worksite manager in sociologist Nicolas Jounin's ethnography of the French construction sector put it, "A Mamadou is never a boss." Some workers remained for decades at the so-called unskilled level, with agencies refusing to certify their attainment of skills on the job. They were aware that temporary work agencies made money this way; they could pay them at a lower rate while extracting valuable specialized labor from them, and then dismiss them from their jobs with no warning.[8]

Temporary work remains unregulated because of construction industry pressure on the government. Since most temporary workers are migrants who do not have French nationality, and many are undocumented, collective mobilization is risky and difficult. The intérim sector occupies the lower tier of a dual labor system in which profitable industries are able to extract labor from migrants in precarious situations. This dual system is not unique to France; it is widespread across the global North, in countries such as Germany and the United States, as well as in Bahrain and the United Arab Emirates, where migrant workers occupy an inferior status and benefit from none of the protections of citizens.[9] The temporary work sector is a primary example of "inclusion through exclusion": it integrates African migrants into the French economy as inferiors with few rights or opportunities for career mobility.

The Gare du Nord, they hope, will help them advance within the intérim. Jal, a Malian in his thirties, started coming to the Gare du Nord after arduous days doing the heavy lifting at a road construction job and (when his contract ended) going from agency to agency to find another job. At the station, he shared his frustrations with other folks in the same situation. He heard about a new hospital being built in the suburbs from a friend there, which still needed workers to prepare the terrain. He showed up at the agency address the next day and was given a job. He began to see the station as an alternative work agency where he might find not only sympathy but also his livelihood. Other men used the station as an entrée into informal economies that were sometimes criminal (drugs and stolen merchandise), or to find a patron as Hafidou did. In an ideal situation, these activities were combined with wage labor, even if short-term positions were all they could find. "Even a poorly paid job was valued," as Keith Hart points out for Frafra migrants in Accra: "It was an island of regularity and predictability in a sea of ephemeral opportunities."[10]

As employment became more difficult to find after the 2008 economic crisis, adventurers turned more and more to the Gare du Nord as a primary worksite (this is how Amadou got his nickname, Security without Salary, showing up for "work" at the station every morning at nine o'clock). It had the added benefit of being located outside the subjugating gazes of construction bosses. Lassana said the station taught him how to get better positions in construction by refusing the subordinate position imposed on him; he became an *étancheur* (roofer) and eventually a team leader. Most of the adventurers I spoke to downplayed workplace subordination and emphasized instead the skills they had gained. At the station, several men told me that they had learned techniques for dealing with difficult bosses, for evaluating which bosses were good to work with, and for holding their bosses accountable when they withheld wages.

Despite his precarious status with a one-year resident permit, Lassana took his long-time boss (whom he had gotten to sponsor his resident permit) to the labor tribunal for unpaid wages. He won. "That's thanks to the Gare du Nord," he told me, "If I stayed in the *foyer*, I might never have done that." It took courage. He got the wages, but through a legal loophole his boss managed to terminate Lassana's employment (by closing his business and opening another one in his wife's name). Lassana was not surprised, but he had lost a valuable long-term contract. Going against dominant wisdom, he said that once he had papers and a skilled worker certification, he preferred temporary work anyway, bragging that he knew the system so well that he could get better pay there. Even when he needed work, he refused at least three jobs he thought were offering inferior pay with respect to his skills. He liked the flexibility of temporary work, which fit with his hopes for a more mobile future. He and his comrades tried their best to dignify undignified work conditions.

Social and family networks are generally seen as playing a more important role in developing countries where there is imperfect information about opportunities and a lack of formal institutions for labor migration.[11] These networks also play an important role in contexts where formal institutions exist, as in France, but where those institutions put some people into inferior positions in the labor market, as Jounin shows is the case for France. Adventurers activate social networks at the station (and create new ones) to create a space where they are less unequal than in the intérim.

After 2008, even decent temporary jobs were hard to find. In October 2009, a group of undocumented temp workers went on strike and occupied several temp agencies in Paris. They pointed to the importance of their work in key French industries, reclaiming resident work permits from the government without raising the issue of poor labor conditions.[12] None of the men I knew at the Gare du Nord were interested in participating in that movement, believing that it would not achieve its goal. They had turned instead to the station, where they would face classic questions: How could they establish a community in an informal context where there is neither kinship nor contract? How could they define an "economic form" where there was a hodgepodge of precarious activities?[13] It was exactly in that space where the adventurers hoped to develop and demonstrate their skills.

## MOBILE INFRASTRUCTURE AND THE ADVENTURE

There is a term in French for the improvisatory strategies used by people who occupy inferior social statuses: the "Système D." The 'D' stands for the noun *débrouillardise* and the verb *se débrouiller* which approximately translates to "to work around" or "to get by." As Libby Murphy points out in her brilliant history of the notion, *se débrouiller* is an art with connotations of improvisational shrewdness and ingenuity, and in its most frequent usage in France it referred to the way that French people bent the rules to get around bureaucratic red tape.[14] Murphy shows that far from being a purely French invention, the Système D is a hybrid creation that arose in Algeria at the beginning of French colonization. It has since emerged in Francophone contexts where inferior social positions and unequal resource distribution lead to precarity and suffering.[15] Although it fell out of very common usage in France in the 1980s, structural readjustment in West Africa led to a reinvigoration of the term as it came to refer to *la débrouillardise* that people in Senegal and Mali had to have to make ends meet when stable employment was scarce.

The Gare du Nord method has much in common with the Système D; it is also about trying to work around systems of migration bureaucracy and labor markets to create new kinds of economic opportunities for adventurers' success abroad. It is also a hybrid, born of adventurers' experiences on the road and their engagement in French urban life. The Système D, like what the adventurers are doing, is reserved for people without power, who cannot control the design of the legal, economic, or urban space around them, but who nonetheless will attempt to influence it. As anthropologist Peter Redfield points out, this bricoleur-like approach rarely has fantastic results for those who use it. Like the bricolage of the Système D, the Gare du Nord method most often just helps migrants to "patch things together, to get through one crisis and on to the next."[16] But even when it is merely reactive to the strategies of those in power, these practices nonetheless manage to produce something new: in this case, an alternative economic and infrastructural space to ensure livelihoods and prove adventurer skills.

This chapter examines the economic practices of the Gare du Nord method: how adventurers use the station for money transfer and saving practices that bypass both official and kin systems, cultivate station networks to find jobs, and develop expertise in the transit system, learning how to communicate that knowledge in order to meet new people. In all of these practices, adventurers examine the gaps within formal infrastructure and apply their knowledge and social relationships to fill those gaps. In this sense, they are acting as what AbdouMaliq Simone calls "people as infrastructure," operating as infrastructural conduits where there were none.[17] As in the contexts that Simone examines in Kinshasa and Johannesburg, social aspects such as "the particularities of an individual's family and ethnic background, their personal character and style, and their location in particular arrangements of residence and circulation with others" affect infrastructural interventions.[18] Unlike Simone's case, their infrastructural interventions are carried out in a place where there is not a penury but rather a surfeit of state-made channels that participate in their marginalization. They must learn to work with and work around those channels.

At the Gare du Nord, transportation infrastructure provides a useful model and focus to examine how migrants engage with urban spaces from multiple social positions: as mobile adventurers, as transnational kin, as the objects of immigration regulation, and as players in official and noninstitutional (also called "informal") economic markets. Focusing on infrastructure—that is, channels that maintain and create relationships between and among places, persons, and things—helps to decenter what Ayse Çaglar and Nina Glick Schiller refer to as the "methodological nationalism" of transnational and migration studies, which often reproduce the notion of a bounded national and ethnic group by focusing on particular communities united by nation or language.[19]

Infrastructure as a subject of inquiry has provided a rich source of anthropological innovation that I build on in this chapter.[20] Ethnographies of the social and political side of infrastructure have illustrated how, in places where the state fails to provide it or where infrastructure is not available to everyone, people often act as the conduits of services and information, taking the place of missing infrastructure, providing social ties that enable its effective delivery, and using systems such as trash disposal to establish what Rosalind Fredericks calls an "ethics of infrastructure." Jennifer Cole illustrates how communication infrastructure may act as both a "metonym" for migrant communities and as a technology that produces those communities, while Xiang and Lindquist consider how low-wage labor migration relies on a set of social and physical channels and intermediaries constituting "migration infrastructure."[21]

Unlike many places examined by these studies, Paris has too much infrastructure, having been produced by centuries of state interventions in planning and urban space. Underground projects tend to go over budget as they are met with the obstructions of existing circuits, a crisscross of electricity wiring, catacombs, sewage, and subway tunnels, built up over centuries. At the same time, there are not enough channels that work against the logic of capital circulation and population control built into the system since the nineteenth century.[22] For example, there are few intra-suburban connections and many suburban residents complain about the Paris-centric design. West Africans at the station are operating in the space between a surfeit of transportation infrastructure fitting the logic of accumulation and a lack of transit lines that do not correspond to this logic. They created alternative communication channels not because the state had failed to do so, but because state infrastructure is embedded in the types of circuits and values, such as security and surveillance, that they want to avoid or use for other purposes.

What does this mean in practice? Much of what West African men who call themselves adventurers do at the station there is talk. They greet each other and size up new arrivals, they have long discussions over coffee, they talk to people coming in on trains, they retell the stories of their travails in France, they share news and debate politics. Such discussions can be a pleasurable break from taxing commutes and jobs. They also study the departure board and the metro map, observe the social flux of people to figure out who is who; they become experts in the various scams and schemes targeting train passengers, and as we saw, they spend a lot of time observing and interacting with police and security teams. It takes a lot of hard work, which they are motivated to do because they want to establish and maintain communication channels that they hope will create value for them.

These activities confound the ways that work and economic activity tend to be defined. It is useful to think about these practices through the lens of what anthropologist Julia Elyachar calls "phatic labor," the work of making and maintaining the ties that bind people in social and economic relationships and that produces "social infrastructure."[23] This notion draws on Roman Jakobson's "phatic function" of language and Bronislaw Malinowski's "phatic communication"; both notions highlight the way that language not only references something that exists in the world but also creates and maintains communication channels.[24] For example, adventurers often engaged in lengthy salutations each time they saw someone they knew, inquiring about their families, health, and homes for several minutes; these interactions were more about maintaining social ties than about conveying information. They offered them respite from an alienating life elsewhere in the capital, including long days on worksites where they had to endure insults from other workers and the strict control of their bosses. But they were about opening social channels and making sure they remained open.

At the Gare du Nord, "social infrastructure" is created through relationships that enable new conduits through old channels.[25] The practice of "hacking" provides a useful way to understand how this process works. Hacking involves knowledge and mastery of system codes, as well as the ability to improvise within that system in order to divert existing channels and create new ones. Similar to the bricoleur, the hacker takes a playful tinkerer's approach to systems and machines. Like the "archetypal hacker selves" of the digital world, West African adventurers employing the Gare du Nord method "have playfully defiant attitudes, which they apply to almost any system in order to repurpose it."[26]

Their hacking activities also involve translating the *débrouillard* techniques they mastered during their migratory journeys onto a French public space. Since Paris already has so much infrastructure, they do this by hacking the existing infrastructures and rechanneling them through the social world they weave at the Gare du Nord. Thus, their success is based on their capacity to put material and social infrastructure together; that is, to use existing infrastructure in new ways in order to make it generate a combination of various kinds of capital (symbolic, social, material). In order to create value, these channels cannot be, as Pierre Bourdieu puts it, like a "beaten path" but rather they must be—or at least, be perceived as—novel modes of communication that enable relationships.[27]

The effects of their tinkering, bricoleur-like practice creates an alternative system of relations than the one for which the infrastructure was initially designed. From a hub of metropolitan transport, the Gare du Nord method makes the station into a hub for West African networks of value creation, whether through money transfer systems, micro-saving networks, providing services where there are infrastructural gaps, or by creating relations with people outside kin communities. To put this method into practice, these men need to master the formal infrastructure and then rechannel it.

## HOW TO: THE GARE DU NORD METHOD

In 1996, a group of sociologists led by eminent urban scholar Isaac Joseph—the French conduit for Erving Goffman's school of sociology—published a collective study of the Gare du Nord, which they called *Gare du Nord: A User's Guide*.[28] The thick tome explored how social interactions occurred in a mass transit hub where hundreds of thousands of strangers brushed elbows each day. It was impressive in scope and coverage and a unique study for French sociology. Aside from professional status (e.g., station employees, metro employees, emergency workers), however, the contributions ignored social differentiations. Like the sociologists who contributed to the volume, Lassana, Amadou, Dembele, and their peers had developed their own methodology and analysis of this complex space. They offer an alternative user's guide to the station: the adventurer's how-to of the Gare du Nord.

### *1. How to Master Hundreds of Trains and Hundreds of Thousands of Square Feet*

The Gare du Nord is an enormous station: four hundred thirty thousand square feet spread across five levels. Even more impressive than its sheer size is the amount of people who traipse through its corridors and step onto its platforms. Between metro, rail, bus, and foot traffic, there are almost seven hundred thousand people who set foot into the station each day. Over five hundred trains arrive and depart from the early morning to the last train around midnight, not counting the metro. Every meeting I had with Lassana or Amadou was a new lesson in how to navigate the station. They illustrated how well they knew it—unlike me—by taking shortcuts and watching me scramble to keep up. They knew where the police would be at various times of the day, and which corners remained uncontrolled and unoccupied.

One day as we took a series of escalators from the basement commuter rail platforms to the international Eurostar terminal on the second floor, Lassana greeted dozens of people he knew along the way. Although he occasionally would see friends and kin from his village on their way to catch the metro, most of the people he said hello to were other young West Africans whom he had met through the Gare du Nord networks. He had a precise social map of the station space and knew where different groups hung out: down in the mall was where the *renois* (French-African youth) met up; the "Congolese" and other central Africans hung out in front of the McDonalds or in the back of the station where the buses came; men from Romania chatted in front of the old stone entrance. He incorporated the rhythms of the station so that he could walk through immensely crowded spaces with ease. When I lost my ticket needed to exit, he helpfully took me to the turnstile that was always broken, where I could pass through without a ticket. His was proud of his expertise, this local knowledge that, he said, good adventurers had to develop.

Many of the young West Africans I spoke to about their activities at the Gare du Nord knew that transit system knowledge was useful to meet people. They knew that travelers, especially those from afar, were likely to get lost and ask for directions. On a cold evening in 2010, a young woman who had arrived from the airport to take the TGV to Maubeuge, a town in northern France, asked Doulaye, the newcomer, if he knew when the next train was leaving. He blinked and stumbled over his words, to the pleasure of his comrades standing nearby, who started laughing. Doulaye turned to Amadou, to ask him if he knew which train line went to that town, but by the time he turned back to the woman, a different young man was whisking her away, pointing at the departure board and the line that would go to that town. Doulaye shook his head in frustration and his new friends laughed, telling him that in order to be successful here he needed to know the *panneau* (the departure board) by heart before trying to meet women or anyone else at the station. "You gotta know the departure board!" they yelled, cracking up.

The *panneau* in the station's main hall is an exalted form of knowledge because it represents the official infrastructure of the French long-distance and high-speed train system. The people they most sought to meet came from farther afield than the left bank, making the metro and commuter rail an important but lesser form of infrastructural knowledge. For some train passengers, the old-fashioned departure board with its manual click and shuffle (now replaced with a digital board) embodied the time-space of railway journeys and the nostalgia of nineteenth-century modernity signified by this sensory experience.[29] "Knowing the *panneau*" was not only about mastering the French transportation system—and thus French ways of classifying spaces and relationships—but also about knowing how to mobilize that knowledge in social interactions.

The moment of Doulaye's embarrassment was not just an opportunity for his friends to denigrate a potential rival; it was an important teaching moment as well. Doulaye went to work memorizing the departure board. It was a moment of cultural transmission, which helps assure the continuity of the station community of West African migrants and the infrastructure produced through the Gare du Nord method. The *panneau* and the train line maps signified this networked knowledge; Lassana would quiz me on which train lines went to which northern towns just to display how much better he knew the *panneau*.

### *2. How to Make and Move Money*

In mid-2013, Lassana was laid off from his long-term work contract as a specialized construction worker laying foundations of residential and public buildings around the Paris region (in retaliation for taking his employer to the labor tribunal). His kin at the immigrant dormitory had been little help, as the connections they had were for positions at the "unskilled" level. But he saw that kind of job as "going backward" (*aller à l'envers*). He approached old friends at the station to widen his chances of finding a suitable position. In part thanks to his reputation as a generous friend and good worker, several of them transmitted his request to other folks they knew in construction. In three weeks, he found a decently paid temporary position laying the groundwork for a new high-speed rail line in the southwest of France, near Bordeaux. In that job, commuting back and forth with a team of workers each week, Lassana contributed in another way to one of the emblematic channels of French state infrastructure: high-speed rail.[30]

"It's too difficult to find a good intérim job these days," Bakary, a Senegalese construction worker, complained to me one day. "You go from agency to agency, all day, they tell you the same thing: there's nothing available. Then they'll tell someone else they have something."[31] Instead, he said, it was better to rely on friends at the station who could tell you which worksites needed people. "What about your cousins and brothers? Don't they help you find work?" I asked. "Only in the beginning," he said. It was preferable to avoid family connections for jobs in France because they would try to take "half your salary," he explained. The Gare du Nord, he said, presented many advantages as a work placement network—the *patrons* were already vetted by fellow adventurers, and so less likely to cheat you, the conditions were better than half of the temporary jobs around, and you got to bypass the temp agencies, where these men often felt humiliated.

In the aftermath of an international economic crisis, adventurers use the social tools at their disposal to meld the temporary job sector with their own networks. Amadou can recall the time when temporary work agencies would come to the front square in the early morning to recruit West Africans as day laborers. He says that for a period in the 1990s and 2000s, the station became known as an easy place to find jobs "that the French don't want."

By 2010, it was much more difficult to find a decent temporary work position. Today, the lack of work and continued influx of new migrants have made it so that recruiters no longer come to the station, and these agencies have much more stringent requirements (still, industry leaders complain about a lack of workers). "Now," said Lassana, "it's become like everything else. You have to go in with your big applicant file and your CV and your diplomas or they won't take you." The station remains a node in migrant labor networks thanks to the work that these men do helping each other find jobs.

The front square of the station has become an improvised and horizontally organized temporary work agency. No one asks for your resume or your diploma, but you have to build a reputation as a serious worker among the station regulars to find a job this way. Lassana, Jal, and Dembele all used Gare du Nord contacts to find new temporary construction jobs. When they did, they made a hybrid out of two strategies for finding work, combining the model of the French-run work agencies with patronage and family networks. The Gare du Nord system bound them to each other: helping someone find a job could help garner a loan down the road. For the adventure, the Ghanaian proverb cited by Keith Hart seems to apply here too: "Familiarity is better than kinship."[32] Ahmed, an older Tunisian migrant, had also made use of the network when he was out of a job. He had worked with Bakary on a construction site. When they ran into each other at the station front square, Bakary introduced him to some of the adventurers and vouched for him. Ahmed left with some leads for agencies with openings for his specialty.

In addition to work agencies, their station community also allowed migrants to set up solidarity banks similar to the widespread practices among West African village associations in France.[33] Fourteen of the men I spoke to at the Gare du Nord participated in some kind of independent micro-savings system based at the station, which offered an alternative to the official banking system *and* to the system that operated among members of a single village or ethnic group. Instead, their affiliation and trust were based on the networks they established at the Gare du Nord. Unlike most "*caisse communes*" (community banking) of West African men, micro-saving here was premised on the right amount of social distance. They sought ties with those outside of their immediate families, towns, and ethnic groups while basing a common understanding and trust on West African cultural repertoires of belonging, migration, Muslim religious commitment, and obligation.[34]

The Gare du Nord method provides alternative models of solidarity and reciprocity through the *caisses communes*, and also draws on cultural idioms of ethnic boundary making. One *caisse commune* was comprised of four regulars at the station: Lassana, Amadou, Jal, and Bakary—three Malian men and one Senegalese of differing mother tongues and ethnicities. They had no common relatives, and their home villages were all several hundred kilometers apart. The adventurers found the key to their belonging in the Gare du Nord community and in many ways transcended ethnic boundaries, but ethnic stereotypes found their way into many boundary-making jokes and discussions at the station. Lassana said his Soninke family would forbid their daughters to marry non-Soninke men because those men would be lazy and not work; Fula communities (like Jal's) insisted that Khassonke men (Amadou) were *feticheurs*, that is, animists and thus not true Muslims; while Bamana elders (Bakary's father's family) said Soninke men were too obsessed with money and thus bad marriage partners. These statements did not reflect actual prohibitions but rather the connections between these groups expressed through a repertoire of jokes and stereotypes.[35] They also used such stereotypes at the station to interpret the behavior of their fellows, especially when someone deviated from the values of solidarity and reciprocity. This was true, for example, when Amadou reneged on his responsibility to the *caisse commune*, dropping out before he had repaid what he had taken. "That's so Khassonke!" (*C'est du Khassonke, ça!*"), exclaimed Jal, and Lassana added, "They're all sweet talkers, but they don't speak the truth" ("*Ils sont des beau-parleurs, mais ils n'ont pas la parole*").

Despite potential risks, these initiatives provided common pools of money that helped migrants gain autonomy both from French migrant networks and from family back home, which often both acted as "negative social capital" draining migrants' resources.[36] As a kind of investment diversification, it allowed them to envision projects outside of the monthly village collection, to which they also contributed. In addition, more than half of the young men I got to know at the station were younger brothers (often of their fathers' second wives), who did not yet have enough sway in their respective family structures to define how the money they contributed would be spent. Finally, the circle of redistribution created by the *caisses communes* enabled migrants to operate as patrons back home—for example, Jal used the money collected during one cycle to help his cousin come to France. His cousin became part of relations of obligation, and in a wider sense, Jal's family became linked to the men at the Gare du Nord. Lassana even ended up visiting Jal's dying mother in Bamako before her own son was able to make the return trip. The station's solidarity banks were detached from kin and village networks, but then reinvested in those networks. Adventurers had to gain trust and also figure out how to switch between reciprocity systems.

Migrant remittances help the station networks enter into circuits of credit, obligation, and exchange in villages. As studies of such remittance and migrant development practices illustrate, they carry with them a host of moral connotations that require translation between multiple circuits of exchange.[37] Remittance that provides prestige and greater resources may also transform the workings of social reproduction. Money transferred through migration has been shown to alter village hierarchies and create generational conflict and inequality, as migrants used remittance and development projects (such as house building) not only to maintain relationships from afar but also to maintain distance.[38] In addition to these effects on villages and family ties, inventing new remittance strategies allows adventurers to show off their skills and creates new relationships outside of the kin-to-kin networks in which remittance is usually analyzed.

For most migrants in France, there are three options for transferring euros to their families: via foreign banks with French locations, through companies like Western Union, or through friends and family. For West Africans, most money gets transferred through a system that Jal, astutely observing its formality, called "Malian Western Union," which operates through immigrant dormitories. They only used the actual Western Union or similar companies if they had a sudden and urgent need to send money.

African banks with offices in Paris played an important part in the accumulation of money for individual migrants and were reserved for saving larger amounts that would be transferred back to purchase land, buy a house, or retire. Migrants rarely talked openly about such bank accounts, for fear that they might attract too much attention. For the eight men I met who had such accounts, they were crucial because they enabled them to make purchases and transfer money without having to go through their family. They combined strategies for individual accumulation with excessive gift giving when they returned in person, performing both largesse and the migrant's successful appropriation of the signs of European modernity, such as Western-style dress, in a display of "conspicuous redistribution."[39]

For the monthly transfers (like many fellow West Africans in France, most of these men reported sending back between 100 and 150 euros per month while employed), even the "Malian Western Union" was seen as a potential sponge on their resources. Bakary preferred to avoid the immigrant dormitory transfer system by trying to find other people through the station who would bring money home for him because he could better manage how the money would be spent without bothering with kin intermediaries and the various "taxes" they would skim from the money he was sending. He and Lassana admitted that this was risky, but he added that it sufficed to "know people" well enough to distinguish those who were trustworthy from those who would cheat you, a skill in discernment that Lassana said he had learned from his grandparents "in the village." That capacity allowed him to skirt those kinship networks of the immigrant dormitory transfers, but making a bad judgment call could cost them a lot, so they had to both make connections at the station and be able to discern who was trustworthy.

When I went to Mali in 2011, Lassana was unable to go because his resident permit was about to expire. He gave me 500 euros to convert into CFA (West African Francs) and bring to his family. Through his involvement with my research, he created a channel to transfer money without going through official services—whether of the formal marketplace or of the kinship ties in immigrant dormitories. He worked hard to maintain that channel: when I first left France, he called me every week just to "*prendre les nouvelles*" (get the news). We did not share much information during these short calls, but rather performed the essential phatic function of keeping communication flowing and open. That way, when the channel was needed, he would not find it disintegrating and blocked.

The skillful manipulation of various money transfer systems displayed the adventurer's skill at making links and social relationships that might prove valuable down the road. They combined transnational banking with informal microfinance, and kin-based money transfer and accounting with money transfer systems that bypassed kin networks. This was the beauty of the Gare du Nord—it was a site where formal and informal economies and infrastructures came together and could be combined.

### 3. *How to Exploit the Gaps*

"The Gare du Nord is a pain in the ass," complained Stéphane, the father of two young children who worked in the security risk sector. He lived between London, where he worked, and Paris, where his wife and children were based, and took the Eurostar train from the Gare du Nord on a weekly basis. He was a business traveler and had a frequent traveler pass, which allowed him to bypass the crowds and sit in the bright but quiet Philip Starck–designed waiting room before boarding his London-bound train. Even though he had about the highest class, most exclusive and comfortable experience that the Gare du Nord could offer, he still found it difficult to navigate. He talked about getting out of the taxi at the front of the station, "There are cars everywhere, no sidewalks, no one knows who has the priority but everyone thinks it's theirs," and then navigating the cobblestones with luggage, a stroller, and two kids. His experience points to a broader problem: many of the intermediate infrastructures that would allow passengers to get where they need to go are cumbersome and slow. Taxi lines are too long, there are no luggage transfer services, and many train transfers are complicated to make, with signage and information difficult to access. Passengers often transfer from the Gare du Nord to the nearby Gare de l'Est, which is a ten-minute walk away, yet there is no clear indication of how to get from one station to the other. Unlike in airports, there are no caddies available for transporting bags, and the crowded entrance makes it difficult for drivers to stop and get out of their cars to help. The few licensed porter services are expensive and difficult to find. This gap in infrastructure to get passengers from the city into the train is where Driss and his colleagues came in.

Driss is a Malian man in his fifties who arrived in Europe in the 1990s. He spent almost twenty years working in Spain, mostly on farms, before deciding to make his way to France with a friend from his village. In 2010, he got to Paris with a Spanish work and resident permit that allowed him to travel to France but not to live and work there. The year he arrived, he heard from some folks at the dormitory that he should go to the Gare du Nord to find a job. It would otherwise be hard to find a position without a work permit, and he was too old to work as a day laborer on construction sites. Even if he wanted the job, they told him, the temporary job agency directors would not give him a chance because of his age. Driss was fine with that—he said he had no interest in working in construction, where he would be controlled by a boss and an overseer.

Once at the station, he and his friend noticed people struggling to get their bags inside and to their trains. It was an opportunity. He requisitioned one of the few SNCF luggage trolleys that could be found at the station, and then stood outside to find clients getting out of taxis with heavy suitcases. Driss operated by proposing his services to the taxi driver first, who would then pass clients on to him. When they asked the cost for the service, he would hold up his hands and shake his head. "There's no price," he would say, "It depends on you." Most often, he got somewhere between 2 to 10 euros, but sometimes he made as much as 20 and once, he said, he received a crisp 50-euro bill. It was rare that he received no money at all, but when it happened, he would wish the travelers a nice day and head back to his spot in front of the station. "The French pay the worst," he said, and "Americans were not great, but not bad." His favorite clients were "from the Gulf." When he spotted a family that he thought came from the Emirates or Saudi Arabia, he would drop whatever he was doing to zoom over to their taxi with a bright, "Assalamu aleykoum!" as he helped their driver unload the bags from the trunk onto his caddie.

Driss's services were modeled on the parallel infrastructures of some West African airports, where there were minimal official commercial amenities and much in the way of informal services for travelers arriving and departing. He had found a space in the gray area between legal and illegal: as long as he did not officially charge for his service, he said, he could be an unofficial porter. As soon as he

FIGURE 8. Driss (L) pushes his luggage caddie across the Place Napoleon III toward the main entrance of the station, accompanied by another unofficial porter, June 2018. Author.

proposed a price, however, he was offering an unlicensed service and could be arrested. "I'm just helping people," he explained to me, "And if they want to give me a gift, they can." He was able to spot a gap in the channel that transferred people from train, to station, to the larger city, and find a solution. The SNCF badge on the trolleys offered an added layer of trust for potential clients. He had the mark of a true *débrouillard.* His frugal way of living allowed him get by in Paris and make enough to send a little back to his wife and children in Mali. He was finding a way to integrate with transportation infrastructure and exploit its insufficiencies.

His evaluation and exploitation of the system's lacks, however, were not enough to make him successful at it. He also had to build social ties at the station. When he first arrived, Driss was modest and friendly, and Lassana and Amadou saw him as an elder to whom they owed respect. He relied on them to help him operate his porter services. Without their protection, he might be hassled for taking another improvised porter's territory, or someone might take his trolley. He had to be able to escape the notice of station workers and railway police, who harassed him for using "SNCF property." He relied on his friends to warn him. I heard a customer service employee at the SNCF call Driss a "cheater" for using the luggage carts, echoing the way Sarkozy described the Congolese man whose ticket check had instigated the station revolt in 2007. The police also bothered him when he had first arrived—they wanted to make sure that he was not participating in any of the station's tourist scams.

In addition to fellow West Africans, Driss relied on several young men who hung out with him at the station—including a few who did not have a stable residence. They kept watch over his trolley when he was not around. The most reliable was Thomas, a thirty-something Portuguese fellow with a well-trimmed beard, who had grown up between Lisbon and the suburbs of Paris. He had been a bartender in Portugal but was unable to find work when he returned to France and could not afford an apartment. He spent his days in the middle of the station's front square, chatting and joking with Driss and their friends as he nursed a tall can of beer semi-hidden in a newspaper. If Driss did very well, he would buy a round of drinks or coffee for everyone.

Thanks to the connections he made at the station and his self-effacing smile that inspired trust, Driss has been working at the station entrance for almost a decade. I went to catch up with him in the summer of 2018, and Lassana told me that Driss worked at the station in the morning in the same place as he had been in 2010, where taxis dropped passengers off for high-speed rail lines. As I approached the front square of the old stone façade on a warm June day, I recognized Abdessalam, a middle-aged Tunisian who was also in the trolley-porter business, and I asked him if Driss was around. He gestured to a space just a few yards from us where several motorcycles were parked. There he was, wearing sunglasses and a tight-fitting polo shirt, leaning against a scooter. He looked about ten years younger than the last time I saw him. He was completely transformed, joking and playfully insulting Abdessalam.

"The police and the SNCF never bother me anymore," he said, smiling again. "They know I'm not into anything criminal and they let me do what I want."

Abdessalam pouted and looked out sadly across the square. "But me, they bother me all the time!" he said, shaking his head.

"It's because you're new here," explained Driss. "But stay with me and you'll learn!" Driss said, always keeping one eye out for potential customers.

In the eight years since he had come to the station, he had transformed, from a quiet man keeping a low profile to avoid police attention to a loud and visible presence who, like Amadou, liked to show off the fact that he "managed" this part of the station. He told me several times that no other porter could work there without his blessing. When Abdessalam "stole" a client that Driss had spotted first, Driss and the other men hanging out with them would harangue him to remind him of his place in the world of unofficial porters.

Many of the local restaurant managers and owners knew Driss and often had lunch at the kebab place across the street. I sat with him and Seydou, his friend from his village, one day as he joked with the manager, a Tunisian who had been working there since 2005. The manager grabbed Driss's luggage caddie and brought it inside to the back of the restaurant. "You're stealing my caddie!" yelled Driss, "And I won't accept that! I'm going to call the police right now, thief!" They all laughed, and the manager explained that he was just protecting it. "We're all friends here," he said. He looked at me and added that at the Gare du Nord "you really have everything." Seydou, who had migrated with Driss from Mali to Spain and then on to France, had come by to check on how the porter business was going. Seydou had his own hustle at the airport, offering overburdened passengers heading for Africa a better deal on overweight luggage fees than they would pay at the counter (the airline personnel were in on it too, he explained, and took their cut). He had gotten Driss's trolley from the airport when the SNCF took the one he used to use.

"This would not work anywhere else," said Driss, "Any other station and I would have been stopped [by the police] a long time ago. But at the Gare du Nord, there's room for everything." It had become a familiar adage. Driss would know—he was friends with many of the different groups of folks at the station, including the most precarious. They sometimes drank together, and often argued about who owed whom, and how much. He was even on good terms with most of the SNCF employees, as well as his compatriots.

Driss refused to tell me how much he made, but based on the mornings I spent with him it seemed he might get two or three clients on a bad day and twice that on a good day, perhaps making between 20 and 50 euros total. It was not a lot, but it was relatively stable income for which he did not have to spend hours canvassing temporary job agencies, enduring insults and—if he a got a job—grueling work. He could take a break when he felt like it. He had gained the respect even of the police who now ignored him. "I'm my own boss here," he said, when I asked him if he liked the work at the station, "And that's important."

Driss had found an infrastructural niche that allowed him to make a small amount of money and "be his own boss" on his adventure. In addition to being socially adept and making the connections that would allow him to build necessary social capital to continue his operations, Driss also had to know the station by heart. In order to bring material and social infrastructure together to create value, then, adventurers needed to learn and build skills—the cleverness to see novel channels in the well-worn routes made by official transportation infrastructure. In a place where a misstep could lead to losing money or even to deportation, it was also crucial to recognize who was trustworthy and who was unreliable.

## SOMEONE TO TAKE AWAY

One evening as we were saying goodbye to Jal on the train platform, Lassana said to him, "Thanks. You're really someone 'to take away' (*quelqu'un à emporter*)." Jal smiled and shook Lassana's hand, then placed his hand over his heart. When he got on his train, I asked Lassana what he meant. It was important, he said, to be able to classify people in the station community according to whether they were "*quelqu'un à emporter*" (someone to take away) or "*quelqu'un sur place*" (someone for here). They borrow this vocabulary (*sur place* and *à emporter*) from the fast-food restaurants surrounding the station: people were either "for here" or "takeaway."

Lassana explained this distinction as follows: People like Omar (of "the bluff") or his friend Massa, both Malians like him, were only "for here"—that is, for the Gare du Nord. They were not people who could be depended on in the future or beyond the confines of the station, "entertaining but not trustworthy." On the contrary, some of the men, like Jal, were "à emporter." Some relationships formed at the station would endure beyond this transient space, and investing in those friendships and the channels they made meant being able to identify trustworthiness. Even if they did not share family or village or even (in many cases) ethnic affiliation, some friendships made at the Gare du Nord were significant and deep social ties. Perhaps this was because these friendships were free of the rivalries and hierarchies that structured the rest of their experience in France and their relations with their own kin. As Keith Hart puts it, they were ties based on "trust generated by shared experience, mutual knowledge, and the affection that comes from having entered a relationship freely, by choice rather than status obligation."[40]

Some "*sur place*" guys like Omar and Massa were necessary to "*faire l'ambiance*" (give the station a lively and entertaining feel), but it was important to put more effort into maintaining connections to those who were "*à emporter.*"[41] The distinction is a moral classification that helps guide these social relationships. Lassana and Jal further elaborated on what they meant by these terms. The "good" adventurer, they agreed, is someone who starts at the Gare du Nord but ends elsewhere. The "bad" adventurer, on the contrary, seeks relationships that reach their consummation within the bounds of the station's social world. *Sur place* stays in the present tense; *à emporter* is about building future relationships, a temporal orientation at the heart of the adventurer's project of creating channels that will enable onward movement.

All of Massa's actions went against the way Lassana and Jal defined the "good" adventurer likely to find happiness. When Massa wanted to find a new apartment, I compiled advertisements for him and called real estate agents. When I asked

Lassana if he knew whether Massa had found anything, he said, "Forget about it. I'm sure that Massa didn't do anything with what you gave him. Massa, he's not serious." Lassana sometimes attributed Massa's personal failing to his ethnicity, which was Khassonke, or to his upbringing (he lacked the quality Lassana called *len siren,* the honor and courage bestowed by how your parents raised you).

"We don't speak the same language," he said. "We are not the same." I pointed out that he did not share a "mother tongue" with Jal either. He berated me for being dense, pointing out that what he meant by language was not *what* language they grew up speaking but rather *how* they used that language—to speak the truth or not, to work hard or not, to be serious about the adventure or not. Those who skirted the rules of reciprocity, hard work, and future orientation risked seeing their status at the Gare du Nord plummet: they did not speak the "truth" and thus did not speak the "same language" as Lassana and Jal did.

Adventurers create more long-term, "takeaway" solutions to find "happiness," which involve creating relationships beyond the ephemera of those who are merely "sur place." They define the moral economy of station social life and try to mitigate potential risks of throwing in their lot with strangers in a public space. The station creates a new community with its own structure of values, norms, and hierarchies, where status and dignity might still be found. The pair of "*à emporter*" and "*sur place*" reveals the tensions of a community defined in part by transience. Men who return to hang out at the station to hit on women even once they have a serious girlfriend, papers, and a job—as Massa did—are seen in a negative light. Yet the story of Hafidou suggests that even those who succeed this way should return just enough to maintain the channels of exchange and reciprocity that helped them get by in the first place. To be serious about the Gare du Nord method meant to use the station's space to forge relationships across difference in it, in order to then pursue these serious relationships elsewhere. Adventurers focused on making connections beyond the station and on making station relationships part of other social worlds—of labor and of kin—that structured their time in France.

And even when they do move on, something remains. In 2014 when I returned to the station with Lassana, he told me that Amadou had met a woman and moved to the countryside. Then he gestured to a young man in cargo shorts and a tight-fitting T-shirt, chatting with friends outside the station and said, "There, that's the new Amadou now. He's the biggest player (*dragueur*)." Ephemeral or not, the relations they form at the station create durable channels where a new generation of adventurers is now operating.

## THE GARE DU NORD: *C'EST L'AFRIQUE*?

The strategies adventurers employ to survive and find dignity abroad creates social infrastructure through the Gare du Nord. Given the racialized boundaries that govern French urban space, this social infrastructure is seen as illegitimate: migrants are accused of taking the station out of French territory and making it part of "Africa," as politician Nadine Morano put it. I heard several white inhabitants of Paris say the same thing about the station, and more than a few people told me that arriving in the area around it was "like going to the Third World." I was having lunch in Chantilly, a small bourgeois town north of Paris whose train lines come into the Gare du Nord, when a retired white Frenchman asked me about my research. When I told him about the Gare du Nord, he chortled and replied, "*Ohla! La Gare du Nord! Plutôt la Gare des Noirs, n'est-ce pas?*" (Oh my, the North station! More like the Noir (black) station, isn't it?).

When I told Lassana about what the man in Chantilly had said, he was unfazed. Of course, as everyone knew, he said, French people are racist. More importantly, he added, the man was wrong; such a statement proved how little he knew the station. Lassana said that it would be worthless to spend so much time there if it were really only a space for Africans or black people. "The thing is that the Gare du Nord is international. There's everything here!" he said, repeating the refrain.

The station was a good site to be an adventurer because of its central location within transportation networks—unlike peripheral suburbs—and the people from all walks of life that transferred through it each day. As such a crossroads, it was also a "difficult" place, Lassana reminded me. In order to activate the potential such a site held, migrants had to master this complex arena and its social world enough to intervene in it. Far from making the station part of Africa, what adventurers are doing instead is making it into a hub of social exchange that brings together the many itineraries of French urban life that meet there: this is why what they are doing, as precarious as it is, is an alternative to the French model of integration.

The official integration model implies that Africans must leave their own community and values and adopt Frenchness (though they will never be considered fully French). Acquiring knowledge about French traditions, learning interactional norms, and gaining the ability to communicate in French are often seen as part of the integration process in which foreigners become citizens. West Africans at the station also emphasized the importance of gaining French linguistic and social knowledge. They did not see it as a linear path to assimilation or citizenship, but rather part of how they sought to expand channels and social relations. Infrastructural know-how overturns presumed hierarchies of knowing based on assimilation, which define Africans as marginal actors who need to assimilate French ways of acting and behaving in public space. Instead, as Lassana said to me several times, "For us, the Africans, we know the Gare du Nord by heart and it's not complicated. For you and for the police, it's complicated, but not for us. Adventurers know all of this, everyone has his place, we understand that."

His claim inverts the hierarchy to elevate what he defines as African adventurer forms of knowledge and mastery. To understand what he means by "African" in this case and how it differs from its derogatory use by Nadine Morano and others, it is important to consider the larger context and history of migrations to France from West Africa. He is not referring to traditional African "culture" that French policy attributes to African-origin residents. What he emphasizes instead is the skill set and practices of adventurers. What Lassana means by "African" here is an ability to master multiple types of infrastructural knowledge, to enable encounters and build lasting social relationships, and to be a good cultural translator. This is what makes the station an African hub.

Despite their efforts and deep knowledge of the region's transportation infrastructure, it is difficult to uphold dignity in a situation where they are subjugated by French laws, the labor market, and policing practices, as well as demeaned in the French public sphere, where Africans are accused of backwardness, overrunning the social order, and refusing to integrate and adopt French customs.[42] Even if they were very good at the Gare du Nord method, their success was precarious and subject to reversal—Hafidou's story reminds us of the danger as well as the promise of encounters across difference. All of the men I met struggled throughout their time in France, going through periods of unemployment accompanied by legal and economic insecurity. The Gare du Nord method did not often work to find dignified and sustainable livelihoods—how could any strategy lead to success in such a context? But it did try to recover some lost dignity and to carve an alternative pathway toward real integration, making a small corner of life where these men could patch together a meaningful existence.

## "GET USED TO IT"

When Doulaye, discouraged, asked Lassana what to do if women avoided his advances and yelled, "Leave me alone!" when he asked "How are you, miss?" or offered to give directions, Lassana encouraged him to keep at it.

"If a girl doesn't want to talk and says so, that's fine, I say, 'Have a nice day' and walk away. If a girl is not polite, if she yells at me to stop talking and leave her alone, I just ask her, 'What, do you have a problem at home or something? That's how it is here, it's a *Gare Internationale.* Get used to it.'" (*T'as un problème à la maison ou quoi? C'est comme ça ici, c'est une Gare Internationale. Faut s'habituer.*)

The reaction Lassana advises is a form of street harassment—insisting that a woman be "polite" and accommodating. But I never saw Lassana, or any of the adventurers, talk to women at the station in that way. Instead, he was giving Doulaye a message about the encounter logic of the Gare du Nord method. The station is an "international" site (i.e., not only a "French" one) where problems "from home" had no place, and where meaningful interactions (not civil inattention) should be the norm. His statement reverses the familiar adage of French debates on immigration, that immigrants should either assimilate to French norms ("get used to it") or leave.[43]

At the Gare du Nord, unlike the rest of France, Lassana is implying that migrants propose a model for interactions and social relations, based on a form of local knowledge combining the lessons of adventure with their knowledge about "French ways of living" and the station's social field. There were many moments in which successful social interaction at the station, a key part of the Gare du Nord method, required infrastructural mastery that included not only knowing the networks that converged upon the station, but also understanding the social makeup of the station population, how people moved through it, and what interactions had potential. Being a good adventurer included embodied performance and linguistic ability that made some men "smooth-talkers" (*beau-parleurs*). Language ability in French had nothing to do with assimilation but rather was part of the adventurers' capacity to act as the "merchants" of infrastructure—middlemen, translators, and cultural brokers—who could put to use the state-centric infrastructure while also getting other people involved in the informal, bottom-up infrastructures that they were in the business of making.

In the face of political and legal marginalization, adventurers are enlivening this international hub through phatic labor. They do so not principally by claiming a place as their own and transforming that space, but by connecting it to other sites and networks. Through this process, they began to transform the station into a space of encounter and boundary-crossing, where value is produced using the adventurer's ethos of branching outward, making connections across difference.[44] They did this by creating channels that connect the networks of West African life in Paris, from the migrant worker dormitories to the West African banks, from construction worksites to village council meetings, and bringing them to meet at the Gare du Nord. Beyond Paris and French integration, this phatic labor, the hard work of adventure, connects the community of the Gare du Nord to the villages of the Senegal River Valley, where they remit money and visit family. The Gare du Nord method makes this train station into a stop along a route, significant and productive because of the channels that meet there as well as those that can be creatively formed through state infrastructure and its gaps.

Nonetheless, adventurers remain in precarious economic positions. The connections they make provide a stop-gap measure, some money, and a temporary job. But can they help migrants achieve the traditional markers of their success abroad—accumulating wealth, getting married, building a home, and contributing to village development projects? The Gare du Nord method is not only a practical set of tools for dealing with the police and their marginalization in the French economy but also an aid in creating a moral community (of "true adventurers") to reconfigure relations to kin at home and elsewhere. In the next chapter we will see how the Gare du Nord becomes part of migrants' affective strategies and intimate lives as they struggle to forge a new pathway for coming of age and finding meaningful success abroad.

# 5

# The Ends of Adventure

## *Coming of Age at the Gare du Nord*

Nous ne savons pas, au moment de partir de chez nous, si nous reviendrons jamais.

Et de quoi dépend ce retour? demanda Pierre.

Il arrive que nous soyons capturés au bout de notre itinéraire, vaincus par notre aventure même. Il nous apparaît soudain que, tout au long de notre cheminement, nous n'avons pas cessé de nous métamorphoser, et que nous voilà devenus autres. Quelquefois, la métamorphose ne s'achève pas, elle nous installe dans l'hybride et nous y laisse.

*At the moment of leaving home we do not know whether we shall ever return.*

*And what does that return depend on? asked Pierre.*

*It may be that we shall be captured at the end of our itinerary, vanquished by our adventure itself. It suddenly occurs to us that, all along our road, we have not ceased to metamorphose ourselves, and we see ourselves as other than what we were. Sometimes the metamorphosis is incomplete. We have turned ourselves into hybrids, and there we are left.*

—CHEIKH HAMIDOU KANE, *L'AVENTURE AMBIGÜE*

Migration is often represented as a journey of departing from home and arriving abroad—a line connecting two places. *Aventuriers*, like many migrants, often experience multiple departures and arrivals. Their voyages are full of false starts and deferrals, returns and reembarking. When they tell the story of their journey to France, they begin with the moment they stepped off the plane with the feeling they had taken a big step up in the global hierarchy of migrant destinations (with North America occupying the top rung).[1] After years of turmoil in West and Central Africa, their adventure was finally bearing fruit. What often followed was an almost immediate dismay to learn that they were subject to the same obligations and hierarchies they hoped to leave behind in the village, compounded by the constraints of the bureaucratic and economic system they became part of in France. Their marginalization in the French system forced many migrants to depend on the solidarity networks of their village or ethnic communities.[2] This is what Lassana called "being on the sidelines"—that is, being doubly marginalized—as if they are only observing and being told what to do (by their elders and by the French state) instead of enacting their adventures in France.

They knew that their time in France would be mostly filled with "work and struggle"; that was part of the point of adventure. Living through that struggle to succeed abroad is how they gained respect and status when they returned home. But it is also true that they were disillusioned. Not because they do not find gold in the streets but because of the discrimination they face, the violent policing, and their exclusion from a decent labor market—all of which makes it more difficult for them to succeed by their own measure and by that of their family.

Drawing on their research among Malian migrants in France, Carolyn Sargent and Stephanie Larchanché-Kim make the point that complex and harsh immigration regulations lead migrants to move back and forth between legality and illegality, caught in a "liminal space" and often hiding their status from their closest family members because of the shame that comes with being undocumented.[3] Migrants are occupying this liminal space more often and for longer periods of time, and much recent scholarship on migration documents the suffering experienced by those in this precarious situation. This problem raises another question: What happens in the liminal space? What do migrants do when uncertainty is their lot, other than suffer? Men of adventure, says Lassana, are also men of action, and so that is the question he and his friends were determined to face head-on.

Heaviest in adventurer hearts was the concern with "getting stuck," as they often put it. Every good adventurer had to deal with being rerouted, but the key was not to let that rerouting make them deviate from the pathway they projected into the future, when they would be welcomed back to their village having gained wealth, knowledge, and life experience on the road. In 2009, just after he finally received a one-year resident permit, Lassana was sure of his future. He described a pathway that would take him beyond France to northern Europe, and imagined advancing in the construction industry, eventually becoming a worksite manager. By 2014, he could no longer envision that pathway, and he complained more about "splitting his head" between France and Mali, using a frequent term I heard adventurers use to describe a general malaise and lack of direction while in France. He was unable to get as good a job as he had in 2011, despite his ten-year resident and work permit. He had not yet been able to break ground on his house-building project in Bamako. His family asked for more money each month, he said—each year the harvest seemed to be worse. He saw that migration routes were getting more dangerous and more people were dying before they made it to Europe. When his resident permit expired, would he be able to get a new one? When he went home for a visit, would he be able to return to France? He was not sure.

Lassana, like many adventurers, began to question the whole undertaking. What was the purpose of adventure? How could migrants find a path out of struggle, in a situation where even if they made it to France, they had to deal with being degraded by the police, their bosses, and the state immigration bureaucracy? They first had to find a way to step out from the sidelines. Entering the social world of the station was yet another departure *en aventure*, this time to a true urban wilderness away from communities of immigrant dormitories. Lassana hoped it would help him to become a "big somebody;" that is, to come of age and build wealth and prestige, gaining knowledge and world experience that only travel to distant lands could offer.

This is what the Gare du Nord method had been building to, what it was ultimately for: not just to get by and find a job, but to help achieve the dignity of adulthood and prove their worth to themselves and to their brethren—to realize what Henrik Vigh has called "social becoming."[4] As part of this quest, they sought relationships with French women and attempted to reposition their relationship to the French state and to their kin. Ultimately, the adulthood they achieved was precarious and required constant (re)achieving.

The stories adventurers told were full of examples of how they learned how to survive in foreign lands, leaving the land of their ancestors and—like a classical hero—striking out on their own. But dig a little deeper, and we see how much their adventures remained a part of kin relations and obligations. Their itineraries show that there are many Gare du Nord methods, including different approaches to combining the social ties they built in France with their kin relationships.

These trajectories also reveal the ambivalent effects of this new mode of social becoming. As days stretched into months and months into years, the mobile ways of life acquired abroad became more difficult to convert into a new life of settlement in the village. Despite their projected futures of return, very few would end up going back to live in their villages before retirement age. Some young men even claim that their experiences at the Gare du Nord encouraged them to delay marriage—and thus for their village kin, entrée into full adulthood—even once they had the means. They found that their positions were precarious and could just as easily be reversed; it took significant toil to maintain their status. Many young men vacillated between *la galère* (struggle) and *le bonheur* (happiness).

As adventurers confront difficulties on their voyage abroad, they seek other socially acceptable ways of becoming a man. They had to operate a careful conversion of the status they could produce through social networks at the Gare du Nord—their "adventure capital"—into the kinds of wealth and authority that signified status and dignity in their communities. As Jennifer Cole shows about the case of Malagasy women migrants, they had to achieve this transformation of value despite meagre income and legal marginalization that is the migrant's lot in France.[5] They multiplied their strategies but remained in a period of transition, often spending a decade coming of age without ever quite arriving at the next stage in life. Their experiences also reveal the way that changing immigration regulations have helped transform paths to adulthood in this migrant community.

## THE ADVENTURER'S DILEMMA

It is tempting to see obligations to village kin as a drain on migrant resources, and indeed many West Africans complain about all the money they had to send home for the endless parade of marriages, funerals, baptisms, and holidays—in addition to the monthly amounts they remit. They complained about mistreatment from siblings or step-mothers. But migrants also depend on these relationships to give meaning to their time abroad, to pull it into a larger life-course trajectory that makes their movement socially significant.[6] Without them, the adventure risks becoming aimless errantry far from home—a disconnection Lassana said would surely lead to failure abroad. Their mobility had to have a purpose.

This is the dilemma. It creates one of the struggles at the heart of the journey abroad. How do they both escape their family and fulfill their obligations to them for longer and longer periods of time? It is a classic conundrum, one which many people will face in different ways, at each stage of their lives.[7] What makes the struggle so acute in this case are the restrictions and paradoxes of French policies that, as we have seen, integrate migrants into inferior and precarious positions. As we have also seen, the Gare du Nord is no exception: it is one of the emblematic public spaces of race-based policing in France. But since that control is not total, and since the station is the place of confluence where the most precarious and the most affluent come together, it has become the site where migrants try to balance the demands of their family and of adventure.

At the station, they build a new pathway toward social becoming, one that follows neither the French state narrative of labor migration nor their family's vision of what that pathway should look like. In searching for the dignity they have lost along the way, in proving themselves, they use the station to find alternative ways to come of age—and in doing so, they must somehow integrate the "migratory circuits" made at the station with their kin relationships in France and at home.[8] They have to maintain a delicate balance of avoiding the burdens of kinship while proving continued investment in their families.

Adventurer social ties, often spanning the world, are kept alive by what Jennifer Cole and Christian Groes call "affective circuits"—that is, the movement not only of money but also of "goods, emotions, ideas, and advice"—that tie migrants to kin.[9] As they begin to build ties also to the Gare du Nord, the station becomes part of these affective circuits. Migrants link the station not only to their home village, but also to several migrant trajectories to Europe and within West and Central Africa. Affective circuits, however, are not necessarily warm and helpful. In the case of the Gare du Nord migrants, they were also sustained by competition and jealousy—the weight of brotherhood.

Adventurers not only had to navigate relationships with their family in France and in their home village, but also with their siblings abroad elsewhere. Their relationships with their brothers and other men from their villages in their age group were not usually characterized by mutual solidarity evoked by the term *fraternity*. They were, rather, caught up in what Mande-language speakers call *fadenya*: intense and sometimes violent sibling rivalry and competition.[10]

Like Lassana, many of the other West Africans at the station were middle or younger brothers, often the children of second wives, who struggled against inferior positions within their family hierarchy.[11] They hoped to use the Gare du Nord method to overcome their marginalization to become what Lassana called a *petit patron* (small boss) and someday, he hoped, a *grand quelqu'un* (a big somebody), a status generally reserved for older, married men who have returned from their journeys abroad.[12] The restrictions and difficulties faced by migrants in France were changing the very definition of what it meant to come of age; how young men marked their arrival at this status; and indeed, what it meant to be a man.[13] These changes affected not only those in Europe, but also their "immobile" brethren at home and their siblings *en aventure* elsewhere.[14]

The time that *aventuriers* spend in the Gare du Nord—talking to women, challenging the police, creating economic and social networks, and tinkering with French infrastructure to suit their own ends—helps them improvise new ways to define their masculinity through which they prove themselves abroad. When Lassana was unable to achieve the traditional markers of manhood and prestige—including marriage, founding a family, and building a modern house in Yillekunda, he tried to imagine and enact an alternative kind of coming of age through the Gare du Nord method, and become an adult without marrying or returning for good. He did this in the company of a transient community of fellow migrants, all trying to get by in France and in the process transforming what it meant to come of age, to be a man and a migrant, and to form relationships on the road.[15]

## ADVENTURES IN THE "FRENCH GENDER SYSTEM"

Marriage, kinship, and masculinity have long been key domains that French law and policy have tried to control, as they are seen as central to the reproduction of the nation.[16] The frequent concern in French public policy about managing African sexuality and family structures—through debates about polygamy, forced marriage, fraudulent marriage, and street harassment—illuminate the ways that entangled notions about race, kinship, and sexuality define French belonging and national borders, in a system Eric Fassin calls "sexual democracy."[17] The station illustrates another aspect of this system: how black men are presented as a sexual threat in public space and especially in public transportation.[18]

"People come to the Gare du Nord either to meet women or to find money, or both, and if they tell you something different, they are lying," proclaimed Ibrahim when I saw him in 2018, after pointing out where at the station he had met his ex-girlfriend (in the tunnel between the commuter rail and the line 4 metro). Indeed, "to meet women" was what most adventurers told me when I asked why they were at the station; they did not talk much about making money. But the simplicity of Ibrahim's pronouncement hid how these two intertwined goals were also the fundamental ingredients of how adventurers sought to come of age and prove their masculinity on the road. As Ibrahim also suggests, these two goals were deeply intertwined in a broader project to solve the adventurer's dilemma and deal with uncertain legal status.

Adventurers combined what they saw as French norms with the know-how they had acquired at the station to get women to talk to them. They had to work hard, and against stereotypes, to prove to those women that they were, as they put it, "serious men." They hoped that the relationships they formed would help them to succeed in France by broadening their social and familial networks and by ensuring their status among their kin at home *and* in France. Starting a family with a French partner offered one of the few remaining pathways toward legalization. Even once they began these relationships, adventurers found that there were many barriers, including racism and suspicions they faced from the French state, their in-laws, and their own families. But, they said, the Gare du Nord was the best place to learn how to overcome those challenges.

The principal goal of "meeting women" was often misinterpreted by the police and other observers as an importation of African gender norms to French public space. Many white station users and store employees I spoke to at the station saw it this way. They accused "the blacks who hang out here" (as one woman working in a station clothing store called them) of ostentatious displays of masculinity considered to be street harassment. The Gare du Nord had become one of the emblematic sites in the fight against street harassment and "the blacks who hang out here" were assumed to be the main perpetrators. The accusation recalls Hugues Lagrange's (2010) widely cited book, written up by several news outlets, arguing that African-French masculine authoritarianism dominates housing project environments. As we have already seen, public debates were full of examples that presented African male sexuality as dangerous and threatening to public order.

When I pointed out that many of the men were looking for more serious relationships and did not engage in catcalling, the response I most often received was exactly what a member of the railway police told me in 2010: "Yes, but if so they're just doing that to get papers, and sometimes the poor woman doesn't even know," a sentiment which echoes French policy directives fighting against so-called "fake marriages" ("green card marriages" in the US context, *mariages blancs* and *mariages gris* in France).[19]

The official stance against fake marriages upheld an idealized separation between romantic love and any material or instrumental concern. Adventurers, like many of their compatriots, recognized that love, status, and money tended to be intertwined.[20] Even if their desire was authentic, the legitimacy of such a union was questioned from another angle. "Most of them already have a wife back at home," another SNCF police officer told me, again echoing the debates about African polygamy, which was banned in France in 1993.[21] West African attitudes toward marriage, much like the attempts to meet women at a place like the Gare du Nord, are seen as evidence of cultural difference and displays of excessive masculinity that are unacceptable in French public space. These representations come from the assumption that these men are invading French spaces with "African" cultural practices, such as the unequal treatment of women.[22]

Migrants' behavior in public spaces like the Gare du Nord are used as evidence that they refuse to play by the rules of the "French gender system." This is ironic because, as Ibrahim, Amadou, and Lassana have all pointed out, they seek to meet French women at the Gare du Nord by doing "like the French" and aligning with what they saw as "white" or "European" attitudes and norms, such as the idea that women in public spaces should be subject to the male gaze. They saw what they were doing as joining the French system of gender relations which, as Joan Scott puts it, "celebrates sex and sexuality as free of social and political risk."[23]

Lassana put it this way: "In France, you can talk to a woman you don't know, and you can have a coffee together, and she might be a serious woman, a woman who thinks about the future. We learn that when we get out of the foyer. We learn . . . to be French, a bit, with women. But for us, *au bled,* ah no! That is not how you meet women," He paused for a moment. "Unless you're a bandit!"

To put it another way, they see the Gare du Nord as a space where they are learning and applying—not contravening—French norms for mixed-gender exchange and interaction. If that seems backwards, it is only because in the last decade French political and media discourse has repeatedly put forth the idea that immigrant communities are to blame for street harassment. This blaming is itself a retooling of the trope of dangerous Arab and African sexuality—a notion forged in the colonial period and reinforced after the Algerian War.[24] This baggage of colonial racism was what made their behavior suspect—otherwise, I rarely saw them engage in cat-calling, and they condemned any of their peers who gained a reputation for taking advantage of women (in part because it hurt their collective reputation). Their attempts to meet women at the station and any resulting relationship, however, were seen as immediately suspect, despite the possibility such relationships offered for social integration.

In addition to the barriers put up by the French state and the police, they also had to contend with their families' expectations for them. These expectations, in the end, concerned them much more. Men told me again and again that they never planned to remain in France for more than two or three years. But after more than a decade, they had become accustomed to their adventure way of life. For many of these men, marrying a woman from their village or accepting a betrothal proposed by an uncle in France contradicted their attempts to carve their own pathway outside of kin circuits. At the same time, they sought social acceptance and needed a way to meaningfully come of age. The serious relationships they sought at the station would, they hoped, provide a solution to the impasse they faced.

Why try to meet women at the Gare du Nord? Given its reputation, it seemed to me like an unlikely place to meet a "serious woman." Amadou said the opposite was true. He said that he was uninterested in meeting Parisian women who, he claimed, were only interested in sex or a brief fling. *Parisiennes* were urbane and worldly; adventurers were looking for what Amadou and his friends called "Amiens girls"—*les filles d'Amiens.* "Amiens girls," named after a small city about one hour north of Paris, designated young women from any of the towns and rural areas north of Paris served by the trains for the Gare du Nord. They were from working-class backgrounds and were seen as having been raised with discipline. "They're not spoiled children like so many of the children here," said Lassana. Like the police officer who had interrogated Lassana about whether it worked to hit on women at the station, I was also skeptical until I met several couples who had met at the Gare du Nord, including three couples who had children together.

## THE MEN OF ADVENTURE MEET THE GIRLS FROM AMIENS

Starting a family was one way to gain respect from their kin, whether it was with a woman from their village or with a white woman they met at the Gare du Nord. Massa, a Khassonke construction worker from the Kayes region of Mali, was about thirty when I met him in 2009. He had a baby daughter with Céline, who was twenty-two and came from a small town near Amiens ("basically a hamlet," she had called it). They had met a few years prior outside the station after she had taken the one-hour train from Amiens to Paris on a Friday evening. Massa had stopped to ask her for a cigarette at the station exit. They had chatted for a bit, he said, before he invited her to get something to eat at the McDonalds across the street. Céline was eighteen and a student in a technical high school. They started seeing each other.

When Céline met him, Massa had been living undocumented in France for several years. When her parents first learned of her involvement with him, they refused to let him past the threshold: "A black man will not enter this house!"

Massa said her parents proclaimed. During the week, Céline worked in her parents' dry-cleaning business, and on the weekends she would save money to take the train to Paris to spend time with Massa. Her relationship with her parents grew more tense as things got more serious with him. She left her hometown and moved into Massa's small apartment that he shared with two other Malian migrants. After a few months, she learned that she was pregnant—nearly two years after their first meeting. "A child is always good news," Massa said.

He imagined that this child would improve his relationship with her parents, now that he would be the father of their grandchild. He also was happy to tell his family about it, as it would illustrate an important milestone in his social becoming: parenthood, what Meyer Fortes called the "*sine qua non* for the attainment of the full development of the complete person to which all aspire."[25] Despite his optimism, he had also been worried because he did not have enough to support a family or provide suitable living conditions. When the baby girl was born, Céline moved back into her parents' home, as Massa's room was too small to house a family. She was also looking for the help and support with a newborn that her family would provide. During the first year, he visited her on the weekends (and her parents let him come inside the house).

His relationship to Céline and in particular the fact that they had a child changed both Massa's status at the station and his legal status in France. When they first started dating, he stopped hanging out at the Gare du Nord. He still greeted his friends when he took the train to Amiens, but he did not hang out there with Céline when she came to Paris. When she had the child, Massa was able to use his declared paternity of a child born in France to get a one-year visa under the status *vie privée et familiale* (private and family life). Like most of the men I met at the station, he did not plan to marry the mother of his child officially, at city hall. Getting a residence and work permit by having a child, instead of by marrying Céline, allowed Massa to circumvent the administrative hassle of measures that made it difficult for foreigners to get papers based on marriage, the logic being that marriage could be faked, but paternity was paternity.[26] Still, he had to renew his temporary *carte de séjour* each year in an arduous process for several years before getting a multiyear resident permit.

For Céline and other young women from the north of France, relationships with West African men could provide their own form of adventure and coming of age. Although I did not have the opportunity to speak at length with Céline, despite several attempts to do so, I understood from several young women in similar situations that they had trouble imagining a future in their small, deindustrialized towns. They came to hang out at the Gare du Nord after taking the train in on a Friday evening, without much of a plan for where they would stay in the capital or what they would do once they arrived. Aurelie, a young woman from Laon who had met two consecutive boyfriends, both from Senegal, at the Gare du Nord, said that the idea of staying in her town forever depressed her. Some of their ideas reproduced colonial stereotypes about African male sexuality, as when Aurelie told me that she was not attracted to "white guys, with their bellies and all that," but preferred "*les noirs,* who are more athletic and take care of how they look." A few young women giggled when I ask them why they wanted to meet "Africans" at the station, nudging each other and saying something like, "Well, it's well-known, that!" (*Ben, c'est bien connu, ça!)* but refusing to elaborate.[27]

Beyond the racist stereotypes, they also shared some of the same hopes as adventurers. Vanessa, a young woman who came to the station one Friday from Maubeuge, said that she knew a few girls from her town who had met their boyfriends at the station, and she hoped they would introduce her to a "nice African man." "Everyone back home, they're all stuck there, but I want to get out," she said, echoing what many West Africans said about the necessity of adventure. This future-oriented vision and the desire to avoid getting stuck provided a common ground in these relationships, but their ideas about gender roles and how to get to the place of self-realization did not always match.

Divergent expectations and interpretations meant that these relationships were characterized by "working mis/understandings," a concept that Jennifer Cole uses to understand the "complex, cross-cutting interests and tensions" among binational couples living in France, who must negotiate their different expectations "in the shadow of state categories."[28] After his child was born and he obtained legal status, Massa was still struggling. He had not yet landed a long-term job (CDI) but relied on interim work and did not make enough money to gain prestige by building a house back home. He reoriented himself toward a future in France, declaring that after he made more money, he would have at least four more children, God willing, and in his mind, Céline would quit her job to care for them. I asked what his family in Mali thought about this plan and he said that, unlike her parents, his family was not against their relationship. He said he could send his children back to the village to be raised if he was worried about them getting a bad education in France (for which he would need Céline's permission).[29] Eventually, his plan was to have enough money to return to his village with his French family, build a nice house there, and find a younger second wife with whom to have more children. Céline would never agree to this plan, Massa acknowledged, but he said he could always take the children and then she would have to come with him.

When I saw Massa in 2010, his daughter was two years old (he showed me a picture of her that he carried in his wallet) and he had started hanging out again at the Gare du Nord. He was tired of going to Amiens every weekend, tired of dealing with Céline's parents, who were still racist, and his plans for making money and getting an apartment on his own had not materialized. Even when he finally found a decent job, it was not a long-term contract, and when he looked for apartments, many of the real estate agents would tell him that they did not have anything available. "They hear your voice, they see your face, and after that it's, 'oh sorry it's been taken,'" he said, repeating a frequent lament about discrimination in the housing market.[30] Like Lassana, his stunted hopes for attaining wealth and prestige had led him back to the Gare du Nord method.

The other problem, Massa said, is that Céline is jealous and does not like him coming to the Gare du Nord when she is not with him. I asked him if he would bring her here when she visits, and he laughed, insisting that he could not do that. "When she comes, I meet her here and then we take the metro to my place; we don't stop here to hang out. I don't want these guys around her!" he said, gesturing to his friends standing around the station entrance. I asked him why he doesn't go to live in Amiens with her, and he explained that it would be embarrassing for him to go live with her parents, who would not accept him anyway, and that it would be impossible to find work there.

"That's not how it works for him, Julie," Lassana scolded when he overheard me ask this question. He meant that there was a patrilocal imperative, which was not only about where one lived but also about masculinity; a man could not let the woman take the lead in where they went. "The woman must follow the man," he said, "That's how it is for Massa."

"But if the woman is taking the man to the USA, that's a different thing!" said Amadou, disagreeing. There were many men who broke the patrilocal imperative if they saw it as part of an onward journey. I had met men who had gone to Brussels and Cologne to live with women they had met at the station, and that was Lassana's initial hope. The problem was not so much with a cultural norm as with the fear that going to a northern village without securing a good living in Paris seemed like something that could compromise their adventure.

Both Massa and Céline used their encounter to fashion an alternative future from the one they saw in their respective hometowns, but these futures quickly diverged from each other and caused rifts in their relationship. Céline imagined Massa would find an apartment for them to live in together in Paris, whereas Massa preferred to pay minimal rent to save money for his house-building project in Mali. While Massa provided money to help raise their daughter, Céline provided all the labor of care. Having a child meant that she became even more tied to her hometown and her parents than she had been before, while Massa continued his adventure. Negotiating relationships with French women, including parents and in-laws, often proved difficult and fraught with misunderstandings, ambivalent outcomes, and opposing visions for the future. There was no happiness without struggle, as Lassana frequently said, and these intimate social relations provided a place where adventurers could prove their masculinity. Given the adventure's extension in time and the novel reproductions (including French-African children) that resulted from these relations, I found that such relations could also compromise reintegration at the moment of return that Massa imagined.

The third time I met Massa, he was with another young woman who came from the Picardy region north of Paris. Amadou and Lassana were very upset about this development. It seemed he had violated some of the main precepts of their community. After all, they had a reputation to uphold. They needed to have enough men who were seen as "serious" to attract other "serious" women, and Massa's actions threatened to give them a bad reputation. As Amadou put it: "You find a girl, you don't come to the station anymore."

"Don't come back here!" Lassana yelled at Massa one evening in front of the McDonalds. "He wants to see his friends, but he shouldn't be here," he said, and his friends agreed. They advised Massa to do what some of their other friends had done and "go to the countryside" (*aller à la campagne*) with Céline to be a true family head.

Even Amadou, the "President of the Gare du Nord," dreamed of going to the countryside with Alice, a woman from the northern French town of Laon whom he had met at the station. Amadou had long refused his older brother's demand that he marry, which began almost as soon as he arrived in France. It was hard for him to do so because he held his brother in very high regard. He had bought Amadou his visa and ticket to France. But Amadou struggled and was often out of work. He told me that he had a ten-year resident permit, but some of his friends said that he had been undocumented before he met Alice at the station.

He dated Alice for a few years, during which he was still known by his peers as a ladies' man at the station. But once he got a better job, he decided to find an apartment in Alice's hometown and move in with her there. She converted to Islam, and they had a religious marriage at the mosque (which is not recognized by the government). They now have three children together, and things are "calm" out in the country. The only thing he could find to complain about was that he had to do the cooking when he arrived late after a long day because Alice, he said, only made "steak and pasta," and he preferred the hearty stews he grew up with. Alice worked at a doctor's office but recently took time off to take care of their youngest child. The only thing he would not accept was to stop working and stay at home with their children; it went against his vision of the masculine role of the provider. He is happy to have left "crazy" Paris, although he still works as an *interimaire* in the construction industry in the capital and has a two-hour commute back and forth each day, stopping to see friends at the station on Friday evenings between trains. I walked him back to his train one Friday in 2018, exchanging pictures of our children as we marveled about how much had changed since the days of "Sécurité Sans Salaire" (which Lassana still insisted on calling him).

Despite their focus on being the provider and household head, many adventurers said that they sought to meet white European women because, Lassana claimed, they were more likely to "work and contribute." "Malian women just want to be supported," he said. "They don't think of the future. I need someone who thinks always of the future." He was repeating a stereotype that African women just wanted to spend money, which I heard as a justification from several other men at the station about why they were looking for "white women" in particular. I pointed out that Lassana's sister and many of her friends worked very hard *and* took care of several children. He wrote this off as an exception to the rule (it wasn't).

After a tumultuous relationship with a white French woman that ended, Ibrahim finally renounced this erroneous notion and told me that he just wanted a "serious woman, white or black or something else." After more than ten years in France, they refused some of the traditional gender roles that they believed would come with a village marriage, but they still wanted to preserve the idea that men were household heads and women took care of children (which, based on their observations, was the case in France). When Lassana failed to meet the European woman he dreamed of, he focused instead on cementing prestige by controlling his brothers elsewhere abroad. He used sibling relations—based on descent instead of alliance—to find ways to assert authority and dignity within his lineage while remaining in the space of adventure.

## MOVING BROTHERS

When Lassana hitched a ride on a truck heading out of his village, Yillekunda, around 1997, it was the moment that he departed from the world of lineage represented by his village and his father's house and entered into the liminal world of adventure. More than twenty years had passed since then, and very little had gone according to plan. He had found a much less independent life than he had hoped for. First, because he had needed to rely on help and finance from family members—usually siblings or uncles—while on the road. Second, he had many obligations to the strong community from his village and region that was already well established in France.

Lassana had several brothers and cousins abroad or trying to get there: Moussa, his older half-brother, became a successful merchant in a Brazzaville market; their eldest brother left for a diamond-mining town in Angola; another brother had gone to Spain; and his cousin Mohamadou ("Momo") had tried to go to Brazzaville soon after Lassana left Yillekunda. He had other cousins in Spain and France. These ties would define his own coming of age trajectory at the Gare du Nord, especially when onward movement and marriage eluded him. His sister and brother-in-law in France had paid for his airplane ticket and helped him get by when he first arrived. Once he found a job and got papers, he repaid those debts by helping to fund other family members' migration. But when his youngest brother Souleymane sought his assistance, Lassana refused.

Souleymane was stuck in his village, stalled and left behind in a place where migration was not available to everyone yet remained an imperative. Many scholars have pointed out that neoliberal reforms and economic restructuring have created more instability across Africa, leading to situations where typical pathways are foreclosed and markers of adulthood are hard to attain.[31] Migration regulations exacerbate these uncertainties, closing off one of the most sought-after paths to build wealth and prestige. This was the situation for Souleymane, who would not inherit much and had few marriage prospects because of his lack of status and migrant wealth. He was stuck "awaiting the passage to adulthood" as Gunvor Jónsson says of the many "immobile" youth in Soninke villages who watch their brothers leave and return bearing gifts.[32] He was in a similar situation to what Dorothea Schulz has called the broader "generation-in-waiting" of Malian youth—and indeed, youth across the continent—often described as feeling stuck and unable to realize their aspirations.[33] The only way out, he believed, was to embark on his own adventure. Côte d'Ivoire was off limits because of the civil unrest and xenophobic violence that had been growing since the early 2000s, so he headed west to Mauritania.

At the same time, Lassana, already in France, was struggling to avoid getting stuck himself. His Gare du Nord method was, so far, moderately effective. Connections made through the station helped him get by while he was undocumented and find a job when he was unemployed. But would it help him go from being a marginalized younger brother beaten up by his siblings to a patron and source of authority for those older brothers, giving him the status and dignity he did not have at home? This was what he was searching for on the adventure, and when his younger brother Souleymane departed from the village against his wishes, it suggested that his status was not yet cemented.

When Lassana legalized his status in France in 2009, it meant that he could finally think about going home, if only for a visit. Migration regulations in France and elsewhere have created the paradoxical situation whereby migrants seek more permanent residency status—implying settlement—so that they will be able to move more freely. Catherine Besteman has observed the phenomenon in the United States among Somali migrants, who joke that the point of getting a green card (US permanent residency) is to be able to return to Somalia.[34] While legal documents create more freedom and mobility, they also create more obligations. Since he was no longer undocumented, Lassana's father expected him to return home for a short time to build him a modern house and to find a wife; that is, to follow the normative trajectory of the Soninke adventure even if Lassana would then return to France to accumulate more wealth.

Precarious legal situations could lead to strained relationships with kin in the village. Although it was an improvement, a one-year resident permit (*carte de séjour*) did not allow Lassana to leave and reenter France as he wished. He waited over six months with a temporary receipt (*récépissé*) and by the time he received the actual permit, he only had a few months left before he had to renew again. He did not want to risk being refused entry after almost a decade spent struggling to obtain legal status. His family members in the dormitory—including several who were still undocumented–pressured him to go home, and during their weekly calls, his father berated him for not returning. His unwillingness to observe Ramadan and his hip-hop "delinquent style" clothes (as he called them) were cited as further markers of poor judgment. His father accepted his remittances but did not hide his distaste for what he heard about Lassana's style and activities from their family in France.

Through the Gare du Nord, Lassana had already begun to carve his own path toward success. Nonetheless, he was still concerned about his elders' perceptions, for they could undermine his authority in his village association. He poured his energy and resources into maintaining the affective circuits that tied him to his siblings and their families. He started emphasizing his social role as maternal uncle to his sister's nine children growing up in the suburbs of Paris. Lamenting the fact that they all seemed to be "lost like a lot of Soninke children growing up in France and not in Yillekunda," he began to visit her more frequently and find ways to help them "find their pathway." Against his sister's wishes, he succeeded in convincing her husband to send their middle-school age daughter to Yillekunda for several months "for education," because of her frequent suspensions from school. He paid particular attention to her older sister, his eighteen-year-old niece, because she was named for his mother. He talked at length with her and gave her advice, enlisting my help to find her a job in retail. He started monitoring what his other older half-brothers were up to, agreeing to send money to them if they would return to the village to be with his aging father. He was still going to the Gare du Nord almost every day. When he was not at work, he was at the Gare du Nord or with his family.

Lassana negotiated his social position in relation to his brothers through the affective circuits created by migration. While remitting money home to his father satisfied an obligation, sending money to his brothers who had left on their own adventures signaled that he had surpassed their status. The older brothers who had once domineered and teased him now relied on him for support. In return for money, Lassana tried and sometimes succeeded in dictating where they would go and when. After a resurgence of armed conflict in Brazzaville and the threat of sudden deportation, his brother Moussa decided to return to Mali in 2009. Lassana remembers Moussa calling him from Brazzaville to ask him for money to make the voyage home.

"I sent him 330 euros," he said, citing the exact amount he wired his brother, "But he didn't do anything for me when I was trying to get to France."

By helping Moussa, Lassana showed that he was a giver and not a receiver, while Moussa had to take the subservient role of accepting money when he should have also been remitting it. Instead of going back to the village where he had a wife and two children, Moussa set up a new shop in Bamako next to some Soninke friends. His store, which sold used clothing and electronics from the United States, was unsuccessful. He went to the village every few months but cited his business as a reason to make a quick return. Lassana began sending some money directly to Moussa, but only on the condition that he use some of it to return to the village for longer stretches of time.

The adventure pathway also changed for Momo, Lassana's cousin who had grown up in Gabon and then had been sent to live with his uncle in the village as a teenager. In 1997, Momo went back to Gabon and then to Congo, but in both places, he failed to make any money. "Now it should be finished," said Lassana, explaining that Momo was not cut out for the adventure because he "likes lively atmospheres too much" (*il aime trop l'ambiance*); that is, he liked to go out dancing and drinking, a taste he had acquired (according to Lassana) because his migrant parents had raised him in Libreville, the capital of Gabon, instead of in their village.

Lassana used the example of his cousin Momo to point out that successful adventure demanded discipline and hard work, which relied on village upbringing. Momo was lacking in the quality called *len siren* (courage) in Soninke. Unlike dignity of birth, age, and status, *len siren* (literally, good child) is an attribute that depends on how a person was raised. "Len siren depends on your mother," explained Lassana, "Your mother has to give you len siren, or you won't have it." Momo was never able to save enough money to pay for the passage to Europe, which Lassana attributed to the fact that Momo had grown up abroad, in a non-Muslim country, and thus was missing the Soninke work ethic and *len siren*. After an unsuccessful attempt to make enough money to get to Europe, Momo returned to Yillekunda in 2003. Under family pressure, he married. But after one year he already wanted to head back on the road. He had fallen in love with a "*métisse*" (a woman of mixed African and European ancestry) he met on a bus in Senegal, he told me, and did not want to stay in Yillekunda. But Lassana refused to help, instead sending him just enough money for a cheap motorbike, which would enable him to make money in the nearby town of Diema.

Lassana made the journey home in 2010, after he had received a second one-year resident card. He spent one month in Bamako before he returned to Yillekunda for the first time since he had left as a teenager, bearing suitcases full of gifts from Paris. Despite this display, Lassana's father remained unsatisfied with his decision not to marry and his refusal to build a new house in the village for his family there. More than remittances, traditional marriage to a woman from Yillekunda or from a nearby village would have cemented Lassana's place in these circles of exchange. According to his relatives, he could have then returned to France and even remained abroad, as long as he continued to send money back. But Lassana refused the clearest marker of his entrée into adulthood, believing that it would interfere with his adventure pathway.

Lassana sees his relative success—signaled by his arrival in France—as the story of an underdog brother who usurped his elder brothers' authority. The position he gained through migration would lead him to attempt to control his brothers' movement. He would attempt to distribute affective roles in his family, such as who would be the dutiful brother and return to care for their father. The Gare du Nord method allowed Lassana to become a breadwinner and patron in relationship to his kin, but in their eyes his bachelorhood confined him to the realm of someone who had not attained full adult status, putting him in the same category as his cousin Momo.

Once he returned to the village, Momo used the motorbike that Lassana paid for to make connections in the nearby town of Diema and start a small phone repair business. When the business failed, he decided to leave town again. He went to Mauritania to find work, with the hope of eventually securing passage to Europe. His back-and-forth movement diverges from the ideal adventure trajectory but resembles migrant pathways that are becoming more common. His kin believe the cause of Momo's problems was stunted growth and attributed his failure to the fact that he had not yet come of age because he had grown up outside the village due to his parents' lengthy adventure in Gabon.

Lassana finally seemed to attain adult status in his community, despite the fact that he was unmarried, when he received a ten-year resident permit in 2014. He began to change his style, growing a beard and getting rid of the braids. He was acquiring the trappings of adulthood and the status it entailed without either returning to the village or marrying. Yet he still needed to cement these acquisitions by buying land and beginning his house-building project in Bamako. Lassana's visit home posed a further predicament: How could he translate the adventurer's mobility into the elder's stasis, of which founding a family and constructing a village house are emblematic?

## UNCERTAIN RETURNS

"This is my house," Lassana said one afternoon in the summer 2014, unfolding a set of blueprints provided by a Senegalese architect that he had met at the Gare du Nord. One evening, I noticed a silver piece of drainpipe sticking out of his bag. "Each day from our worksite, I take one piece like this home," he explained. "It's for my house in Bamako. Eventually, it will create a high-quality drainage system like the one you see on the building over there." He gestured across the street to a row of typical Parisian apartment buildings. Between the material he took back from his worksite and the blueprints, his Bamako house was becoming more concrete. Like all adventurers, he had a plan. Like most of these house projects, it was a very long process.[35]

"My father wants me to build a new house for him in Yillekunda," he explained, "But I'm not ready to do that." At that point, he had already spent years trying to make his Bamako house a reality. House-building is central to questions of status and achievement, but it does not always signify imminent return. As Luke Freeman observes, migrant house projects are sometimes a proxy for physical return; they help to maintain distance from home and defer the end of adventure by giving migrants a presence while absent.[36]

Lassana's blueprints and drainpipes helped him to project himself into the future and imagined return without forsaking his adventure. As soon as he received his resident permit, he started planning for purchasing land in Bamako. Unlike his sister's unfinished house built by a cousin contractor who had "eaten" half the money she sent him, Lassana was determined to avoid family networks. His house took shape through the connections he had made at the Gare du Nord.

In 2011, he got a loan from an African bank with a Paris office. He then bought land outside the city through a Malian cooperative, ignoring his half-brother Moussa's advice to buy in a more central neighborhood. The house planning and building was a source of constant anxiety over getting ripped off (as he could only watch over the process from afar). Lassana spent hours poring over the possible architectural plans. He planned to include small stores on the ground floor, one of which he would run and the others which he would rent out.

He planned to go look at the land and sign the deed in person in Bamako in 2012, but the planned trip coincided with a hearing in a drawn-out court battle against the owner of the construction company where he worked, whom he accused of withholding pay. He canceled his trip. When I went to Mali in 2012, he sent me to visit the land he had bought, sign the deed as his proxy, and bring it back to him in Paris. The entire transaction became part of a larger performance of his status: he made his older half-brother Moussa take a day off from work to come with me to visit the land, almost an hour outside of the capital.

Millet fields surrounded demarcated plots of land in which nothing had been built; most of them were owned by migrants abroad like the young man from Kayes who accompanied us on the visit. While we are there, Moussa disparaged the site for being too remote, but was reassured when he found out that "the Chinese" will be building a highway from Bamako to another city that will run right by it. As the clerk handed the deed to me, he said, "The buyer insists that you and only you may sign in his place." He was talking to me but looking pointedly at Moussa, who watched me sign it. Lassana's encounter with me allowed him to circumvent kin networks throughout his house-building process and thus to maintain his status as a patron who did not depend on his older brothers.

In addition to building houses in Bamako, many of these adventurers plan and implement village projects as a replacement for physical return. Through these projects, which can include mosques, water towers, wells, and other structures, they maintain a connection to the village and gain prestige for their families.[37] The most prestigious villages in the area near Lassana's hometown were two neighboring locales that had sent many sons to the United States. Unlike most of the other villages, these two had electricity, an infrastructural display of their modernity as well as a source of local prestige.[38]

The onward mobility that Lassana emphasized about his adventure contrasted sharply with the fixedness and settlement that return demanded.[39] More than two years after I signed the deed, ground had still not been broken on the house plans, just as Moussa's shop in Bamako remained unfinished concrete, and the village house they began for their father was only a shell. In theory, the adventure process involves a transition from mobile to stable, from the network to the dwelling. In reality, however, the fixed abode remains incomplete and empty, and plays a role less as a space for living than as a space for imagining a return that does not forsake adventure. As Caroline Melly shows in the case of Senegal, migrant-built houses resist the assumption that dwelling is the only way to make a house meaningful. She points instead to the incompleteness and instability of these "inside-out houses."[40] The process of building helps maintain the channels that connect the adventurer to the country, but does so as a future prospect of an always-deferred return, as part of their becoming while on the road.

In 2014, Lassana received a ten-year residency and work permit. I accompanied him to Mali, where he planned to spend three months between Bamako and Yillekunda. The trip was another chance to display his status. I visited him at Moussa's shop when he came to Bamako. In the three years since I had first visited, the shop was still exposed concrete, with clothes for sale hanging from wires strung on the walls. Moussa was outside sweeping the front porch and looking for potential clients when I arrived. Lassana was inside reclining on the store's only chair, surveying the street from behind his shaded glasses. Despite the 95-degree heat, he was wearing heavy, shiny jeans, a polo shirt, and a black corduroy blazer, which contrasted with his French wardrobe that consisted of a few T-shirts and hoodies and a couple of old pairs of low-slung jeans. He kept his big earphones on as I approached, nodding his head to the music, and looked up to shake my hand and then return his gaze to the street. He was now the patron to his older, married brother, who was sweeping on the sidewalk.

Return and marriage are meant to end the phase of adventure, with society reintegrating the adventurer as a man. Yet this phase—meant to be liminal—has become more permanent, sometimes encompassing most of migrants' adult lives. This has made dispositions formed during the migratory journey more difficult to shed once migrants return to the village. Moussa spent minimal time in the village, returning infrequently to see his wife and children, and was trying to find ways to leave for the United States. But Lassana was insisting he stay in Mali and return more frequently to see their father. I found Yillekunda full of other long-term adventurers, all seeking ways out of the village.

## THE NEVER-ENDING ADVENTURE

A few months before we first met, Lassana had learned that he was finally going to get a resident permit. He had also found out that his youngest brother had made it onto a boat in Mauritania, bound for the Canary Islands, with two other men from

FIGURE 9. Lassana in 2014, sitting in his brother's store in Bamako, Mali. Author.

their village. The boat hit rough waters, and sank. Some of the men were rescued by another boat, perhaps the coast guard—he wasn't sure.

But Souleymane did not make it. When Lassana told me of his brother and this tragedy at sea, Lassana said, "He was too weak. He failed." He used the French word *échouer*, meaning "to fail," but also, concerning boats, "to run aground, to cause a wreckage." "That was his path," he said, his eyes clouding over. It was a refrain I often heard in response to the death of loved ones.

"What is my path?" he wondered aloud.

When Lassana spoke of his brother's tragic "failure" at sea, he emphasized Souleymane as the stopped trajectory, the wreckage, and the failure. Souleymane was a foil to his own narrative of success. He fashioned his own "destiny" as the opposite of "God's will" for his brother:

> You think you arrived because you made it to France. France is not the end. It's not even the goal. You think you arrived because you got papers? Papers are not the end. You think you arrived because you got a long-term work contract? Well then you're stuck. You think if you get sent back (*refoulé*, deported) that's the end of your path? Then you're going to fail. Me, I have papers. I'm in France. I had a long-term contract. But have I found my happiness? No, my path is not done. I'm not satisfied with my boss; I'm going to find a better one. I'm going to get a better salary. Maybe I'll go back to temporary work if I can get good pay. The problem with French people and some of these Africans is that they think if they have these things they are *done*. They're content. Not me. That's why I'm at this station. . . . It's an international station. Maybe I'll meet a girl from Germany and go there. And then somewhere else. And then who knows.

He sought incremental progress, made through constant movement and strategizing. This version of his pathway seemed to forgo the endpoint of village prestige, marriage, and return. In the wake of his brother's death at sea, Lassana reimagined his becoming as a continuation of social and physical mobility. If not in space, at least in terms of his work and status in France.

Born of the legal restrictions on migration, collapsing labor markets, and the policing of black men in French public space, the Gare du Nord method provides some West African young men with a way of confronting ever more "ambiguous adventures," to use the still apt title of Cheikh Amadou Kane's 1961 novel about a Senegalese student's existential crisis spurred by migrating to France.[41] As more family members spend longer and longer periods of their lives abroad, the way of being *en aventure* may change the long-term social reproduction of home communities, just as migrants have transformed this cultural framework to fit the demands created by EU policies and Fortress Europe. Migrants adapt to the new requirements of contemporary journeys of migration and fashion new ways to become adults. Several of the men from Yillekunda, including his brother Moussa, seemed stuck in the adventure even after returning home. They were still seeking to create channels that take them outside of village circuits of accumulation and relation, only to reinvest in those circuits in new ways. When migrants enact these new forms of investment, they reshape the affective circuits among siblings, changing adventurers' relationships to each other and to the villages to which they will never fully return.

While Lassana's experience suggests that some men are able to convert their methods at the Gare du Nord into long-term social ties, creating new ways to become a Soninke man, it also reveals how the legal and economic precariousness experienced by African migrants in France makes this conversion more fragile and subject to reversal. Despite Lassana's display of success and embodiment of *grand quelqu'un* dispositions in Mali, when he returned to France, he had to go back to a life on the margins that was less secure than before. Having lost his job, he led a precarious existence, despite his legalization. There were a few months where he could not pay his rent and almost had to go back to living at the foyer. He performed his arrival as a big somebody in Mali but returned to France to find he had no job to maintain that status and no wife or finished house to confirm to his kin that he had become a man. Even as young men attempt to leave the constraints of village hierarchy and depart from their communities to come of age abroad, their becoming remains a collective affair constituted through their negotiation of affective circuits that tie them to kin both near and far. In a situation where many siblings migrate—which is increasingly the case across sub-Saharan Africa—this renegotiation occurs not only between home and abroad, but also among several relatives attempting to find success through migration.

When I saw Lassana in the summer of 2015, he was fasting for the month of Ramadan for the first time since he arrived in France. When I asked what made him fast this year in particular, he said it was to satisfy his father's wishes. His father had always wanted him to fast, he said, but he never bothered him about it because Lassana braided his hair, a sign that he was still an errant youth for whom observing Ramadan would have been an incongruous practice. Growing a beard and fasting would show that he was still on the socially sanctioned pathway, despite all of the detours and winding roads he had taken to achieve what moderate success he had found on his adventure. Like many underemployed adventurers at the Gare du Nord, he still lacked the funds to realize his house-building dreams in Mali, and finally he settled for building his father a "modern"—that is, concrete—house in Yillekunda during a return visit in 2015. This was what his father had long wanted him to do, but he had resisted, fearful of getting stuck in the village or of deviating from the forward-moving pathway he had in mind. His father enjoyed the new home, where Lassana installed a TV that we had laboriously gotten onto an Air France flight to Bamako.

## BEYOND FRANCE

In the summer of 2016, I met Lassana at the shiny new Starbucks café seating area in the front square of the Gare du Nord. It had replaced the bike racks where many of his peers used to hang out and have run-ins with the police. Lassana's situation in France was more or less the same. He was thirty-five and still had not found a long-term job. He had been getting by as a day laborer and on unemployment checks. In 2015, he traveled several hundred kilometers every week as part of a work team building a new high-speed train line near Bordeaux. That project had ended, and from our sporadic phone discussions it seemed that he had only a few temporary short-term jobs that year. He and his friend Idris, a stylishly dressed "Malian with French papers" (as Lassana put it), about the same age as Lassana, lamented the contemporary reality for Malians.

"Everyone is fed up," said Idris, "Everyone wants to go back to Mali, they're fed up with France."

"Why don't they go back?" I asked.

Idris and Lassana looked at me incredulously. "They can't!" Idris said, "Even if they have papers now. They haven't done what they wanted to do, they haven't even built a house in Bamako yet and so they would have to deal with renting if they go back." Renting, he said, was a mark of shame. They would never be able to come back, he added, to complete their adventure, unless they found a way to maintain their residency permit in France. To do that, they have to stay most of the year in France and try to find work so that when it's time to renew it they are able to do so. "We are not like our fathers' generation, are we?" Lassana pointed out. "We don't want to just migrate, work as an unskilled laborer (*manoeuvre*) for forty years, marry up to four women, and go back to retire in the village. No, we have projects! We want to build houses, build *something*. It's not just about marriage and children for us."

As they distanced themselves from their fathers' projects, they also distinguished their tactics from the more recent arrivals. As routes changed, so did the migrants. Idris and Lassana discussed the "new generation" of West Africans arriving in France with a mixture of awe and disapproval. They had endured such risk and hardship that they were "broken."

"But what they've seen, it changes them. And they're all about themselves. They forget about the villages, forget about sending money back." His words reminded me of what his father said to me about Lassana when I had gone to Yillekunda.

Lassana and Idris were aware of the strange disconnect between the representations of life abroad and the reality they faced every day, and also aware that the risk today's migrants faced surpassed anything they had confronted on their adventure. Based on my limited conversations with some of the men who had arrived recently, they also had much in common. They too were scared of getting stuck in France. They yearned for an elsewhere that would offer more opportunities for carrying out the hard work they demanded of themselves. Idleness was the enemy of adventure.

"If I could go home now, I would," Lassana said. But his trips home rarely lasted more than a few months each year. He was worried about losing his residency status in France or being out of the temporary labor market for too long, which would make it more difficult for him to get a better interim job.

Migration regulations—for some, the impossibility of returning to France at all—keeps many migrants from going back, even when they would like to. Returning meant potentially getting stuck at home. They strove to prove their success and come of age, as their fathers and grandfathers also had, but all the hurdles that they had confronted on these lengthy adventures made their destinations shift. The pathway they had envisioned, of onward mobility abroad and prestige at home, was crumbling before their eyes, and they had to scramble to find a new one before it was too late. The places they came from—Mali, Senegal, Côte d'Ivoire—were shifting; new conflicts and ethnic divisions were arising that contrasted with the multilingual, multiethnic communities they had grown up with before leaving. And as they were trying to figure all of this out, their brothers and nephews were calling them, asking for help to cross the sea.

## THE GARE DU NORD, IT'S US

I caught up with Ibrahim in the summer of 2018. He had given up his neon green tracksuit for more neutral tones and covered his braids with a du-rag. Instead of posting photos on social media of fistfuls of euros and fancy watches, he was posting pictures of himself operating heavy machinery on a worksite—one of the more noble tasks in the construction industry. He said that things were now very different from when we had first met, when he had suspected that I was working with the police. At the time, he had been involved in minor drug dealing. But that, he said, was for younger folks, and "it was no way to become somebody."

Ibrahim had achieved some traditional markers of success but was reconfiguring others. He had built a house in his native Tambacounda, in Senegal. Since his father had already been a migrant to France when Ibrahim was a child, he had more means and fewer obligations. He fulfilled basic demands of his kin, but he also said he used his status as the youngest brother to avoid excessive family responsibility in France. It was why, he said, he could get away with the hip-hop-inspired style that he had adopted since his time in Dakar and direct his "conspicuous redistribution" toward his friends—I saw him buy rounds of drinks at cafés, and he insisted on paying when I saw him. He knew all the waiters and cooks at the nice bistro where we were sitting, across from the station, who shook his hand and joked with him. It was a far cry from the young man I had met almost a decade earlier, often needing to borrow cash and ostentatiously switching between four cell phones. He was neither married nor a father—two of the key signals of coming of age that he was still searching for. He said he planned to return to Senegal, but he was not sure when. He wanted to construct a house in Saly, an upscale French-dominated beach resort town south of Dakar. First, he had to find the "serious" woman he could marry.

As we walked toward the station entrance across the front square, we crossed in front of a few police officers. One of the officers recognized Ibrahim and they greeted each other warmly. "I haven't seen you around for a while!" the officer said, "You've changed!"

"I don't come to the Gare du Nord anymore," Ibrahim explained to me. "Well, I come, but it's not like before. I come to see friends or watch a football game. *Le bizness*, it's not good. Once you get a job, you grow up, things are different. I work now; I can't come here. You stop drinking, stop messing around. I'm more serious now. But I still come; everyone knows me here. I am an *ancien* now. Someone's always going to buy me a coffee; everyone knows me here because we're the ones who know the Gare du Nord. The Gare du Nord, it's us."

I remembered that he had once called the Gare du Nord "the real wilderness"; this was the role the station had in the initiatory journey of some West Africans in France. Their family members were skeptical, concerned that they had deviated from the right path. But for these men, their path had led them to the big glassy entrance of the station. It was the real unknown, where they would have to prove themselves, to use all their know-how to figure out how to do so despite the police, the job market, and a baffling bazaar that hundreds of thousands of people passed through each day.

Do they eventually achieve some kind of stable adulthood this way? Rarely. Many times, the status they gain at the station is not as portable as they would like it to be. They keep going back there, in part because they have a community, as Ibrahim does, where they find recognition, where they are less marginalized, and finally, where they belong. Although they were not able to achieve everything they hoped, neither were they stuck. Almost everything changed for them, just as it was changing for their families back home. They came out of the Gare du Nord transformed. This change did not occur according to the progression proposed by the initiatory journey of their parents or according to the narrative of French integration and assimilation. Adventures rarely went to plan. As they confronted risk, suffering, and danger, they also remade the station into a meaningful social world.

# Conclusion

In July 2018, the French national railway company announced that the Gare du Nord would undergo a reconstruction "as major as the renovation of Jacques Hittorf in 1864," which would triple the current surface area.[1] At the projects' completion, projected to be in time for the 2024 Paris Olympic Games, a private company will become the majority stakeholder of the Gare du Nord, for the first time since the railways were nationalized. The project highlights the goals stressed in earlier renovations, including improved circulation, reinforced security, and better "luminosity" and "clarity." It adds environmental responsibility measures and leisure activities such as coworking spaces and a jogging track on the roof. According to the video simulation presenting the project, passengers in the Gare of the future will be comprised almost exclusively of white, well-heeled urbanites.[2] The project announcement was full of ambition, promising a structure that would attain all the unrealized goals of the exchange hub and then some, correcting the errors of the past.

But the Gare du Nord is also—and will remain—an unfinished product that does not match these models and expectations. The confluence of many itineraries over more than one hundred fifty years have made the station into a significant public space in the intersecting histories of modernization and migration in Paris. It was conceived through a nineteenth-century vision of hope, progress, and international exchange embodied in the railways, combined with fears over difference and "dangerous" classes. The station was given life by more than a century of migration, with workers arriving and building their world around it before leaving to make way for more newcomers. It is the result of infrastructural dreams and infrastructural violence, of French urban planners seeking democracy and transparency combined with a security imperative multiplying policing and surveillance techniques, and a commercial attempt to create new spaces for consumption and leisure. The station's history shows how inequality has been built into French public spaces, shrouded first in cloaks of imperial industrial progress and then in the ideals of democratic living together.

The top-down logic of planners, architects, railroad barons, and politicians could not plan or predict what the station would ultimately be; it is a concrete, lived, experienced place of transit that will always be shaped and reshaped by unpredictable encounters that lie outside of the planners' purview. The accumulated work of adventurers like Lassana, Amadou, Ibrahim, Yacouba, Jal, Omar, Dembele, and many others have produced the station too, making a transit hub into a social and economic destination. It is a place where many circuits and channels meet, and it is precisely those channels that West Africans at the station have learned to uncover and then rewire. The Gare du Nord as a public space has been shaped by these new circuits.

I have proposed that by tracing adventurer pathways and practices at the Gare du Nord we can reframe the way we tend to think about migration, French public space, and living together. More than any other discipline, anthropology allows us to produce what Jean and John Comaroff call "grounded theory," the kind of analysis that emerges from lived experience in specific locations and historical contexts.[3] "Adventure," I have argued, is not only the way West Africans at the Gare du Nord describe their voyages, but also a way of theorizing who they are and what their situation in France is, as well as who they might become. It is grounded theory par excellence, moving between the "epic and the everyday" of migrant lives.[4] The adventurer's imaginary situates them in a long historical tradition but is also forward looking. It offers a form of grounded theory that is concerned, as the Comaroffs put it, "not merely with how social worlds are constituted, but how they might conceivably have been different, and how their present might give rise to better futures."[5] And in particular, from an adventurer's perspective, how those better futures depend on reconfiguring integration, social relationships, and their own coming of age.

Better futures may depend on radically changing the current political economic system. In the current system, migrants provide a reserve pool of labor that keeps wages down, while the political capital of xenophobic anti-migrant discourse is what gets many candidates elected to public office. Immigration control is also a key element in defining the boundaries of nationality and citizenship, and deportation has become "a pervasive convention of routine statecraft," as Nicholas De Genova puts it.[6] This system ensures the continuation of labor migrants' "differential inclusion" into Europe.[7] Many scholars have documented how this process happens in France, showing how inequality is inherited by the French citizens who are descendants of African immigrants despite universalist rhetoric.[8] Migrants—for all their creativity and effort—have an uphill battle when it comes to changing the unequal structure that circumscribes their possibilities and leads to suffering. The practices of migrants and other marginalized and racialized populations do, however, provide alternative frames, futures, and ideas for what can be done in the interstices and fissures that all the planning and policing in the world cannot eliminate.[9]

The perspective of adventure—the way West Africans at the Gare du Nord understand and theorize not only their own existence but also the current predicaments of France and Europe—offers another way of seeing the way migration works and what integration might look like, and it highlights the new social worlds that migrants create at places like the Gare du Nord. In lieu of concluding these unfinished projects and journeys, I would like to propose how the adventures discussed in this book can help productively displace the commonsense thinking about migration and its relationship to ideologies of race, nationalism, difference, settlement, and what it means to belong somewhere.

## ON MARGINALIZATION AND ETHNOGRAPHIC ATTENTION

Many excellent studies of African migration to Europe examine the periphery of urban and political life, such as housing projects, *banlieues,* camps, detention centers, undocumented workers' movements, ethnic community associations, and immigrant dormitories, illustrating both migrants' inventiveness and the suffering caused by marginalization.[10] Yet migrants and their descendants remain relegated to the marginal slot reserved for them by European states' discourse and policy. The focus on the margins reproduces the classification schema developed in the colonial encounter and reinforces the idea that African migrants and other visible minorities are out of place elsewhere (for example, in the middle class, in the government, or in the center of Paris) despite their incontestable presence in those spaces.[11] It appears as if they live in quasi-isolation because of social marginalization, never quite part of the center of European and French urban areas.[12]

The view from the Gare du Nord blurs the line between periphery and center and sheds light on the control measures put into place in an effort to maintain their distinction. Adventurers refuse to be consigned to the outer cities and immigrant dormitories or to be defined by the way they are marginalized spatially, economically, and politically.[13] Instead, they occupy a space not meant for them, and they enliven it. They keep showing up and insisting they belong, that they make that place what it is, despite the many attempts to plan them away (culminating in the station's 2024 project). They are not exceptional in this sense but a prime example of many people across France—and Europe—who every day refuse to be "sidelined," as Lassana always put it.

Adventurers have a lot to teach us about the modes of attention of ethnographic critique when it comes to migrant communities. The excellent work on "altermobilities" and much literature on migrant resistance stress the political mobilizations and rights-based claims of migrants, such as the many social movements that have come out of migrant organizing in France and elsewhere. Anna Tsing's observation, "Mobility means nothing without mobilization," emphasizes that the fact of moving from one place to another is not enough to enact change.[14] But the problem with privileging mobilization is that the forms of mobility unaccompanied by political claims can be seen as "meaning nothing"—or as less worthy of attention.

Adventurers would turn this idea on its head. "Mobilization," they would say, "means nothing without mobility." That is, any rights achieved through social movements mean little if they do not also gain the possibility of continued mobility. Seeing themselves as adventurers and not as immigrants helps to understand why several men insisted that they were not seeking the rights of citizenship (another reason was because they recognized that they would still be treated as "second-class" citizens).[15] They offer another model of migrant trajectories, questioning the idea that attaining papers is the ultimate goal of migrants, and that the only way to integrate somewhere is to *settle* there.

Their perspective suggested to me that the notion of settlement (which they seemed to be forced into against their wishes) as the end of migration was misguided and parochial, the product of a Western imperial worldview that arose out of settler colonialism.[16] This view imposes settlement as the precondition for belonging—part of what Liisa Malkki calls a "sedentarist metaphysics."[17] Unlike the many critiques of the "arboreal" model of the nation-state inspired by Malkki's work, however, adventurers are not wandering nomads who resist the notion of rootedness. As we have seen, they remain tied to agrarian backgrounds even when on the road. Mobility does not oppose their rootedness but reinforces it; through a focus on enabling onward movement while investing in place-making where they are, they create a form of integration that does not envision settlement as the end goal. Their version of integration necessarily rethinks the categories of difference assumed in most of the French discourse about it.

## ON DIFFERENCE

Adventurers make us question the stubborn categories we use to sort and divide people into groups, to define who belongs and who does not, who is threatening, who can be assimilated, and who must be controlled by the police or circumscribed to the periphery. In some cases, they propose an alternative set of boundaries that are no less divisive, but help to illustrate that the categories states use are the products of long histories of interaction and so subject to manipulation and change. They expose the contingency of the current system of national belonging and migration management. It does not have to be this way.

In France, a long history of ostensibly refusing to recognize difference in theory while reproducing it in practice has led many to denounce government attempts to "eradicate difference" while also critiquing the way that radical difference and inequality gets produced by state actors.[18] An adventurer lens focuses in on difference and the way it has shaped French urban landscapes, laws, and what it means to be French. But adventurers also emphasize the value of difference, refusing to regard it as a pure construction of French policy and discourse.[19]

"We are not the same," Lassana said, referring to the French police, but also to his friends Amadou and Ibrahim. That difference, they point out, is not a barrier to be overcome, but a source of value. This is a trader's logic: trading demands some kind of difference to establish the potential of exchange.[20] Difference becomes a source of opportunity. The problem, they suggest, is when differences crystallize into a hierarchy instead of providing the grounds for exchange. It should thus not be a handicap; policy does not need to domesticate it or plan it out of existence. Rather, we might see that the everyday use and appropriation of urban spaces like the Gare du Nord can provide more opportunities for valuable encounters across difference to arise.

## ON ROOTING AND UPROOTING

In proposing alternative categories of difference, adventurers also disturb the meanings given to those categories. Lassana and Amadou once proposed to counter French racial mappings of urban space that can only see "in black and white," as in media and political debates about the 2007 revolt. Instead, they denounced racism and proposed the distinctions of *renois* and *bledard*. As we saw, their description of the "renois" aligned with the way the government tends to represent young African-French men in peri-urban areas. Instead, let us focus here on their self-designation as bledards.

On the surface, bledard maps directly onto common sociological understandings of Sahelian African migrant populations, designating "uneducated labor migrants from rural areas."[21] It is often assumed that those who possess such characteristics are unlikely to accept French values or be politically engaged by participating in Republican projects of citizenship or voting.[22] Bledards like Lassana, Amadou, and their peers occupy the slot of the culturally different, not-yet-modern Other who might be incapable of adopting modernity.[23] This frequent trope in the racist representations of Africa and the continent's inhabitants is based on taken-for-granted hierarchical distinctions between rural and urban, Qur'anic-school-educated and French-educated, traditional and modern—distinctions inherited from modernization that have little purchase on the social worlds of West African adventurers.

Adventurers' itineraries upend the idea that their "African villages" are traditionally insular and that Paris is the apex of cosmopolitan modernity. Most adventurers have a Qur'anic school education and speak multiple languages; once they arrive in France, they learn French. They expose the flawed colonial assumption that French education is the pathway to development and instead emphasize that it is Qur'anic education that prepares one for migration abroad.

The "uprooting thesis" imagines that migrants' cultural pathology and mental suffering come from being torn from the traditional soil of their "African village" and transplanted directly into the urban *anomie* of Paris.[24] Adventurers narrate an utterly different process, by which self-realization and social reproduction is achieved through migration—not stunted by it. Problems occur because this pathway is blocked, not because the pathway exists. *Aventuriers* seek a balance; they invest in the reproduction of rural communities while creating new urban social relations. They do not have to choose between being a "ruralist" migrant devoted to the village or becoming a "cosmopolitan" devoted to city life.[25]

The uprooting narrative fails to capture their already mobile lives, in which they spend years voyaging abroad before arriving in Paris. Many men I met were born abroad—in Congo, Côte d'Ivoire, or Gabon, the children of *aventuriers*. Their home villages in the Senegal River Valley have been shaped by mobility in a region of West Africa forged by long-distance trading routes that have existed since Paris was a Roman outpost on the Seine River.

From this perspective, adventurers help to build what James Ferguson has called "an anti-teleological set of concepts and tools" able to make sense of a world in which a linear narration of developmental progress does not correspond to the reality of migration.[26] We cannot invert the narrative of modernity, placing multilingual West Africans at the summit of cosmopolitanism and their provincial French hosts at the (monolingual) bottom (even if there may be some provocative truth to that).[27] The point that adventurers make is rather that these distinctions—like those of periphery/center, rural/urban, rooted/mobile, social/individual—and their placement on rungs of a ladder leading to enlightened modernity, are misguided, and they dissolve when confronted with mobile itineraries that straddle them. These distinctions had no purchase at the Gare du Nord; what mattered instead were questions of moral worth: how to know whether someone is only "for here" (*sur place*) or might merit the commitment of being "to go" (*à emporter*).

## ON INTEGRATION

Seeing migration as an initiatory journey (the heart of what "adventure" means) displaces the narrative proposed by citizenship and assimilation in which migrants adapt the ways of life of the host country, for which they are rewarded with legal status in a ceremony of naturalization. At the Gare du Nord, they practice an alternative form of integration by getting to know and mastering French transit systems and urban spaces to be able to meet people from outside of their communities.

The temporality of being an adventurer cannot be squared with the permanence of identity and naturalization presumed in discourses about citizenship, for migration here is about a moment in the life course, the transition from childhood to adulthood. Migrants maintain a status of in-between cultural brokers who see their voyages abroad as pathways to status at home and abroad: home and away, Paris and African village, are united in a single goal of social becoming. Similarly, relationships to kin and meaningful self-realization on the road—often seen as opposing forces—reinforce each other when conditions are right.

Adventurers help to rethink the classical social theory distinction between structure and agency, based on a Western imaginary in which social constraint opposes self-realization.[28] How would an adventurer journey take flight and become meaningful without the reinvestment in kin relations, such as the way Lassana rearticulates his relationship to his brothers? The adventure is a constant renegotiation between breaking away (beginning with the dramatic village escape) and returning to the fold, of reproducing circuits of reciprocity built in West African villages and cities by making new ones in the French capital.[29]

Adventurers at the Gare du Nord might be overlooked because they do not correspond to the categories or sites of typical inquiry—the Gare du Nord itself is a place of ill-repute, of danger, and of annoyance for its "average users." Migrants who hang out there are seen as suspect even by compatriots. By seeing the Gare du Nord from an adventurer's eyes, we see something else: its social potential for helping migrants eke out a meaningful life in Paris, where they practice their own form of infrastructural and social integration. Through these efforts, the Gare du Nord has become a living hub of exchange.

Integration in its most elemental form, as its architects in France imagined but never could achieve—"the process of interactions and reciprocities, made possible on the basis of common principles"—leaves the abstract realm of laws and political speeches to be enacted on a public space.[30] Unsurprisingly, migrants' form of integration is singled out as an illegitimate occupation of French public space by the police, residents, and some urbanists, who suggest that they do not belong at the station. Adventurers respond by improvising mutual belonging founded on respect and exchange.

## NATIONALISM AND THE "PERILS OF BELONGING"

Adventurers offer alternatives to the exclusionary ethnic identities being promoted by West African and European political leaders. The adventure experience provides a framework for social relationships that values difference, exchange, and boundary-crossing. There has been a rise in parts of West Africa of what Peter Geschiere calls "autochthony" projects, which promote policies that give full rights only to those who can claim ancestral rootedness to a particular soil.[31] When adventurers departed their villages in the 1990s, they left countries newly democratic (in the case of Mali) and in periods of transition (Côte d'Ivoire, Senegal, and Guinea). Resource depletion and economic crisis would lead to xenophobic policies in Côte d'Ivoire. Large populations of people with Malian or Burkinabe backgrounds fell victim to policies emphasizing *ivoirité* that sought to limit citizenship to those who could claim rooted belonging in an Ivoirian village. As a result, millions of people who identified as Ivoirian but had no such claim to *ivoirité* had to return to their countries "of origin" in the 2000s.[32] There was a similar process in Cameroon that focused on ethnic difference, and Mahmood Mamdani argues that the same native/settler distinctions coming from colonial rule are what led to the Rwandan genocide.[33]

The inspiration for these exclusionary politics is the fantasy of an "Otherless universe," a term Geschiere borrows from Achille Mbembe to describe a place "marked by an almost paranoiac drive toward purification and a never-ending search for foreign elements hiding inside."[34] This "Otherless universe" is exactly the vision that adventurers are fighting against. Their practice offers a clear counterpart to autochthony politics, which, as Geschiere and others point out, are on the rise in Europe and elsewhere too.

Against the drive for ethnic sameness, adventurers seek out the possibility of difference, their very histories and practices a testament to the potential of multiplicity. Adventurers bragged about their ability to speak multiple languages and operate across stylistic registers, skills that were useful when they sought to meet new people and survive abroad. On the flipside, this drive for encounter does not diminish their belonging to their homes, villages, and ethnic groups, which provide the grounds on which their voyages can take flight. Theirs is the opposite of an elusive and untethered cosmopolitan identity where the migrant belongs everywhere and nowhere. It is a precise constellation of connections creating channels between the villages of the Senegal River Valley, the metropolises of West and Central Africa, and French cities such as Paris and Amiens. These are channels that need to be maintained through significant labor; adventurers are ruralist cosmopolitans in action.

All of what I have proposed here suggests that the adventure remains a hopeful trajectory toward social becoming, driven by migrants' improvisation and creativity in carving out a space of freedom in grim circumstances to realize their goals. They do offer some important pathways out of the dead-end thinking about migration and security dominating EU debates in the twenty-first century. But the tangible results for West African adventurers at the Gare du Nord are ambivalent at best.

How can they reconcile the desire for rootedness and connection to home villages with hopes for self-realization on the road when policy does everything to make holding those two things together impossible? How are migrants to make the connections they seek when their existence in public spaces is controlled and repressed by the police and French laws? It would be a mistake to see adventurers as living out a heroic narrative; seeing migration as adventure does not offer redemption or save migrants from the problems of an unequal labor market and rising xenophobia that drives the kind of migration and policy we see today. It cannot stop the demonization of Muslims in France or solve the built-in inequalities that marginalize migrants and their children. But it offers a flicker of light, of hope, in a concrete template for moving forward and for finding meaningful social and economic opportunities in a sea of stifling regulations.

Adventurers may not seek citizenship—that is, belonging in a community defined in political terms—but that does not mean that they give up claims for equal treatment. They seek to work and be treated fairly by their employers and the French state, to continue affective ties and maintain social and kin relationships, and to be allowed to travel, to embark on new voyages. Is that too much to ask, they often wonder, in exchange for the labor they provide, building the infrastructure that will continue to symbolize French progress?

## (STILL) DWELLING IN MOTION

For several years, when I spoke to Lassana on the phone, I would apologize for not yet having finished my book. He would compare it to his Bamako house-building project, still underway. "The important thing is that you're working, you're serious, you're thinking about the future," he reassured me several times, echoing the advice he had been giving all along. His gaze was always on the horizon, on the lookout for a better job, a better apartment, and more opportunities. As he started to go back more frequently to Mali, his attention turned also toward planning potential business ventures in real estate and construction, two of the country's most flourishing sectors where he hoped to show off the skills he had gained abroad. His vision started to move beyond the Gare du Nord, and he was also spending time scouting other railway stations and public places around the capital. When I saw him in 2018, he still had not found anywhere with the right mix of international conjuncture that he had always lauded at the station.

We had coffee at a bar-tobacco shop a block away, where Lassana had become a regular; we ran into several people he knew, and he joked with the Chinese owner and his son at the bar. We talked about how much the Gare had changed since we had met. It now had many upscale shops and restaurants, including several well-known international chains, and even the American burger café Five Guys. Gone were the basic rest stop cafés like Autogrill, where we used to sit and drink coffee in tiny plastic cups. They had been replaced by a Starbucks and a fancy Italian café, leading the people I knew to find other places nearby, like the bar where we were sitting. Lassana told me that he saw these changes as positive signs of the station's continued growth, and his friends agreed. Ibrahim sent me a picture he had taken of the fancy brasserie built where one of the police stations used to be. The Gare du Nord was gentrifying.

The social scene in the front square was still a lively one. There was a "new generation" (as Amadou put it) of young African migrants who met there, leaning on the fence separating the station from the Starbucks outdoor seating area. Several of the teenagers I used to see around the mezzanine mall had grown up and "come up" from below, and many of the *anciens* whom I knew from my fieldwork still showed up to greet their old friends. But they were no longer at the center of things. They hung back, observing from behind the big glass doorways of the entrance, as Dembele used to do, watching passengers arrive and depart as a police patrol walked slowly across the square. Some things have not changed: despite court decisions condemning the police for racial profiling and laws that have made large-scale profiling illegal, young black men are still disproportionately targeted for ID checks, as they are elsewhere in French public space.[35]

Many of the migrants I knew were leaving the interim sector and going into commercial activities—starting electronics importing from China or real estate speculation in Bamako, often in cooperation with their brothers at home.[36] Some announced "the end of migration," suggesting that West African wage labor mobility that had begun in the colonial period was no longer a tenable system. What will come out of this change remains to be seen—it could be more repressive measures and more uncertainty. France, the European Union, and West African adventurers—they are all at the edge of a threshold, looking to see what the future will hold and finding the models they have insufficient.

When I think of them this way, on the threshold, I am reminded of that glassy entrance of the Gare du Nord, where I would watch Lassana, Amadou, and Ibrahim, who would pause there, surveying the movement and interactions playing out across the front square. How do they know who is who or whom to trust or where they belong in this rush of people? The French model failed to provide a pathway—French laws and political discourse grasp at Enlightenment values and universal citizenship while their humanistic referent is forever retreating over the horizon, giving way to the exclusionary tactics of xenophobia and police repression in the name of maintaining French identity. They had to reinvent the road taken by their elders, finding ways to connect themselves to their lineage while promoting mobility abroad. The adventure frame helps them navigate the thorny nest of this French public space: of social relations, livelihoods, and encounters with the police. Adventure-as-resource provides a flexible guide for their voyages, malleable enough to be molded to fit new situations, yet retaining enough of its shape to be recognized across generations. Despite the many walls now being built, adventurers will continue to depart. And as they do, they will seek ways to build a meaningful life, to come of age, to make connections across many borders, to renew their home communities through journeying, and to gain prestige at home by going abroad.

We might learn a thing or two from adventurers' toolkits about dwelling in that space that hangs between the here and there, rural and urban, traditional and modern, rooted and uprooted, home and away. It is the unstable space of a transit hub, where boundaries shift and migrants find a space for dwelling in motion. From that place, departure need not entail rupture. New connections do not mean the erosion of the past. Migrant existence in that in-between provides a space of invention, as Victor Turner put it, where new kinds of belonging are forged.[37]

# NOTES

## INTRODUCTION

1. I have replaced the names of research participants with pseudonyms.

2. See Bredeloup (2014), Canut (2014), and Canut and Sow (2014) for terminologies of adventure.

3. See Dougnon (2013, 40) for a list of these terms in Malian/Mande-speaking contexts. These terms offer similar meanings to the idea of "bush-falling" in Cameroon, also used to indicate migratory journeys today (Alpes 2014, Geschiere and Socpa 2017, Nyamnjoh 2011). On the broader structure of the rite of passage, see Turner (1969), van Gennep (1960).

4. Manchuelle (1997).

5. Bredeloup (1994, 2007); (see also Barou 2002, Bredeloup 2014, Canut 2014, Dougnon 2013).

6. As Sylvie Bredeloup (2014) points out, this was the dominant assumption of migration scholarship in the Marxist tradition (cf. for example, Adams 1977, Amselle 1976, Diarra 1968).

7. Dougnon (2013, 40).

8. Tsing (2005, 4).

9. See the International Organization for Migration (IOM) Missing Migrants Project: http://missingmigrants.iom.int/ for information on the many migrants who remain unaccounted for.

10. As Ruben Andersson (2014) illustrates, the European criminalization of migration has created an entire industry and a multibillion-euro military-style border security apparatus that extended well into the African continent. As Hein de Haas (2008) points out, despite policy based on the myth of African invasion, the E.U. is not interested in stopping the flow of migration.

11. These estimates are higher than official figures published by the E.U. and its member states; as many scholars point out, migrant deaths in the Mediterranean are significantly

underreported (Brian and Laczko 2014; see also Albahari 2016). The International Office for Migration reports on their website that documented deaths for 2018 are fewer than in previous years.

12. See Dougnon (2013); Jónsson (2012). As Gaibazzi (2015, 3) points out, even those who stay behind constitute an "integral element of migration"; they and their villages are drawn into the structures created by mobility.

13. Cf. De Léon (2015) on the U.S./Mexico border and the deadly policy of "prevention through deterrence." On the way European migration policy creates the problems it purports to solve and the deadly consequences of these policies, see Feldman (2012); Jeandesboz and Pallister-Wilkins (2016); Kobelinsky and Le Courant (2017); Landau and Freemantle (2018).

14. Ana Minian (2018) has documented a similar process in Mexico-U.S. migration patterns, where immigration reform killed the circulatory migration patterns of Mexican labor migrants and trapped undocumented Mexicans in the United States.

15. See Schmid (2014).

16. Recent artistic attention to the Gare du Nord includes novels (Djemaï 2003, Sorman 2012), and Claire Simon's two films *Gare du Nord* and *Géographie Humaine.*

17. See, for example, the popular "Secrets of Paris" website about the district: http://www.secretsofparis.com/10th-arrondissement/.

18. Djemaï (2003).

19. Mehta (1997).

20. E.g., Fassin (2005). For a critical appraisal of media and humanitarian representations of border violence and refugees, see Ticktin (2016); in the wider European context, see Cabot (2014) on Greece.

21. De Genova (2013).

22. Michael Wieviorka (2014) argues that "integration" as an analytical term is no longer fit for use in contemporary sociology but must itself be explained (cf. Schnapper 2007; see also Wieviorka 2008). See Barou (2014) for a historical account of how the term has been used in France. Cf. Hinze (2013) on the relationship of integration policy and urban space in Berlin.

23. The first restrictions on this migration came into effect in the 1970s during the economic crisis. While the more extreme policies that emerged during this period were initially defeated or repealed after massive strikes and protests among immigrant and French workers, by the 1990s the government had succeeded in implementing restrictions aimed at stopping the flows of migration from Africa (see Hargreaves 1995, Raissiguier 2010).

24. Marine Le Pen, the leader of the extreme right-wing party Rassemblement National (formerly Front National), received one out of three votes in the May 2017 presidential elections. Those votes were widely believed to have been motivated by anti-immigrant, anti-Muslim sentiment (see Faye 2017). See also Silverstein (2018) on the construction of "crisis" in postcolonial France.

25. Beaman (2017, 18). See also Fernando (2014, 130) on the way Muslims in France are excluded from being full partners in *le vivre ensemble.* Although, as Mostafa Dikeç (2007) points out, the accepted way to talk about race in France is through the idioms (or euphemisms) of culture and geography (e.g., "banlieue youth," "immigrant origin," "African origin," "issued from immigration," etc.), there are also many explicit references to race in the public sphere, as public intellectual Rokhaya Diallo (2012) has pointed out in several articles

and interviews. On the persistence and history of racialization in France, see Fleming (2017), Keaton (2013), Khiari (2006, 85), Knox (2016), De Rudder, Poiret, and Vourc'h (2000), Stovall (2006), Thomas (2013).

26. Durkheim ([1893] 1997); Bourdieu and Sayad (1964); Sayad (1991, 1999); cf. Silverstein (2004a) for a critical interpretation of the "uprooting" discourse.

27. Xenophobic rhetoric is deeply connected to maintaining cheap migrant labor, as Seth Holmes (2014, 13) and others have pointed out.

28. Several politicians, government officials, and scholars pointed to "African" family structure as a cause of the infamous 2005 riots that spread across the country's urban periphery. The French Employment Minister blamed polygamy, as did the general secretary of the Académie Française, historian Hélène Carrère d'Encausse (See *Le Monde/AFP* 2005). The leader of the majority party in the French congress, Bernard Accoyer, said that polygamy was "in part the cause of the disorders that we have had" (see Accoyer 2005).

29. As a headline in the newspaper *Le Figaro* put it, "The map of November 2005 rioters confirms the profound malaise of African immigrants," referring to sub-Saharan Africans in particular (Gabizon 2006). Quoting geographer Hugues Lagrange's (2010) controversial research, the article detailed how the "traditional African system" clashes with urban French life. These representations are similar to French colonial discourse that configured "African culture" as a danger or obstacle to the French civilizing mission (see Conklin 1997).

30. Bredeloup (2014), Timera (2001). On the role of hope in West African migrant pathways, see Bjarnesen (2009); Kleist and Thorsen (2016).

31. On the importance of rethinking the way anthropologists use native discourse, categories, and speech, see Trouillot (2003), Bonilla (2015). As Yarimar Bonilla (2015, xvii) points out, the repositioning of informants' voices in anthropology requires "taking seriously their arguments and their native categories: elaborating on them, theorizing with them, and questioning and departing from them as necessary—as one does with all theorists."

32. For further reflections on the existential indeterminacies that immigration law produces, see Khosravi (2011); Navaro-Yashin (2007); Menjívar (2006).

33. See Soumaré (1993) on the presumed cultural barriers to sub-Saharan migrant integration.

34. See Beaud and Pialoux (2005) for an exploration of these themes in Nicholas Sarkozy's discourse.

35. See Fassin (2005).

36. Çaglar and Glick Schiller (2018).

37. When asked in interviews why she made two films about the Gare du Nord, Claire Simon responded that it was the Parisian station "where the most different social classes meet each other."

38. According to the SNCF press booklet, "Gare du Nord 2015–2023: Transformations" (SNCF Gare & Connexions 2015).

39. The Gare du Nord has its own customs police, often dressed in civilian clothes and standing at the exit of Thalys trains from Belgium and the Netherlands.

40. An SNCF user pamphlet from 2010 outlines these "incivilités," which otherwise include insulting an employee, smoking inside, and traveling without a ticket.

41. I use the English translation adventurer and the less clunky French term *aventurier* interchangeably throughout the book.

42. Many people also see a connection between the notion of adventure and the oral history epic of Sunjata/Sundiata, which retells the story of the thirteenth-century emperor of Mali who went into exile and then returned to vanquish his enemies and become king.

43. Bredeloup (2017). See also Cohen and Sirkeci (2011) on "cultures of migration" for similar cases.

44. Whitehouse (2012, 88). *Tunga* is the Bamanakan/Malinke term; given how widespread this language and its close cousins (such as Jula) are throughout Mali, Côte d'Ivoire, eastern Senegal, Guinea, and Gambia, it is often used among West Africans of various ethnolinguistic backgrounds as a lingua franca in migratory contexts.

45. I thank Professor Abdoulaye Sow for providing information about these words and their translations. See Dougnon (2013, 40) for an analysis of these terms in Malian and Mande-speaking contexts; see Gaibazzi (2015, 81) for a discussion of the meaning of *gunne* (bush, wilderness) and its relation to migration in Gambian Soninke contexts.

46. Gaibazzi (2015).

47. Philip Curtin's (1975) investigation of the precolonial era of Senegambia illustrates that a culture of mobility was established through caravans and exchange with the Arab world from at least the sixteenth century.

48. See Stoller (1992, 1999, 2016). See also Rouch (1956).

49. See Geschiere and Socpa (2017, 177); Alpes (2014).

50. For an overview, see Eickelman and Piscatori (1990).

51. See Dougnon (2007) on how colonial forced and migratory labor practices in Mali created new destinations and ideas about labor and dignity as related to "black man's work" and "white man's work."

52. Manchuelle (1997, chap. 2).

53. See Dougnon (2007, 2016) on Malian migrants to Ghana in the early twentieth century, who showed off their new status by returning with "Western" clothing and a bicycle; Jean Rouch documents the same phenomenon among Nigerien migrants to Ghana in his 1967 documentary film *Jaguar*.

54. The Soninke poet and biologist Thierno Tandia illuminated this proverb for me in an interview in 2018.

55. Bayart (2009, 69).

56. Melly (2017, 140, 38).

57. Smith (2017, 18). See also Bjarnesen (2009); Buggenhaggen (2012); Daum (1998); Dicko (2014); Kane (2002).

58. See Vigh (2006) on "social becoming." See Piot (2019) for an examination of how Togolese visa lottery recipients imagine and experience their lives in the United States. See also Castles, de Haas, and Miller (2013) on the importance of looking beyond push-and-pull factors to understand migration.

59. Sylvie Bredeloup (2014) has argued that the adventure serves as an "interpretative frame" for many West African migrants.

60. Mann (2015).

61. See Mann (2006, Introduction), on the multiple meanings of caste and hierarchy in Mali.

62. Whitehouse (2012), personal communication.

63. I thank Abdoulaye Sow for providing this translation, and Thierno Tandia for his insights into the concept of courage or *len siren,* which, as in the Bamanakan version (*den nyuman*), translates literally as "good child."

64. See Bondaz (2013) and Ouattara (2003) on the social aspects of the *grins*; see Banégas, Brisset-Foucault, and Cutolo (2012) for an overview of the *grin*-like structures throughout the region.

65. Besteman (2016, conclusion); Mbodj-Pouye (2016, 296). On emplacement and migration in conflict situations, see also Vigh and Bjarnesen (2016); Vigh (2018). For the broader tradition of studying emplacement at the crossroads of urban migration studies, see Çaglar and Glick Schiller (2018); Englund (2002); Smith (2005).

66. Cissé (1997), Mbodj-Pouye (2016).

67. Marc Augé (1995, 103) used large-scale commercial transit areas as examples of "non-places," that is, spaces lacking in meaningful social ties and historical grounding: "The space of non-place creates neither singular identity nor relations; only solitude, and similitude."

68. Low (1996, 2008, 2017). The work of Stéphane Tonnelat and William Kornblum (2017) on the 7 train in New York City also provided an approach to studying encounters and urban transportation.

69. Stoller (2002, 179).

70. White (2000, 49–50).

71. See Cole (2010), Meiu (2017).

72. The Nigerien merchants in Paul Stoller's *Money Has No Smell* (2002, 176) have a similar notion of a "path" that structures experiential as well as professional orientations toward migration.

73. Redfield (2000, 18); see also Lévi-Strauss (1962, 21–22).

74. Augé (2002, 59–60).

75. See Geertz (1973); Marcus (1995).

76. Miano (2017, introduction).

77. On women migrants from the same region, see Nehara Feldman's (2018) pathbreaking study. In addition to the frequently studied and cited roles that women play in migration and social reproduction as wives and mothers, less examined is the fact that they also work independently, provide money to enable their brothers' adventures, engage in their own house construction projects, and confront the difficulties of French racism and migration policy in their own ways. See Sargent and Cordell (2003); Sargent and Larchanché-Kim (2006).

78. Desjarlais (1997); Stoller (2002).

## 1. DANGEROUS CLASSES

1. Brice Hortefeux, minister of the interior from 2009 to 2011, in his opening remarks upon a visit to the Gare du Nord on June 14, 2010.

2. See Bourgoin (2013), Demiati (2007), Sainati (2007). Boubeker (2009, 72), however, questions this lament of the diminishing French welfare state, pointing out that even at its height the postwar French welfare social model incorporated white French workers at the expense of immigrants.

3. The "color-blind" version of French history that gained popularity in the 1980s–90s debates about the "Republican model" has been criticized by much scholarship yet persists in the public sphere. On the history of racialized divisions in France, see Chapman and Frader (2004), Ndiaye (2008), Peabody and Stovall (2003), Stovall and Van den Abbeele (2006). For an examination of how particularism and racial boundaries do not contradict but rather have constituted French family law, nationality, public spaces, and universalism, see Bancel, Blanchard, and Lemaire (2005); Davidson (2012); Dorlin (2006); Saada (2012); Scott (2007); Wilder (2005).

4. See Green (1991) for an overview of these comparisons.

5. Both Beaman (2017) and Scott (2007) point out that France has long been a country of immigration, with proportionally more immigrants than the United States as early as the 1910s. See also Noiriel (1996), Weil (2005).

6. The Immigration museum at the Porte Dorée, built by Nicolas Sarkozy when he was president, offers the clearest representation of this national narrative.

7. Hage (2000, 22).

8. See De Rudder, Poiret, and Vourc'h (2000) for an examination of the widespread idea that race and multiculturalism are "American" imports; see Chabal (2013) on the "Anglo-Saxon" model as a French construction.

9. Chapman and Frader (2004, 4), Fredrickson (2002).

10. As historians have documented, anti-Semitism was another racial ideology of the nineteenth century that helped shape ideas about race and difference in France. See Conklin (2013), Chapman and Frader (2004) on the connection between anti-Semitism and anti-black racism that emerged in the nineteenth and twentieth centuries. These two are not the same thing, however; as Schreier (2010, chap. 5) illustrates, Jews *were* adopted as part of the French Republic, although their citizenship never meant the same thing as it did for non-Jews.

11. Peabody and Stovall (2003). See also the large body of work on the "colonial fracture" in France examining this question (Bancel et al. 2006).

12. See Camiscioli (2009) and Ndiaye (2008) for historical accounts of racial formations in France, to which the construction of whiteness has also been central, as Didier Gondola (2009) points out. Olivier le Cour Grandmaison (2008) has traced contemporary French "state racism and xenophobia" to early twentieth-century policies toward colonial subjects and immigrants.

13. See Silverstein (2018, chap. 2) for a discussion about how postcolonial immigrants and their descendants become configured as a "problem" or "challenge" to French Republicanism.

14. Newman (2015, 11).

15. Carmona (2002, 8).

16. Marx ([1939] 1971).

17. Sauget (2009, 10).

18. See Berman (1982).

19. Schivelbusch (1987).

20. Berman (1982, 40).

21. Zola (1890).

22. Saint-Simonianism was a utopian socialist movement founded in the early nineteenth century and based on the ideas of the Count of Saint-Simon. Its leaders proposed a

vision of society wherein technological progress and industry would unite nations and create harmony (see Picon 2002).

23. See Abi-Mershed (2010).

24. Railway planning was not entirely terrestrial. In 1902, the government and North railway company began a project for the France-England railway of the Trans-Manche (a project imagined in the 1830s by Saint-Simonian disciple Michel Chevalier), though it would not be realized until the Chunnel was completed in the 1990s.

25. Reynaud (1850).

26. Peter Soppelsa (2013) similarly observes that the universal exposition in 1900 had to reconcile the potential of disaster and breakdown with the hopeful modernity that the exposition was meant to embody.

27. Sauget (2009).

28. Noiriel (2007).

29. Frégier (1840, 2:29, 140); see also Chevalier (1958), Khalifa (2004). These images of Paris's poor would be reproduced by Victor Hugo in *Les Misérables*, published in 1862 (see Noiriel 2007 for a discussion of Hugo's amalgamation of "poor" and "criminal").

30. See Lorcin (2014), Staum (2003).

31. Weber (1976).

32. Sauget (2009, 162), also see Schivelbusch (1987).

33. Pratt (1992, 7). See also Clifford (1997, 193).

34. In his discussion of creolization, Stuart Hall ([2003] 2015) warns against an uncritical celebration of mixing and contact, placing the emphasis on the power and hierarchy present in Pratt's "contact zone." See Hall and Rosner (2004) for a critical overview of Pratt's work on contact zones and how it has changed.

35. See Harvey (2003, 280).

36. Noiriel (2007).

37. The initial plans for the Gare du Nord began in 1837, the concession and construction in 1843, and the embarcadère's inauguration occurred in 1846.

38. Karen Bowie's (1999) study suggests that the placement of the station resulted from a rivalry between railway tycoons Pereire and Rothschild. Before the government settled on this site, the tycoon Emile Pereire lobbied for an alternate site that would unite the northern railways to his western station, the Gare Saint Lazare, but his proposal was met with local protest.

39. Sauget (2009, 22).

40. Schivelbusch (1987, 172).

41. This separation that masks industrial modernity with neo-classical dressing was an emblem for wider Haussmannian reforms of Paris, a modernization project that harkened back to the civilizational past of antiquity. See Wakeman (2004) on "nostalgic modernism."

42. Anderson (1983).

43. This quote appears in *L'Illustration*'s issue on the *Chemin de Fer du Nord*, date unknown.

44. Centre des Archives du Monde du Travail (CAMT), Series 48 AQ, Box 12.

45. Perdonnet (1855).

46. Perdonnet (1855, 129). Greet de Block (2011) shows that the nineteenth-century Belgian rail development shared these international aims.

47. Perdonnet (1855, 142).

48. Centre des Archives du Monde de Travail (CAMT), Series 48 AQ Box 12.

49. Centre des Archives du Monde de Travail (CAMT), Series 48 AQ Boxes 3303 b, 3303 c.

50. Centre des Archives du Monde de Travail (CAMT), Series 48 AQ Box 3340.

51. Sauget (2009, 75).

52. The disjunction between the projected use of trains and their actual use seems to be a characteristic of many infrastructure projects, as Brian Larkin (2008, 20) shows for the case of Nigeria and Mrazek (1997) for colonial Indonesian roads built by the Dutch.

53. Harvey (2005, 37).

54. See Newman (2015).

55. Foucault ([1977] 2007, 18). See also Papayanis (2004).

56. Chevalier (1958).

57. See Chevalier (1958) for an overview of the representations of these "dangerous and working classes."

58. See Price (1975).

59. Soppelsa (2011).

60. Weber (1976, 3).

61. Chevalier (1958, 182).

62. See De Gobineau (1853). In parallel to the metropolitan case, colonial offices classified "Berbers" as ideal subjects for the civilizing mission, while "Arabs" were seen as further from European races and more likely to disrupt the colonial order; see Camiscioli (2009), Lorcin (2014).

63. Urban planning in Algeria and France in the nineteenth century was seen as a method to instill modern ways of being through the built environment. See Rabinow (1989).

64. See Merriman (1991, chap. 2) for an analysis of the bourgeois discourse equating "peripheral" and "fearsome" populations in Paris in the first half of the nineteenth century.

65. See Douglas (1966). The historical representation of these groups has been overshadowed by Louis Chevalier's (1958) controversial tome. Chevalier treats migration to Paris in the first half of the nineteenth century as a crisis to be explained and a threat to manage, thus accepting the bourgeois representation of these groups as true.

66. Both Papayanis (1996) in his study of Parisian omnibuses and Soppelsa (2012) in a study of the construction of the metro show that anxiety concerning social mixing was built into these transportation developments.

67. Ratcliffe (1991, 549). See also Andrew Israel Ross (2019).

68. Delaroy (1854, 13).

69. Delaroy (1854, 19).

70. Spaces of intense social mixing have long been sites for the elaboration of urban governance measures to quell the potential danger of encounters (cf. Konove [2018] on the history of the Baratillo market in Mexico City).

71. Delaroy (1854, 107).

72. Delaroy (1854, 18). Delaroy's pamphlet tries to reinforce boundaries by developing a classification scheme, based on a genre of nineteenth-century text—the *Physiologie*—that used early biological writings as a template to classify new inventions, technologies, and social types as the "flora and fauna" of the industrial age (see, for example, Siebecker 1867).

73. *Revue du XIXe siècle*, Nouvelle Serie, T.3, juillet-septembre 1837, 533, as cited in Sauget (2009, 148).

74. The difference between criminal action and political action on railways was often blurred, similarly to what Lisa Mitchell (2011, 492) highlights in her study of passenger political action on Indian trains, where trains become sites of popular politics for marginalized users, as passengers use the technically illegal action of pulling the emergency stop to communicate a political message.

75. Sauget (2009, 169).

76. Sauget (2003) and Ross (2019) explore further the different undesirable populations that came to occupy railway stations in the nineteenth century.

77. Sauget (2009, 169).

78. See Gastineau (1861, 20–24).

79. France was no different from colonial situations in which difference was explicitly institutionalized. Studies show that railway systems expanding simultaneously in British colonial domains led to similar anxieties about the dangerous effects of mixing, on the part of colonial officials as well as on the part of the colonized elite. See, for example, Manu Goswami on India (2004, 118) or Frederick Cooper (1987) on Kenya. Chandra Bhimull (2017) illustrates that imperial racism shaped commercial aviation development in Great Britain.

80. See Noiriel (2007).

81. Noiriel (2007).

82. These distinctions were not handed down from on high in the metropole, as it often seemed, but rather emerged in particular historical circumstances in the colonies and in France. See Saada (2003) on the ways that distinctions between citizen and indigène and citizen and subject emerged in colonial legal situations. See Camiscioli (2009) on the development of hierarchies of difference in the twentieth century.

83. See Rabinow (1989), Wright (1991).

84. Noiriel (2007); see also Lewis (2007) on migrants' position in France during the second part of the Third Republic.

85. For more on the process of how these *classes populaires* obtained rights and "became French folks," see Noiriel (2007). This process did not erase the distinctions between Parisians and provincials; people from rural areas and working classes are still marginalized and seen as culturally different and "backward" (Reed-Danahay and Anderson-Levitt 1991, Rogers 1995). For a study on the changing status of French Jews, see Schreier (2010).

86. "Reglementation des chemins de fer" (pamphlet). Archives du Monde du Travail (CAMT), Series 48 AQ, Box 3548.

87. Purseigle (2007, 440). See also Grayzel (1997, 78) on prostitution around the station in the same period. Today, refugees from Syria, Iraq, and Afghanistan have established temporary settlements near the Gare du Nord and have been similarly targeted by the police.

88. Jennifer Boittin (2010) estimates that "134,000 West African and Malagasy soldiers, as well as numerous North African, Chinese, and Indochinese soldiers and workers, fought or labored in France. . . . In 1926, according to police, there were as many as 10,000 to 15,000 black men in Paris" (xvii–xviii).

89. As Didier Gondola (2009, 172) puts it, "Whiteness and Frenchness have been conflated as an exclusionary social category that enabled scores of European migrants to be assimilated at the expense of immigrants and French citizens of African descent."

90. See Gruson (2011), Stevens (2009). Noiriel stepped down from the museum committee along with eight other scholars when the Cité Nationale de l'Histoire museum was built and Nicolas Sarkozy announced the creation of a new ministry for "Immigration and National Identity."

91. See Boittin (2010), Peabody and Stovall (2003), Wilder (2005). See also El-Tayeb (2011) and Gutierrez-Rodriguez and Tate (2015) on the myth of a white Christian Europe.

92. Noiriel (2007).

93. The station played a significant role in the German occupation, the Resistance, and World War II. It is beyond the scope of this book to examine this history; see Broch (2017), Caron (1997), Chevandier (1997), Immelé (2005) on the role of railways and railway workers in these events.

94. The process of regional incorporation has a longer history and more of a recent shift, which suggests that that these groups gained ground by appealing to a more widespread politics of belonging, emphasizing autochthony and rootedness a particular land, which serves to further exclude immigrant populations. See Geschiere (2009) for a comparative case in the Netherlands.

95. Silverman (1992, chap. 3). The Algerian War (1958–1962) also had a lasting effect on French migration policy and attitudes toward foreign workers (Shepard 2008).

96. In my survey of major French daily newspapers *Le Monde* and *Le Figaro* during the 1981 presidential campaigns, debates focused on problems defined as "social"—housing, poverty, education—and did not reference immigrants or immigration.

97. See Beaud and Pialoux (2004), Cannon (2017), Silverstein (2005) on the development of new "dangerous classes" in France.

98. Balibar and Wallerstein ([1991] 2011).

99. Clozier (1940)

100. SNCF Gare & Connexions 2015.

101. See Davidson (2012, chap. 1).

## 2. THE EXCHANGE HUB

1. See Rivière and Tissot (2012) for a summary of media representations of the suburbs during the 2007 presidential campaign.

2. The first immigrant urban revolts that were called "riots" occurred in the 1980s. For a critical review of the term *riot* and its use in France, see Murphy (2011). See also Tshimanga, Gondola, and Bloom (2009), who choose the term *uprisings* to characterize the 2005 events called "riots" by the media.

3. See Fassin (2013) for a detailed account of how the police carry out this daily subjectification.

4. Brice Hortefeux, minister of the interior from 2009 to 2011, said this in his opening remarks upon a visit to the Gare du Nord on June 14, 2010.

5. Moore (1987, 730). See also Foucault et al. (1991, 76). On the anthropological uses of the event for providing new understandings of conflict situations, see Caton (2006).

6. Setha Low (1996) calls this approach the "social production and social construction" of urban space, which is inspired by Henri Lefebvre's now classic text, *The Production of Space* ([1974] 1991). Or, as Doreen Massey (2005, 9) puts it, space is a "product of interrelations."

7. The Paris Urban Planning Agency (APUR), as cited in Newman (2015, 7).

8. See Silverstein (2004b).

9. The Goutte d'Or in particular has been seen as an "immigrant hub" and a center of commercial exchange for African communities. See Lallement (2010), Messamah and Toubon (1990), Milliot (2013).

10. See Toledano (2012, 174), Newman (2015, introduction).

11. Newman (2015, chap. 1).

12. See, for example, *Le Parisien* (2007).

13. Keaton (2006) points out that "suburb" is an inadequate translation of *banlieue*, because the French term is often used to refer to poor areas with high concentrations of public housing and immigrant populations. More accurate is Keaton's translation, "outer-city," which has some of the same connotations of the US term "inner city," but corresponds to the French case in which such districts occupy the periphery of urban areas.

14. See also Silverstein (2004b), Stovall (2001).

15. The Eurostar terminal and the Chunnel project juxtaposed the hopes of interconnection and the fears of transgressing this natural border, as Eve Darian-Smith (1999) illustrates. The new terminal added airport-like security measures.

16. Richer (2008).

17. Christian Lallier's 1995 documentary *Changement à Gare du Nord* highlights the difficulty of transferring from one form of transport to another, as do the findings of Isaac Joseph's (1995) sociological study.

18. See Epstein (2011) for an exploration of how *le vivre ensemble* and *mixité sociale* played a role in urban planning in suburban housing projects in the postwar period. For Newman (2015), public space—often parks—were also part of this vision, and such spaces have been carefully planned to foster a Republican order of social mixing and community.

19. Epstein (2011).

20. Newman (2015, 71).

21. See Kleinman (2012).

22. According to Anderson (2007), the debated term "Web 2.0" refers to a set of emerging principles for internet technology, guided by principles of participatory data building and collaboration, sociability, openness, and "user-generated content."

23. See Dang Vu and Jeaneau (2009).

24. In 1975, the station was legally classified as a historical monument, placing it in the realm of protected national patrimony.

25. See Perrot (1987) for a discussion of how transparency has come to influence the notion of democracy in France. On transparency and democracy, see Garsten and Lindh de Montoya (2008); see also Rosalind Morris's critique of transparency language in Thailand (2004).

26. The *Transilien* is the SNCF's name for the suburban transport network of the Paris region, Ile-de-France. It is a play on the word *Francilien*, which is the name for an inhabitant of the Ile-de-France.

27. These models can be consulted on AREP's website, as well as in the press releases for the rebuilding meant to be completed in 2023.

28. Kanna (2011, 79).

29. De Certeau (1984).

30. Goffman (1963). Terzi and Tonnelat (2017, 521) examine how "civil inattention" is a dominant norm especially in crowded public transit spaces; see also Gayet-Viaud (2011) on "urban civility."

31. Dikeç (2007, 4).

32. Sorman (2011).

33. Mauger (2007).

34. Negroni (2007).

35. See Gas (2007) for an overview of each candidate's reaction to the Gare du Nord riot.

36. See Vanderbeck and Johnson (2000) on youth socializing in malls.

37. These measures echo other attempts in Europe and North America to install devices in commercial areas like malls to stop youth and other undesirables from loitering, or round benches that make it impossible for homeless people to sleep in public spaces.

38. Dikeç (2007). On the way infrastructure becomes part of political struggle for what Henri Lefebvre (1967) called the "right to the city," see Chance (2018).

39. The relationships between Afro-Caribbeans and Africans in France is much more complex than this discussion suggests, and it has been the subject of many examinations, as Remy Bazenguissa-Ganga (2012) points out. Tracing the transforming relationships between these groups in France, he shows that working-class Afro-Caribbeans and Africans first resisted the common identification black/noir as it was ascribed to them by white French and then came to recognize themselves as Black in a globalized context starting in the 1970s. Though their attitudes toward each other sometimes "use and exemplify the racist themes used by whites to describe Blacks," they also often simply suggested a difference in where they came from, as Bazenguissa-Ganga (153) points out about the Malinké word for Afro-Caribbeans meaning "those who come from the other side of the water."

40. Recent scholarship illustrates how "black" has been reconfigured to be relevant as an identity category for political and social action in the present. See, for example, Etoke (2010), Gueye (2006), Keaton et al. (2012), Soumahoro (2014).

41. See Keaton (2013).

42. Trouillot (1995).

## 3. THE GARE DU NORD METHOD

1. Fassin (2013, chap. 3).

2. See Bonelli (2005), Fassin (2013), Jobard (2002), Schneider (2014) on policing and inequality in France.

3. Fassin (2013, 94). In his ethnography of a French anticrime police unit in the suburbs, Fassin found that identity checks were motivated by police attempts to harass, humiliate, provoke, and force submission. See also Jobard et al. (2012).

4. See Ticktin (2016).

5. There are several cases of police brutality in France that have begun with an ID check and have led to critical injury and deaths of young men of color. See, for example, Le Cain (2017).

6. Luc Poignant, police union representative, said that the term *bamboula* was "more or less appropriate" on a French talk show, a comment that the Interior Ministry was quick to condemn. See *Le Monde*/AFP 2017.

7. Treps (2017).

8. See also Miano (2017), Guénif Souilamas and Macé (2004), Faure and Fofana (2017) for a critical appraisal of the way African men are represented in France.

9. Probable cause has had a very broad definition since 1993, when the Penal Procedure Code was revised to allow police to do a legal identity check "whatever [the subject's] behavior, in order to prevent a breach in public order, in particular an attack on the security of persons or of property." (From the Penal Procedure Code, as cited in Fassin [2013, 91]). Fassin points out that there are several state bodies that have condemned the overuse of identity checks, but that these condemnations have no effect on police practice because there are no sanctions when they stop someone without cause.

10. Fiske (1998, 81).

11. Browne (2015, 16).

12. Castagnino (2016, 50).

13. The police officers in Fassin's study also use *tu* with many of the subjects they interpolate, which he points out is a seemingly small impoliteness that opens the door for further aggressiveness and subjection.

14. Scholars have emphasized how legal suspension of rights creates an ongoing "state of exception" to the rule of law (Agamben 1998). See Fassin 2005; Ticktin 2011 for how the state of exception works in relation to immigration policy and politics in France.

15. The Open Society Justice Initiative study showed that police at the Gare du Nord were far more likely to stop those who appeared to be "Black" or "Arab."

16. As journalists Alice Géraud and Fanny Lesbros (2012) observe, the identity checks and brief searches almost never result in the police arresting anyone or bringing anyone in; they are meant to humiliate and harass the young men who are stopped. Internal directives from Parisian police commissariats call on police to target groups of young black and North African men in places like the Gare du Nord to dissuade them from using those spaces, and the police have admitted that they do so because those groups "bother" other travelers (see Ploquin 2019).

17. See Kleinman (2012).

18. For an overview of the concept of precarity in anthropology, see Muehlebach (2013). For comparative analyses of the effects of precarity, see Allison (2013), Ives (2014), Standing (2011), White (2012).

19. Foucault (1979), Davis (1990).

20. For a critical reinterpretation of the Panopticon and its place in surveillance studies, see Browne (2015).

21. De Certeau (1984, 97).

22. Newman (2015, 140–41).

23. Newman (2015, 138).

24. cf. Ferguson (2015).

25. Stuesse and Coleman (2014).

26. See *Le Nouvel Observateur* (2013); the report is based on the railway workers' union, SUD-Rail, issuing a statement denouncing the directive from the SNCF for its subsidiary not to send any "black or Arab" baggage porters for the Israeli prime minister's arrival, a directive *Le Point* journalists confirmed with the personnel director of the subsidiary company (Zemouri 2013).

27. See Ferguson and Gupta (2002) for a critique of this spatializing discourse.

28. I was reminded of these interactions when I read the Togolese rapper and activist Elom 20ce recount the strategy of an Ivoirian friend of his who, when asked for his papers, did not give them but instead gave the police the name of one of his illustrious ancestors, Sunjata Keita (the Malian emperor) or Samory Touré (the Wassalou emperor and resistor of French rule); the police duly noted these names without any understanding of who they were. "I liked that in response to these daily aggravations," comments Elom 20ce, "he brandishes the shield of our grandeur" (in Miano 2017).

29. Foreigners must have passports and resident permits, if applicable, on them at all times or be subject to a verification at the police station, according to French laws established in 1986, with earlier precedents. The regulation comes from the French Code of Penal Procedure (Livre I, Titre II, Chapitre III, Article 78-3, modified in 1993, 1999, and 2006).

30. Newell (2012).

31. Open Justice Society Initiative (2009).

32. This goal speaks directly to recent discussions about street harassment (such as public catcalling) in France, which have pointed to the Gare du Nord as a particularly masculine space where women are made to feel uncomfortable by the men who hang out there.

33. Fula (or Fulani or Fulɓe), often referred to as Peul in French, from the Wolof word, and Soninke are two of the main ethnic groups in the Senegal River Valley area, and both Lassana and Ibrahim had grown up in multiethnic villages with mixing between Fula and Soninke communities. While Fula are traditionally pastoralist herders and Soninke are agriculturalists, a difference that has led to conflicts in some parts of the region, in this case their history is one of cooperation.

34. Herzfeld (2009, 232).

35. The assumption on the part of these young men that white French authority figures cannot tell black people apart was often referenced. It influences the strategies of African migrants, such as when they exchange visas or resident permits with the hope that no one will notice. The police at the Gare du Nord do employ initiatives to more easily recognize these men, such as by taking pictures of station regulars among this group and posting them inside their station.

36. See Aidi (2014) on the sometimes-controversial influence of styles associated with hiphop in the United States on young people in France. Samir Meghelli (2012) argues that hiphop culture in France offered a form of transnational engagement for Afro-French youth.

37. Newell (2012).

38. See Ferguson (1999, 94) on cultural styles; as he points out, cultural styles are "practices that signify differences between social categories," or, in other words, they are the "performative enactment of social categories." On urban styles as a form of seeking dignity and respect in a situation of marginalization, see Bourgois (2003).

39. On these styles as resistance and in relation to policing, see Ralph (2014, 57).

40. The *double peine* refers to the law that allows France to deport immigrants who have been convicted of certain offenses.

## 4. HACKING INFRASTRUCTURES

1. As Bruce Whitehouse (2012) observes among West Africans in Brazzaville, kin are often a sponge on resources more than they provide resources. Distinguishing between bonding and bridging social capital, Robert Putnam explains, "Whereas bonding social

capital is to 'get by,' bridging social capital is to 'get ahead'" (as cited in Lancee 2018). Bram Lancee's 2018 study of immigrant social networks in the Netherlands supports this idea, showing that bridging social capital had more positive economic outcomes for immigrants than bonding social capital.

2. Contact zones often provide such opportunities for translating social into financial capital, as Crystal Biruk (2018, 89–93) shows is the case in rural Malawi, where research survey fieldworkers produce new forms of value outside of their insufficient wage labor through connection to foreign researchers.

3. As anthropologist Keith Hart (2000, 177) observes, for example, Frafra migrants in Accra expended great energy in informal economic activity despite the "inevitability of long-run failure for all but a handful."

4. See Dougnon (2007), Newell (2012), Whitehouse (2012) for analyses of migration from West Africa and changing notions of dignity and work.

5. Jounin (2008, 58); see also Campinos-Dubernet (1985).

6. *Loi du 3 Janvier 1972 sur le Travail Temporaire*. See Jounin (2008, 61n14) for a discussion of this law's effects.

7. Jounin (2008) similarly finds that racist insults were endemic in the world of the intérim, and often used to subjugate foreign workers.

8. Jounin (2008, 39); see also Morice and Potot (2010).

9. See Gardner (2010), Surak (2013), Vora (2013).

10. Hart (2000, 177).

11. Nordman and Pasquier-Doumer (2015). See Fafchamps (2007) for an overview of the role of social capital in developing economies.

12. See Barron et al. (2010).

13. Hart (2000, 177). See also Granovetter (1973) on the importance of "weak ties" in creating community integration.

14. Murphy (2015, 353), see also Wylie (1957).

15. Murphy (2015), Redfield (2000), See Reed-Danahay (1993, 225). As Murphy points out, the System D now exists in English to describe what people are doing in the growing "gig economy."

16. Redfield (2000).

17. Simone (2004). See also De Boeck and Baloji (2016) on the way urban residents in Kinshasa engage in what they call "suturing" to create the "junctions and seams" that tie otherwise disconnected parts of a city together.

18. Simone (2009, 125).

19. Çaglar and Glick Schiller (2011, 2018). This examination of infrastructure builds on geography and urban studies that have examined multi-scalar, urban sites of "interconnectivity" as useful arenas to think beyond models of ethnically bounded diasporas. See also Smith (2005) on interconnectivity, Farias and Bender (2010) on urban assemblages, and Brenner (2001) on scale-making.

20. See Amin (2014); Anand, Gupta, and Appel (2018); Star (1999). Larkin (2013) provides an excellent overview of work on the anthropology of infrastructure. Exemplary ethnographic studies of infrastructure and its attendant politics in this growing field include Anand (2017), Chalfin (2017), Chance (2018), Chu (2014), Elyachar (2010), Von Schnitzler (2016).

21. Fredericks (2014), Cole (2014c), Xiang and Lindquist (2014).

22. Kleinman (2012), Soppelsa (2011).

23. Elyachar (2010); see also Sopranzetti (2014, 2017).

24. Jakobson (1981).

25. Kleinman (2014); cf. Novak (2011).

26. Coleman (2013, 7).

27. Bourdieu (1977).

28. Joseph (1995).

29. Schivelbusch (1987).

30. The reliance on temporary labor to build the types of foundational infrastructure that has long symbolized French modernity points to the overall "flexibilization" or informalization of the state sector, in which employment in state services is more and more flexible, precarious, and privately managed (for more on how this change has developed in France, see Appay 2010).

31. Jounin's (2008) study bears out Bakary's observation about the temporary work sector.

32. Hart (2000, 186).

33. See Daum (1998), Dieng (2002).

34. Cf. MacGaffey and Bazenguissa-Ganga (2000), Stoller (2002). Adventurers are not alone among West African migrants in seeking ties outside of their kin communities. Keith Hart (2000) has examined how trust between strangers emerges among Frafra migrants in Accra, in the space between kin and contract, and Lauren Landau (2018) has explored how friendship and community emerge among diverse migrants in what he calls "urban estuaries" in Kenya and South Africa. Charles Piot (2010) offers a parallel account of the emergence of these new forms of socioeconomic labor in Togo, which eschew kinship and village ties in favor of creating new institutions such as charismatic churches.

35. These jokes and stereotypes emerge from a cultural repertoire of joking kinship (cousinage in French or senenkunya in Mande languages), widespread in everyday interactions across many parts of West Africa (see Whitehouse 2012, 17; Galvan 2006), and also used for various social, economic, and political ends (Smith 2006). For a critical appraisal of joking cousinage as part of the colonial library and now global discourses of conflict resolution, see Canut and Smith (2006).

36. Whitehouse (2012, 25).

37. On remittance, see Cliggett (2005), Cohen (2011), Trager (2005). See also Bloch and Parry (1989), Groes-Green (2014).

38. See Åkesson (2013), Quiminal (1991), Freeman (2013) on the meanings of house building and village projects for African migrants.

39. Smith (2017, 18). See also Newell (2012) on the meanings of migrant gifts.

40. Hart (2000, 185).

41. See Bob White's commentary on *ambianceurs* (in Lingala, *atalaku*) in Congo-Kinshasa, discussed in *Rumba Rules* (2008, 141). Cf. Skinner (2015), chapter 2 on *ambiance*.

42. See Tshimanga (2009) for an overview of this kind of rhetoric.

43. "Integrate or leave" is what former interior minister Claude Guéant suggested in 2011, when he claimed that "immigrant origin communities . . . have little knowledge of French ways of living" and suggested that they did not belong in France if they were unable to integrate.

44. These strategies are similar to what Achille Mbembe (2010) qualifies as Afropolitanism and what Ryan Skinner (2015) further developed as "Afropolitan ethics."

## 5. THE ENDS OF ADVENTURE

1. Whitehouse (2012, 223), Newell (2012). While immigration to France from the Senegal River Valley increased after the Second World War, the vast majority (between 85 and 90%) of African migrants continues to migrate to destinations within Africa. See Whitehouse (2012, 4), World Bank (2011).

2. The failure of the French integration model, the withdrawal of the state and welfare programs, and the effects of French migration regulations thus contribute to "communitarianism"—precisely what the French state criticizes among West African migrants.

3. Sargent and Larchanché-Kim (2006). On the way regulations make it difficult for migrants both to return home and to remain in France, see Timera and Garnier (2010).

4. Vigh (2006).

5. Cole (2014a).

6. Cf. Feldman-Savelsberg (2017).

7. Jonathan Parry and Maurice Bloch (1989) use the notion of short- and long-term cycles of exchange to conceptualize this problem from a social perspective. Short-term cycles characterize the relationships they form at the Gare du Nord, aimed at individual accumulation and pleasure. As Christian Groes-Green writes, such cycles "are allowed only as long as they remain subordinate, over time, to kin-related patronage governed by moralities of social reproduction and ancestral principles" (Groes-Green 2014, 239).

8. See Newell (2016).

9. Cole and Groes (2016, introduction).

10. Depending on the situation, *fadenya* can be negative (*fadenya jugu*) or positive; on the notion of *fadenya* and its many social and cultural functions, see Hoffman (2002), Keita (1990). For an example of how both its negative and positive aspects work in contemporary Bamako, see Skinner (2015).

11. At the same time, they were able to leave and make it to France. By itself, this fact gives them a superior position to their family members and peers who were "stuck" at home (cf. Gaibazzi 2015, Jónsson 2012).

12. The term *un grand quelqu'un* is most often used in Ivoirian French to refer to someone who has achieved a high social status (Kouame 2012).

13. Remaining *en aventure* for a long period of time can change resource distribution and status relations in home communities, similar to what George Meiu (2014, 3) shows is the case in coastal Kenya, where the "normative life course" gets sped up or even inverted when young men migrate. See also Kleinman (2016b).

14. Gunvor Jónsson (2012) shows that young Soninke men who are unable to migrate have difficulty marrying and are often marginalized, illustrating that the impetus to migrate does not affect everyone in the same way, and often exacerbates inequalities.

15. This situation is not exclusive to migrants or produced through migration. As Smith (2017) points out, men in urban Nigeria have to confront changing expectations about masculinity and find ways to negotiate personal aspirations and familial obligations.

16. The regulation of kinship and marriage is part of how all states function, but as several scholars have shown, it has long taken on a particularly central part in the explicit attempts to reproduce nationhood in France, as Jennifer Cole (2014b) points out in her discussion of mixed marriages in France. This is not a recent phenomenon; Judith Surkis

(2006) illustrates that masculinity was a key site of nation building in the nineteenth century, while Camille Robcis (2013) has shown how a structuralist model of French family and kin relationships came to be central to French law in the twentieth century.

17. Fassin (2012); see also Scott (2017).

18. See Miano (2017), Tshimanga et al. (2009).

19. Fraudulent marriages were defined by a directive given to the police in 2005 as "any marriage that is not founded on the free and enlightened desire to take one another as husband and wife and has been arranged exclusively with the goal of migration, professional interests or social, tax or inheritance advantages in mind" (cited in Cole 2014a, 89). Cole points out that it was assumed that only *immigrants*—never native-born French—could be in fraudulent marriages. See Robledo (2011) for a discussion of the legal regime surrounding "fake marriage" and the state's criteria for determining "conjugal truth."

20. Cf. Cole and Thomas (2009).

21. Carolyn Sargent and Stéphanie Larchanché-Kim (2006) have illustrated the devastating effects of this ban on Malian women already in France who were not first wives and who thus lost many of their rights when this ban was enacted. Hélène Neveu-Kringelbach (2016) has shown that French immigration policy makes polygamy more likely among Senegalese migrants, because marriage is one of the only remaining ways to gain legal status.

22. See Tshimanga (2009, 248) for a summary of the many public figures who have made such statements.

23. The same logic was used in the arguments to ban the Muslim headscarf in French schools. When psychoanalyst and public intellectual Elisabeth Roudinesco testified to the government commission examining the potential headscarf ban, she emphasized that the problem with the headscarf was that it "covers over a sexual dimension" and takes away the possibility for women to be "objects of desire" of men, thus interfering with their proper social becoming as women (Scott 2007, 157).

24. See Cohen (1980), Shepard (2018).

25. Fortes as cited in Smith (2017).

26. President Emmanuel Macron's 2018 immigration reforms notably made getting legal status through one's French children more difficult.

27. These ideas fetishizing and objectifying black men are part of French popular culture. There is a song by the white French singer Anaïs that was released while I was in France called "She Only Dates Blacks" ("Elle sort qu'avec les blacks"). The lyrics mocked a white French woman's fetishization of black men and listed many stereotypes (smelling good, knowing how to dance, etc.), but ended with the line "Et elle a bien raison!" (And she's right to do so!).

28. Cole (2014b, 533).

29. See Razy (2007) on the circulation of Soninke girls between Mali and France.

30. The difficulties that people of color, especially of African descent, have in finding housing in France has been well documented; see Préteceille (2011).

31. See Cole (2010), Comaroff and Comaroff (1999), De Boeck and Honwana (2005), Groes-Green (2009), Honwana (2012), Mains (2011), Masquelier (2005), Piot (2010), Weiss (2004).

32. Jónsson (2012, 115). See also Gaibazzi (2015).

33. Schulz (2002). Caroline Melly (2017) proposes the related but distinct idea of "embouteillage," or bottleneck, to describe the way people deal with and get around being

slowed or stuck in Senegal. Jonathan Echeverri Zuluaga (2015) develops the notion of "errance" to capture how African migrants in Dakar experience waiting and acceleration in their journeys.

34. Besteman (2016, 282).

35. Cf. Melly (2017, chap. 3).

36. Freeman (2013).

37. See Daum (1998) for further examples of such return projects.

38. Cf. Larkin (2008) on the way infrastructure displays and performs modernity and prestige.

39. See Lubkemann (2005).

40. Melly (2017, 85). As Melly argues about these "inside-out houses," the Bamako houses migrants build do not depend only on their builders' visions; these unfinished structures have a life made by the people who interact with these always in-process spaces.

41. Kane (1961).

## CONCLUSION

1. From the press release of the new station posted on Parisfutur.com.

2. According to the video simulating the future Gare du Nord at http://www.leparisien.fr/info-paris-ile-de-france-oise/transports/vous-n-allez-pas-reconnaitre-la-gare-du-nord-09-07-2018-7813650.php, it will be a place to "exchange," "relax," and "emerge."

3. Comaroff and Comaroff (2012, 48).

4. Comaroff and Comaroff (2012, 48).

5. Comaroff and Comaroff (2012, 7).

6. De Genova (2010, 34); see also Balibar (2004), Kanstroom (2007), Ngai (2014) on the way states uses immigration control to define national belonging.

7. Mezzadra and Neilson (2010) use the idea of "differential inclusion" to suggest the unequal ways migrants are incorporated in Europe. See also Könönen (2018).

8. See Silverstein (2018); Beaman (2017); De Rudder, Poiret, and Vourc'h (2000) among many others.

9. The Gare du Nord is, of course, not the only site where we might find such alternative configurations. They are to be found in many parts of postcolonial France, as Paul Silverstein (2018, 153–57) points out, from hip-hop to activist political movements that propose "revolutionary love" against the exclusionary logic of the French state.

10. See, for example, Agier (2018) on the migrant camps in Calais; Kobelinsky and Makremi (2009) on detention centers; Lepoutre (1997) and Tetrault (2015) on the *banlieue*; Mbodj-Pouye (2016) and Timera (1996) on immigrant dormitories.

11. Three recent studies challenge this trend of focusing on the margins: Jean Beaman's (2017) work on the French-North African upwardly mobile and middle class, Sarah Mazouz's (2017) study of everyday racism and minorities working in the French civil service, and Fodié Tandjigora's (2018) examination of Malian graduate students in French universities.

12. Cf. Ralph (2014, 171) on overcoming the notion of social isolation in Chicago.

13. It is important to note that unlike US "ghettos," French outer-cities, as sociologist Loïc Wacquant (2007) points out, are not racially or ethnically homogenous; residents have also made them into spaces of integration (see Silverstein 2018).

14. I thank Claudio Sopranzetti for pointing out Tsing's notion. In his study of motorcycle taxi drivers in Bangkok (2017), Sopranzetti underlines this adage to show that the drivers' work of connecting the city becomes meaningful when they mobilize in a political resistance movement.

15. Many West Africans also seek citizenship and legal status; it is beyond the scope of this conclusion to examine the complex meanings that French citizenship and papers have for West African migrants.

16. See Veracini (2013).

17. Malkki (1992, 31).

18. Scott (2007). See Kleinman (2016a) on the way teachers produce cultural difference in public schools; see Mazouz (2017) on civil servants reproducing inequality using racial and cultural categories.

19. Cf. Fernando (2014, 98) on the way Muslim French "pluralize difference" and disturb the "normative center" of the French state's politics of difference.

20. As anthropologists have long noted, systems of exchange involve the necessity of difference, from gift exchange (Mauss 1925) to exogamous marriage (Lévi-Strauss 1949) and the kula ring (Malinowski 1922). The value created is not only economic; as Nancy Munn (1986) illustrates, the Massim of Papua New Guinea went to great lengths to create ties to other islands in order to produce "fame," which only accumulates by cultivating relationships with outsiders.

21. See Poiret (2010) for a critique of such representations.

22. See Tshimanga, Gondola, and Bloom (2009); Senghor (2005) for an overview of these representations.

23. This is similar to what Mahmood Mamdani (2005) argues about the way US policy sees a subset of some Muslims in relation to modernity.

24. See, for example, the French Assemblée Nationale report from 1996, *Rapport d'information sur la mission effectuée par une délégation de la Commission au Mali*. For a critical overview of such representations, their colonial origins, and the way they were used to diagnose the 2005 riots, see Cole (2007), Fassin (2006), Ossman and Terrio (2006), Todd (2005).

25. Ferguson (1992); see Silverstein (2018) who highlighted the relevance of these categories in the context of migration to France. Their cosmopolitanism has parallels in what Diouf (2000) has called "vernacular cosmopolitanism," referring to the Senegalese Mouride trade diaspora.

26. Ferguson (1999, 20); see also Vigh 2008 on the ways that crisis disrupts linear models. As Larkin (2017) points out and adventure narratives reveal, the kinds of disruptions that many thinkers of "crisis" point to are not new, nor can they be located in a particular series of events (e.g., the 2008 economic crisis, structural readjustment), but are continual features of life.

27. See Comaroff and Comaroff (2012) for an example of the generative potential in thinking about "Africa" and the "South" as at the height of an evolutionary model.

28. Elizabeth Povinelli (2006) characterizes this perspective as drawing a contrast between "genealogical society" and the "autological subject."

29. In-depth research among migrants elsewhere suggests that many migrants learn to navigate adeptly between home and host; as Peggy Levitt (2001) shows for "transnational villagers" in the United States, integration and investment in home communities do not need to be opposed to one another.

30. This definition comes from Jacqueline Costa-Lascoux (one of the members of the former High Council for Integration) who wrote an apologia for integration "à la française" in 2006.

31. See Geschiere (2009).

32. See Gary-Tounkara (2008).

33. Mamdani (2002).

34. Geschiere (2009, 224), Mbembe (2000, 25).

35. The court ruled that ID checks were legal but that they could not be carried out in massive operations targeting a large area unless there was a concrete reason related to an ongoing investigation; also, that suspected undocumented status did not provide a justification for such operations. The rulings have not changed profiling practices; a 2017 study found that men perceived as "Black" or "Arab" were twenty times more likely to be stopped for ID checks across public spaces than those perceived as white.

36. On Malian migrant entrepreneurship in France, see Dicko (2011).

37. Turner (1974, 64).

# REFERENCES


Abi-Mershed, Osama. 2010. *Apostles of Modernity: Saint-Simonians and the Civilizing Mission in Algeria*. Stanford, CA: Stanford University Press.

Accoyer, Bernard. 2005. "Interview de M. Bernard Accoyer, président du groupe parlementaire UMP à l'Assemblée nationale," RTL, November 16, 2005. Accessed November 9, 2014. http://discours.vie-publique.fr/notices/053003086.html.

Adams, Adrian. 1977. *Le long voyage des gens du fleuve Sénégal*. Paris: Maspero.

Agamben, Giorgio. 1998. *Homo Sacer: Sovereign Power and Bare Life*. Translated by Daniel Heller-Roazen. Stanford, CA: Stanford University Press.

Agier, Michel, ed. 2018. *The Jungle: Calais's Camps and Migrants*. Medford, MA: Polity.

Aidi, Hisham. 2014. *Rebel Music: Race, Empire, and the New Muslim Youth Culture*. New York: Vintage.

Åkesson, Lisa. 2013. "The Queue Outside the Embassy: Remittances, Inequality and Restrictive Migration Regimes." *International Migration* 51: e1–e12.

Albahari, Maurizio. 2016. *Crimes of Peace: Mediterranean Migrations at the World's Deadliest Border*. Philadelphia: University of Pennsylvania Press.

Allison, Anne. 2013. *Precarious Japan*. Durham, NC: Duke University Press.

Alpes, Maybritt Jill. 2014. "Imagining a Future in 'Bush': Migration Aspirations at Times of Crisis in Anglophone Cameroon." *Identities* 21 (3): 259–74.

Amin, Ash. 2014. "Lively Infrastructure." *Theory, Culture & Society* 31 (7–8): 137–61.

Amselle Jean-Loup. 1976. "Aspects et significations du phénomène migratoire en Afrique," *Les Migrations africaines: Réseaux et processus migratoires*, edited by Jean-Loup Amselle, 9–39. Paris: Maspero, Dossiers Africains.

Anand, Nikhil. 2017. *Hydraulic City: Water and the Infrastructures of Citizenship in Mumbai*. Durham, NC: Duke University Press.

Anand, Nikhil, Akhil Gupta, and Hannah Appel, eds. 2018. *The Promise of Infrastructure*. Durham, NC: Duke University Press.

Anderson, Benedict. 1983. *Imagined Communities: Reflections on the Origin and Spread of Nationalism*. London: Verso.

Anderson, Paul. 2007. *What Is Web 2.0? Ideas, Technologies and Implications for Education*. JISC Technology and Standards Watch Report. http://www.ictliteracy.info/rf.pdf /Web2.0_research.pdf.

Andersson, Ruben. 2014. *Illegality, Inc.: Clandestine Migration and the Business of Bordering Europe*. Oakland: University of California Press.

Appay, Beatrice. 2010."Precarization" and Flexibility in the Labor Process. In *Globalization and Precarious Forms of Production and Employment: Challenges for Workers and Unions*, edited by Carole Thornley and Steve Jefferys, 23–39. Cheltenham, UK: Edward Elgar Publishing.

Augé, Marc. 1995. *Non-Places: Introduction to an Anthropology of Supermodernity*. Translated by John Howe. New York: Verso.

———. 2002. *In the Metro*. Translated by Tom Conley. Minneapolis: University of Minnesota Press.

Balibar, Étienne. 2004. *We, the People of Europe? Reflections on Transnational Citizenship*. Princeton, NJ: Princeton University Press.

Balibar, Étienne, and Immanuel Wallerstein. (1991) 2011. *Race, Nation, Class: Ambiguous Identities*. New York: Verso.

Bancel, Nicholas, Pascal Blanchard, and Sandrine Lemaire, eds. 2005. *La fracture coloniale: La société française au prisme de l'héritage colonial*. Paris: La Découverte.

Banégas, Richard, Florence Brisset-Foucault, and Armando Cutolo. 2012. "Parlements de la rue." *Politique africaine* 3 (127).

Barou, Jacques. 2002 "Les Immigrations africaines en France au tournant du siècle." *Hommes et Migrations*, 1239 (September–October): 6–18.

———.2014. "Integration of Immigrants in France: A Historical Perspective." *Identities* 21 (6): 642–57.

Barron, Pierre, Anne Bory, Sébastien Chauvin, Nicolas Jounin, and Lucie Tourette. 2010. "L'intérim en grève: La mobilisation des travailleurs sans papiers intérimaires." *Savoir/Agir*, no. 12: 19–26.

Bayart, Jean-Francois. 2009. *The State in Africa: The Politics of the Belly*. 2nd edition. Malden, MA: Polity.

Bazenguissa-Ganga, Rémy. 2012. "Paint It 'Black': How Africans and Afro-Caribbeans Became 'Black' in France." In *Black France / France Noire: The History and Politics of Blackness*, edited by Trica Danielle Keaton, T. Denean Sharpley-Whiting, and Tyler Stovall, 145–72. Durham, NC: Duke University Press.

Beaman, Jean. 2017. *Citizen Outsider: Children of North African Immigrants in France*. Oakland: University of California Press.

Beaud, Stéphane, and Michel Pialoux. 2004. *Violences urbaines, violence sociale: Genèse des nouvelles classes dangereuses*. Paris: Fayard.

———. 2005. "La 'Racaille' et les 'vrais jeunes': Critique d'une vision binaire du monde des cités. *Liens Socio* 2 (November).

Berman, Marshall. 1982. *All That Is Solid Melts into Air: The Experience of Modernity*. New York: Simon and Schuster.

Besteman, Catherine. 2016. *Making Refuge: Somali Bantu Refugees and Lewiston, Maine.* Durham, NC: Duke University Press.

Bhimull, Chandra D. 2017. *Empire in the Air: Airline Travel and the African Diaspora.* New York: New York University Press.

Biruk, Crystal. 2018. *Cooking Data: Culture and Politics in an African Research World.* Durham, NC: Duke University Press.

Bjarnesen, Jasper. 2009. "A Mobile Life Story Tracing Hopefulness in the Life and Dreams of a Young Ivorian Migrant." *Migration Letters* 6 (2): 119–29.

Bloch, Maurice, and Jonathan Parry. 1989. "Introduction." In *Money and the Morality of Exchange*, edited by Jonathan Parry and Maurice Bloch, 1–32. Cambridge: Cambridge University Press.

Boittin, Jennifer Anne. 2010. *Colonial Metropolis: The Urban Grounds of Anti-Imperialism and Feminism in Interwar Paris.* Lincoln: University of Nebraska Press.

Bondaz, Julien. 2013. "Le thé des hommes. Sociabilités masculines et culture de la rue au Mali." *Cahiers d'études africaines* 53 (209–210): 61–85.

Bonelli, Laurent. 2005. "The Control of the Enemy Within? Police Intelligence in the French Suburbs (Banlieues) and Its Relevance for Globalization." In *Controlling Frontiers: Free Movement into and within Europe*, edited by Didier Bigo and Elspeth Guild, 193–209. Aldershot, UK: Ashgate.

Bonilla, Yarimar. 2015. *Non-Sovereign Futures: French Caribbean Politics in the Wake of Disenchantment.* Chicago: University of Chicago Press.

Boubeker, Ahmed. 2009. "Outsiders in the French Melting Pot: The Public Construction of Invisibility for Visible Minorities." In *Frenchness and the African Diaspora: Identity and Uprising in Contemporary France*, edited by Charles Tshimanga, Ch. Didier Gondola, and Peter J. Bloom, 70–88. Bloomington: Indiana University Press.

Bourdieu, Pierre. 1977. *Outline of a Theory of Practice.* Cambridge: Cambridge University Press.

Bourdieu, Pierre, and Abdelmalek Sayad. 1964. *Le déracinement: La crise de l'agriculture traditionnelle en Algérie.* Paris: Éditions de Minuit.

Bourgoin, Nicolas. 2013. *La révolution sécuritaire.* Paris: Champ Social Editions.

Bourgois, Philippe. 2003. *In Search of Respect: Selling Crack in El Barrio.* 2nd edition. Cambridge: Cambridge University Press.

Bowie, Karen. 1999. "Polarisation du Territoire et Développement Urbain: Les Gares du Nord et de l'Est et la transformation de Paris au XIXe siècle." Association pour l'histoire des chemins de fer en France.

Bredeloup, Sylvie. 1994. "L'aventure des diamantaires sénégalais." *Politique africaine* (56): 77–93.

———. 2007. *La diams'pora du fleuve Sénégal: Sociologie des migrations africaines.* Toulouse: Presses Universitaires du Mirail, IRD Editions.

———. 2014. *Migrations d'aventures: Terrains africains.* Paris: CTHS.

———. 2017. "Migratory Adventure as Moral Experience." In *Hope and Uncertainty in Contemporary African Migration*, edited by Nauja Kleist and Dorte Thorsen, 134–53. London: Routledge.

Brenner, Neil. 2001. "The Limits to Scale? Methodological Reflections on Scalar Structuration." *Progress in Human Geography* 25 (4): 591–614.

Brian, Tara, and Frank Laczko, eds. 2014. *Fatal Journeys: Tracking Lives Lost during Migration.* Geneva, Switzerland: International Organization for Migration (IOM).

Broch, Ludivine. 2016. *Ordinary Workers, Vichy and the Holocaust: French Railwaymen and the Second World War.* Cambridge: Cambridge University Press.

Browne, Simone. 2015. *Dark Matters on the Surveillance of Blackness.* Durham, NC: Duke University Press.

Buggenhagen, Beth A. 2012. *Muslim Families in Global Senegal: Money Takes Care of Shame.* Bloomington: Indiana University Press.

Cabot, Heath. 2014. *On the Doorstep of Europe: Asylum and Citizenship in Greece.* Philadelphia: University of Pennsylvania Press.

Çaglar, Ayse, and Nina Glick Schiller. 2011. "Locality and Globality." In *Locating Migration: Rescaling Cities and Migrants,* edited by Ayse Çaglar and Nina Glick Schiller, 60–84. Ithaca, NY: Cornell University Press.

———. 2018. *Migrants and City-Making: Dispossession, Displacement, and Urban Regeneration.* Durham, NC: Duke University Press.

Camiscioli, Elisa. 2009. *Reproducing the French Race: Immigration, Intimacy, and Embodiment in the Early Twentieth Century.* Durham, NC: Duke University Press.

Campinos-Dubernet, Myriam. 1985. *Emploi et gestion de la main-d'oeuvre dans le BTP: Mutations de l'après-guerre à la crise.* Paris: Documentation française.

Cannon, James. 2017. "La zone entre classes laborieuses et classes dangereuses: Les marges parisiennes de la Belle Époque à la fin des années 1970." *Espaces et sociétés* 171 (4): 37.

Canut, Cécile. 2014. "On m'appelle le voyageur . . ." In *La migration prise aux mots: Mise en récits et en images des migrations transafricaines,* edited by Cécile Canut and Catherine Mazauric, 261–78. Paris: Le Cavalier Bleu.

Canut, Cécile, and Alioune Sow. 2014. "Les voix de la migration. Discours, récits et productions artistiques," *Cahiers d'études africaines* 1–2 (213–14): 9–25.

Canut, Cécile, and Étienne Smith. 2006. "Pactes, alliances et plaisanteries." *Cahiers d'études africaines* 46 (184): 687–754.

Carmona, Michel. 2002. *Haussmann: His Life and Times, and the Making of Modern Paris.* Translated by Patrick Camiller. Chicago: Ivan R. Dee.

Caron, François. 1997. *Histoire des chemins de fer en France.* Paris: Fayard.

Castagnino, Florent. 2016. "Séparer pour mieux surveiller. Spatialité des risques et pratiques de surveillance en Gare du Nord." *Flux* (103–104): 44–56.

Castles, Stephen, Hein de Haas, and Mark J. Miller. 2013. *The Age of Migration: International Population Movements in the Modern World.* London: Macmillan International Higher Education.

Caton, Steven C. 2006. *Yemen Chronicle: An Anthropology of War and Mediation.* New York: Hill and Wang.

Chabal, Emile. 2013. "The Rise of the Anglo-Saxon: French Perceptions of the Anglo-American World in the Long Twentieth Century." *French Politics, Culture & Society* 31 (1): 24–46.

Chalfin, Brenda. 2014. "Public Things, Excremental Politics, and the Infrastructure of Bare Life in Ghana's City of Tema." *American Ethnologist* 41 (1): 92–109.

Chance, Kerry Ryan. 2018. *Living Politics in South Africa's Urban Shacklands.* Chicago: University of Chicago Press.

Chapman, Herrick, and Laura Levine Frader. 2004. *Race in France: Interdisciplinary Perspectives on the Politics of Difference*. New York: Berghahn Books.

Chevalier, Louis. 1958. *Classes laborieuses et classes dangereuses à Paris pendant la première moitié du XIXe siècle*. Paris: Plon.

Chevandier, Christian. 1997. "La résistance des cheminots: Le primat de la fonctionnalité plus qu'une réelle spécificité." *Le mouvement social*, no. 180: 147–58.

Chu, Julie Y. 2014. "When Infrastructures Attack: The Workings of Disrepair in China." *American Ethnologist* 41 (2): 351–67.

Cissé, Madjiguène. 1997. *The Sans-Papiers: The New Movement of Asylum Seekers and Immigrants without Papers in France: A Woman Draws the First Lessons*. London: Crossroads Books.

Clifford, James. 1997. *Routes: Travel and Translation in the Late Twentieth Century*. Cambridge, MA: Harvard University Press.

Cliggett, Lisa. 2005. "Remitting the Gift: Zambian Mobility and Anthropological Insights for Migration Studies." *Population, Space and Place* 11 (1): 35–48.

Clozier, René. 1940. *La Gare Du Nord*. Paris: J.-B. Baillière et fils.

Cohen, Jeffrey H. 2011. "Migration, Remittances, and Household Strategies." *Annual Review of Anthropology* 40 (1): 103–14.

Cohen, Jeffrey, and Ibrahim Sirkeci. 2011. *Cultures of Migration: The Global Nature of Contemporary Mobility*. Austin: University of Texas Press.

Cohen, William Benjamin. 1980. *The French Encounter with Africans: White Response to Blacks, 1530–1880*. Bloomington: Indiana University Press.

Cole, Jennifer. 2010. *Sex and Salvation: Imagining the Future in Madagascar*. Chicago: University of Chicago Press.

———. 2014a. "Producing Value among Malagasy Marriage Migrants in France: Managing Horizons of Expectation." *Current Anthropology* 55 (S9): S85–94.

———. 2014b. "Working Mis/Understandings: The Tangled Relationship between Kinship, Franco-Malagasy Binational Marriage, and the French State." *Cultural Anthropology* 29 (3): 527–51.

———. 2014c. "The Télèphone Malgache: Transnational Gossip and Social Transformation among Malagasy Marriage Migrants in France." *American Ethnologist* 41 (2): 276–89.

Cole, Jennifer, and Christian Groes. 2016. *Affective Circuits: African Migrations to Europe and the Pursuit of Social Regeneration*. Chicago; London: The University of Chicago Press.

Cole, Jennifer, and Lynn M. Thomas, eds. 2009. *Love in Africa*. Chicago: University of Chicago Press.

Cole, Joshua. 2007. Understanding the French Riots of 2005: What Historical Context for the "crise des banlieues"? *Francophone Postcolonial Studies* 5 (2): 69–100.

Coleman, Gabriella. 2013. *Coding Freedom: The Ethics and Aesthetics of Hacking*. Princeton, NJ: Princeton University Press.

Comaroff, Jean, and John L. Comaroff. 1999. "Occult Economies and the Violence of Abstraction: Notes from the South African Postcolony." *American Ethnologist* 26 (2): 279–303.

———. 2012. *Theory from the South: Or, How Euro-America Is Evolving toward Africa*. London: Routledge.

Conklin, Alice L. 1997. *A Mission to Civilize: The Republican Idea of Empire in France and West Africa, 1895–1930*. Stanford, CA: Stanford University Press.

———. 2013. *In the Museum of Man: Race, Anthropology, and Empire in France, 1850–1950*. Ithaca, NY: Cornell University Press.

Cooper, Frederick. 1987. *On the African Waterfront: Urban Disorder and the Transformation of Work in Colonial Mombasa*. New Haven, CT: Yale University Press.

Costa-Lascoux, Jacqueline. 2006. "L'intégration 'à la française': Une philosophie à l'épreuve des réalités." *Revue européenne des migrations internationales* 22 (2): 105–26.

Curtin, Philip D. 1975. *Economic Change in Precolonial Africa: Senegambia in the Era of the Slave Trade*. Madison: University of Wisconsin Press.

Dang Vu, Hélène, and Hubert Jeaneau. 2009. "Concevoir un espace de transit et de consommation: La gestion de site dans les gares parisiennes." *Espaces et sociétés* 135 (4): 45–62.

Darian-Smith, Eve.1999. *Bridging Divides: The Channel Tunnel and English Legal Identity in the New Europe*. Berkeley: University of California Press.

Daum, Christophe. 1998. *Les associations de Maliens en France: Migrations, développement et citoyenneté*. Paris: Karthala.

Davidson, Naomi. 2012. *Only Muslim: Embodying Islam in Twentieth-Century France*. Ithaca, NY: Cornell University Press.

Davis, Mike. 1990. *City of Quartz: Excavating the Future in Los Angeles*. New York: Verso.

De Block, Greet. 2011. "Designing the Nation: The Belgian Railway Project, 1830–1837." *Technology and Culture* 52 (4): 702–32.

De Boeck, Filip, and Sammy Baloji. 2016. *Suturing the City: Living Together in Congo's Urban Worlds*. London: Autograph ABP.

De Boeck, Filip, and Alcinda Honwana, eds. 2005. *Makers & Breakers: Children & Youth in Postcolonial Africa*. Trenton, NJ: Africa World Press.

De Certeau, Michel. 1984. *The Practice of Everyday Life*. Berkeley: University of California Press.

De Genova, Nicholas. 2010. "Introduction." In *The Deportation Regime*, edited by Nicholas De Genova and Nathalie Peutz, 1–30. Durham, NC: Duke University Press.

———. 2013. "Spectacles of Migrant 'Illegality': The Scene of Exclusion, the Obscene of Inclusion." *Ethnic and Racial Studies* 36 (7): 1180–98.

De Gobineau, J. A. 1853. *Essai sur l'inégalité des races humaines*. Paris: Firmin Didot.

De Haas, Hein. 2008. "The Myth of Invasion: The Inconvenient Realities of African Migration to Europe." *Third World Quarterly* 29 (7): 1305–22.

De León, Jason. 2015. *Land of Open Graves: Living and Dying on the Migrant Trail*. Oakland: University of California Press.

De Rudder, Véronique, Christian Poiret, and François Vourc'h. 2000. *L' inégalité raciste: L'universalité républicaine à l'épreuve*. Paris: Presses Universitaires de France.

Delaroy, Eduard de Rautlin. 1854. *Des moyens de contenir les classes dangereuses*. Paris: Imprimerie Centrale des Chemins de Fer.

Demiati, Nasser. 2007. "Nicolas Sarkozy, ministre de l'Intérieur et pompier-pyromane." In *Quand les banlieues brûlent . . . retour sur les émeutes de Novembre 2005*, edited by Veronioque Le Goaziou and Laurent Mucchielli, 58–76. Paris: La Découverte.

Desjarlais, Robert R. 1997. *Shelter Blues: Sanity and Selfhood among the Homeless*. Philadelphia: University of Pennsylvania Press.

Diallo, Rokhaya. 2012. "The Guerlain Affair: Odorless French Racism." *Palimpsest: A Journal on Women, Gender, and the Black International* 1 (1): 135–39.

Diarra, Souleymane. 1968. "Les travailleurs africains noirs en France." *Bulletin de l'Institut fondamental d'Afrique noire* 30 (3): 884–1004.

Dicko, Brema Ely. 2011. *Les immigrés maliens en France*. Saarbrücken: Université Européenne.

———. 2014. "Après La France: Les investissements économiques de migrants de retour." In *Mobilités dans l'espace ouest-africain: Ressources, développement local et intégration régionale*, edited by Elisabeth Boesen and Laurence Marfaing, 61–86. Paris: Karthala.

Dieng, Seydi Ababacar. 2002. "Pratiques et logiques de l'épargne collective chez les migrants maliens et sénégalais en France." *Africa Development / Afrique et Développement* 27 (1–2): 144–74.

Dikeç, Mustafa. 2007. *Badlands of the Republic: Space, Politics and Urban Policy*. Malden, MA: Wiley-Blackwell.

Diouf, Mamadou. 2000. "The Senegalese Murid Trade Diaspora and the Making of a Vernacular Cosmopolitanism." *Public Culture* 12 (3): 679–702.

Djemaï, Abdelkader. 2003. *Gare du Nord: Roman*. Paris: Seuil.

Dorlin, Elsa. 2006. *La matrice de la race : Généalogie sexuelle et coloniale de la nation française*. Paris: La Découverte.

Douglas, Mary. 1966. *Purity and Danger: An Analysis of Concepts of Pollution and Taboo*. London: Routledge & K. Paul.

Dougnon, Isaie. 2007. *Travail de Blanc, travail de Noir. La migration des paysans dogon vers l'Office du Niger et au Ghana (1910–1980)*. Paris: Karthala.

———. 2013."Migration as Coping with Risk: African Migrants' Conception of Being Far from Home and States' Policy of Barriers." In *African Migrations: Patterns and Perspectives*, edited by Abdoulaye Kane and Todd H. Leedy, 35–58. Bloomington: Indiana University Press.

———. 2016. "Reinterpreting Labor Migration as Initiation Rite: 'Ghana Boys' and European Clothing in Dogon Country (Mali) 1920–1960." *African Economic History* 44: 73–90.

Durkheim, Emile. (1893) 1997. *The Division of Labor in Society*. Translated by W. D. Halls. New York: Simon and Schuster.

Echeverri Zuluaga, Jonathan. 2015. "Errance and Elsewheres among Africans Waiting to Restart Their Journeys in Dakar, Senegal." *Cultural Anthropology* 30 (4): 589–610.

Eickelman, Dale F., and James P. Piscatori. 1990. *Muslim Travellers: Pilgrimage, Migration, and the Religious Imagination*. Berkeley: University of California Press.

El-Tayeb, Fatima. 2011. *European Others: Queering Ethnicity in Postnational Europe*. Minneapolis: University of Minnesota Press.

Elyachar, Julia. 2010. "Phatic Labor, Infrastructure, and the Question of Empowerment in Cairo." *American Ethnologist* 37 (3): 452–64.

Englund, Harri. 2002. "The Village in the City, the City in the Village: Migrants in Lilongwe." *Journal of Southern African Studies*. 28 (1): 135–52.

Epstein, Beth S. 2011. *Collective Terms: Race, Culture, and Community in a State-Planned City in France*. New York: Berghahn Books.

Etoke, Nathalie. 2010. *Melancholia Africana: L'indispensable dépassement de la condition noire*. Paris: Éditions du Cygne.

Fafchamps, Marcel. 2006. "Development and Social Capital." *Journal of Development Studies* 42 (7): 1180–98.

Farias, Ignacio, and Thomas Bender. 2010. *Urban Assemblages: How Actor-Network Theory Changes Urban Studies*. London: Routledge.

Fassin, Didier. 2005. "Compassion and Repression: The Moral Economy of Immigration Policies in France." *Cultural Anthropology* 20 (3): 362–87.

———. 2006. "Riots in France and Silent Anthropologists." *Anthropology Today* 22 (1): 1–3.

———. 2013. *Enforcing Order: An Ethnography of Urban Policing*. Cambridge: Polity Press.

Fassin, Éric. 2012. "Sexual Democracy and the New Racialization of Europe." *Journal of Civil Society* 8 (3): 285–88.

Faure, Sonya, and Balla Fofana. 2017. "Black-out sur l'homme noir." *Libération*, September 19.

Faye, Olivier. 2017. "En vue du premier tour, Marine Le Pen mise tout sur le discours anti-immigration." *Le Monde*, April 18, 2017.

Feldman, Gregory. 2012. *The Migration Apparatus: Security, Labor, and Policymaking in the European Union*. Stanford, CA: Stanford University Press.

Feldman, Nehara. 2018. *Migrantes: Du bassin du fleuve Sénégal aux rives de la Seine*. Paris: La Dispute.

Feldman-Savelsberg, Pamela. 2017. *Mothers on the Move: Reproducing Belonging between Africa and Europe*. Chicago: University of Chicago Press.

Ferguson, James. 1992. "The Country and the City on the Copperbelt." *Cultural Anthropology* 7 (1): 80–92.

———. 1999. *Expectations of Modernity: Myths and Meanings of Urban Life on the Zambian Copperbelt*. Berkeley: University of California Press.

———. 2015. *Give a Man a Fish: Reflections on the New Politics of Distribution*. Durham, NC: Duke University Press.

Ferguson, James, and Akhil Gupta. 2002. "Spatializing States: Toward an Ethnography of Neoliberal Governmentality." *American Ethnologist* 29 (4): 981.

Fernando, Mayanthi. 2014. *The Republic Unsettled: Muslim French and the Contradictions of Secularism*. Durham, NC: Duke University Press.

Fiske, John. 1998. "Surveilling the City: Whiteness, the Black Man and Democratic Totalitarianism." *Theory, Culture & Society* 15 (2): 67–88.

Fleming, Crystal Marie. 2017. *Resurrecting Slavery: Racial Legacies and White Supremacy in France*. Philadelphia: Temple University Press.

Foucault, Michel. (1977) 2007. *Security, Territory, Population (Lectures at the College De France)*. Translated by Graham Burchell. New York: Palgrave Macmillan.

——— 1979. *Discipline and Punish: The Birth of the Prison*. Translated by Alan Sheridan. New York: Vintage Books.

Foucault, Michel, et al. 1991. *The Foucault Effect: Studies in Governmentality*. Edited by Graham Burchell, Colin Gordon, and Peter Miller. Chicago: University of Chicago Press.

Fredericks, Rosalind. 2014. "Vital Infrastructures of Trash in Dakar." *Comparative Studies of South Asia, Africa and the Middle East* 34 (3): 532–48.

Fredrickson, George. 2002. *Racism: A Short History*. Princeton, NJ: Princeton University Press.

Freeman, Luke. 2013. "Separation, Connection, and the Ambiguous Nature of Émigré Houses in Rural Highland Madagascar." *Home Cultures* 10 (2): 93–110.

Frégier, H.-A. 1840. *Des classes dangereuses de la population dans les grandes villes: Et des moyens de les rendre meilleures.* (2 vols.). Paris: J.-B. Baillière.

Gabizon, Cecilia. 2006. "La carte des émeutes de novembre 2005 confirme le profond malaise des immigrants africains." *Le Figaro*, June 29.

Gaibazzi, Paolo. 2015. *Bush Bound: Young Men and Rural Permanence in Migrant West Africa.* New York: Berghahn Books.

Galvan, Dennis. 2006. "Joking Kinship as a Syncretic Institution." *Cahiers d'études africaines* 46 (184): 809–34.

Gardner, Andrew. 2010. *City of Strangers: Gulf Migration and the Indian Community in Bahrain.* Ithaca, NY: Cornell University Press.

Garsten, Christina, and Monica Lindh De Montoya, eds. 2008. *Transparency in a New Global Order: Unveiling Organizational Visions.* Cheltenham, UK: Edward Elgar Pub.

Gary-Tounkara, Daouda. 2008. *Migrants soudanais/maliens et conscience ivoirienne: Les étrangers en Côte d'Ivoire (1903–1980).* Paris: L'Harmattan.

Gas, Valerie. 2007. "Présidentielle 2007: Des émeutes et des candidats." *RFI*, March 28.

Gastineau, Benjamin. 1861. *Les romans du voyage. La vie en chemin de fer.* Paris: Editions Dentu.

Gayet-Viaud, Carole. 2011. "La moindre des choses. Enquête sur la civilité urbaine et ses péripéties." In *Du civil au politique ethnographies du vivre-ensemble*, edited by Mathieu Berger, Carole Gayet-Viaud, and Daniel Cefaï. Bruxelles: PIE-Lang.

Geertz, Clifford. 1973. "Thick Description: Toward an Interpretative Theory of Culture." In *The Interpretation of Cultures: Selected Essays*, 3–32. New York: Basic Books.

Géraud, Alice and Fanny Lesbros. 2012. "Les contrôles au faciès, une réalité gare du Nord." *Libération*, September 27.

Geschiere, Peter. 2009. *The Perils of Belonging: Autochthony, Citizenship, and Exclusion in Africa and Europe.* Chicago: University of Chicago Press.

Geschiere, Peter, and Antoine Socpa. 2017. "Changing Mobilities, Shifting Futures." In *African Futures: Essays in Crisis, Emergence, and Possibility*, edited by Brian Goldstone and Juan Obarrio, 167–80. Chicago: Chicago University Press.

Goffman, Erving. 1963. *Behavior in Public Places; Notes on the Social Organization of Gatherings.* New York: Free Press.

Gondola, Didier. 2009. "Transient Citizens: The Othering and Indigenization of Blacks and Beurs." In *Frenchness and the African Diaspora: Identity and Uprising in Contemporary France*, edited by Charles Tshimanga, Ch. Didier Gondola, and Peter J. Bloom, 146–66. Bloomington: Indiana University Press.

Goswami, Manu. 2004. *Producing India: From Colonial Economy to National Space.* Chicago: University of Chicago Press.

Grandmaison, Olivier Le Cour. 2008. "Colonisés-immigrés et 'périls migratoires': Origines et permanence du racisme et d'une xénophobie d'état (1924–2007)." *Cultures & Conflits* 69 (April): 19–32.

Granovetter, Mark. 1973. "The Strength of Weak Ties." *American Journal of Sociology* 78 (6): 1360–80.

Grayzel, Susan R. 1997. "Mothers, Marraines, and Prostitutes: Morale and Morality in First World War France." *International History Review* 19 (1): 66–82.

Green, Nancy L. 1991. "L'immigration en France et aux Etats-Unis. Historiographie comparée." *Vingtième Siècle. Revue d'histoire* 29 (1): 67–82.

Groes-Green, Christian. 2009. "Hegemonic and Subordinated Masculinities: Class, Violence and Sexual Performance among Young Mozambican Men." *Nordic Journal of African Studies* 18 (4): 286–304.

———. 2014. "Journeys of Patronage: Moral Economies of Transactional Sex, Kinship, and Female Migration from Mozambique to Europe." *Journal of the Royal Anthropological Institute* 20 (2): 237–55.

Gruson, Luc. 2011. "Un musée peut-il changer les représentations sur l'immigration? Retour sur les enjeux de la Cité nationale de l'histoire de l'immigration et sur son occupation par les sans-papiers." *Hommes & migrations: Revue française de référence sur les dynamiques migratoires* 1293 (September): 12–21.

Guénif Souilamas, Nacira, and Éric Macé. 2004. *Les féministes et le garçon arabe*. Paris: Éd. de l'Aube.

Gueye, Abdoulaye. 2006. "De la diaspora noire: Enseignements du contexte français." *Revue européenne des migrations internationales* 22 (1): 11–33.

Gupta, Akhil, and James Ferguson, eds. 1997. "Beyond Culture: Space, Identity and the Politics of Difference." In *Culture, Power, Place: Explorations in Critical Anthropology*, 33–51. Durham, NC: Duke University Press.

Gutierrez Rodriguez, Encarnación, and Shirley Anne Tate. 2015. "Introduction." In *Creolizing Europe: Legacies and Transformations*. Liverpool: Liverpool University Press.

Hage, Ghassan. 2000. *White Nation: Fantasies of White Supremacy in a Multicultural Society*. New York, NY; Annandale, NSW: Routledge; Pluto Press.

Hall, R. Mark, and Mary Rosner. 2004. "Pratt and Pratfalls: Revisioning Contact Zones." In *Crossing Borderlands: Composition and Postcolonial Studies*, edited by Andrea A. Lunsford and Lahoucine Ouzgane, 95–109. Pittsburgh: University of Pittsburgh Press.

Hall, Stuart. (2003) 2015. "Creolité and the Process of Creolization." In *Creolizing Europe: Legacies and Transformations*, edited by Encarnación Gutierrez Rodriguez and Shirley Anne Tate, 12–25. Liverpool: Liverpool University Press.

Hargreaves, Alec. 1995. *Immigration, "Race" and Ethnicity in Contemporary France*. London: Routledge.

Hart, Keith. 2000. "Kinship, Contract, and Trust: The Economic Organization of Migrants in an African City Slum." In *Trust: Making and Breaking Cooperative Relations*, edited by Diego Gambetta, 176–93. Oxford: Blackwell.

Harvey, David. 2003. *Paris, Capital of Modernity*. New York: Routledge.

———. 2005. "The Political Economy of Public Space." In *The Politics of Public Space*, edited by Setha Low and Neil Smith, 17–34. New York: Routledge.

Herzfeld, Michael. 2009. *Evicted from Eternity: The Restructuring of Modern Rome*. Chicago: University of Chicago Press.

Hinze, Annika Marlen. 2013. *Turkish Berlin*. Minneapolis: University of Minnesota Press.

Hoffman, Barbara G. 2002. *Griots at War: Conflict, Conciliation, and Caste in Mande*. Bloomington: Indiana University Press.

Holmes, Seth M. 2014. *Fresh Fruit, Broken Bodies Migrant Farmworkers in the United States*. Berkeley: University of California Press.

Honwana, Alcinda Manuel. 2012. *The Time of Youth: Work, Social Change, and Politics in Africa*. Sterling, VA: Kumarian Press.

Hugo, Victor. 1862. *Les Misérables*. Paris: A. Lacroix, Verboeckhoven & Cie.

Immelé, Coralie. 2005. "La Résistance des cheminots entre 1940 et 1944: Une histoire à la croisée des engagements individuels et collectifs." *Gazette des archives* 198 (2): 139–49.

Ives, Sarah. 2014. "Uprooting 'Indigeneity' in South Africa's Western Cape: The Plant That Moves." *American Anthropologist* 116 (2): 310–23.

Jakobson, Roman. 1981. *Six Lectures on Sound and Meaning*. Cambridge, MA: MIT Press.

Jeandesboz, Julien, and Polly Pallister-Wilkins. 2016. "Crisis, Routine, Consolidation: The Politics of the Mediterranean Migration Crisis." *Mediterranean Politics* 21 (2): 316–20.

Jobard, Fabien. 2002. *Bavures policières? la force publique et ses usages*. Paris: La Découverte.

Jobard, Fabien, René Lévy, John Lamberth, and Sophie Névanen. 2012. "Mesurer les discriminations selon l'apparence: Une analyse des contrôles d'identité à Paris." *Population* 67 (3): 423–51.

Jónsson, Gunvor. 2012. "Migration, Identity and Immobility in a Malian Soninke Village." In *The Global Horizon: Migratory Expectations in Africa and the Middle East*, edited by Knut Graw and Samuli Schielke, 106–20. Leuven: Leuven University Press.

Joseph, Isaac, ed. 1995. *Gare du Nord, mode d'emploi: Programme de recherches concertées, Plan urbain-RATP-SNCF.* Paris: Editions Recherches-RATP.

Jounin, Nicolas. 2008. *Chantier interdit au public: Enquête parmi les travailleurs du bâtiment*. Paris: La Découverte.

Kalifa, Dominique. 2004. "Crime Scenes: Criminal Topography and Social Imaginary in Nineteenth-Century Paris." Translated by Martine Andreoli. *French Historical Studies* 27 (1): 175–94.

Kane, Abdoulaye. 2002. "Senegal's Village Diaspora and the People Left Ahead." In *The Transnational Family*, edited by Deborah Bryceson, 245–63. Oxford: Oxford University Press.

Kane, Cheikh Hamidou. 1961. *L'aventure ambiguë*. Paris: Julliard.

Kanna, Ahmed. 2011. *Dubai, the City as Corporation*. Minneapolis: University of Minnesota Press.

Kanstroom, Dan. 2010. *Deportation Nation: Outsiders in American History.* Cambridge, MA: Harvard University Press.

Keaton, Trica Danielle. 2006. *Muslim Girls and the Other France: Race, Identity Politics and Social Exclusion*. Bloomington: Indiana University Press.

———. 2013. "Racial Profiling and the 'French Exception.'" *French Cultural Studies* 24 (2): 231–42.

Keaton, Trica Danielle, T. Denean Sharpley-Whiting, and Tyler Stovall, eds. 2012. *Black France / France Noire: The History and Politics of Blackness*. Durham, NC: Duke University Press.

Keita, Cheick Mamadou Chérif. 1990. "Fadenya and Artistic Creation in Mali: Kele Monson and Massa Makan Diabaté." *Research in African Literatures* 21 (3): 103–14.

Khiari, Sadri. 2006. *Pour une politique de la racaille: Immigré-e-s, indigènes et jeunes de banlieues*. Paris: Textuel.

Khosravi, Shahram. 2011. *"Illegal" Traveler: An Auto-Ethnography of Borders*. New York: Palgrave Macmillan.

Kleinman, Julie. 2012. "The Gare du Nord: Parisian Topographies of Exchange." *Ethnologie française* 42 (3): 567–76.

———. 2014. "Adventures in Infrastructure: Making an African Hub in Paris." *City and Society* 26 (3): 286–307.

———. 2016a. "'All Daughters and Sons of the Republic'? Producing Difference in French Education." *Journal of the Royal Anthropological Institute* 22 (2): 261–78.

———. 2016b. "From Little Brother to Big Somebody: Coming of Age at the Gare du Nord." In *Affective Circuits: African Journeys and the Pursuit of Social Regeneration*, edited by Jennifer Cole and Christian Groes, 245–68. Chicago: University of Chicago Press.

Kleist, Nauja, and Dorte Thorsen. 2016. *Hope and Uncertainty in Contemporary African Migration*. New York: Routledge.

Knox, Katelyn E. 2016. *Race on Display in 20th- and 21st-Century France*. Liverpool: Liverpool University Press.

Kobelinsky, Carolina, and Stefan Le Courant, eds. 2017. *La mort aux frontières de l'Europe: Retrouver, identifier, commémorer*. Neuvy-en-Champagne: Le Passager Clandestin.

Kobelinsky, Carolina, and Chowra Makaremi. 2009. *Enfermés dehors: Enquêtes sur le confinement des étrangers*. Paris: Editions du Croquant.

Könönen, Jukka. 2018. "Differential Inclusion of Non-Citizens in a Universalistic Welfare State." *Citizenship Studies* 22 (1): 53–69.

Konove, Andrew. 2018. *Black Market Capital: Urban Politics and the Shadow Economy in Mexico City*. Oakland: University of California Press.

Kouame, Koia Jean-Martial. 2012. "La Langue française dans tous les contours de la société ivoirienne." *Collection Note de Recherche de l'ODSEF*. Québec: Observatoire démographique et statistique de l'espace francophone/Université Laval.

Lagrange, Hugues. 2010. *Le déni des cultures*. Paris: Seuil.

Lallement, Emmanuelle. 2010. *La Ville Marchande, Enquête à Barbès*. Paris: Téraèdre.

Lancee, Bram. 2018. "The Economic Returns of Immigrants' Bonding and Bridging Social Capital: The Case of the Netherlands." *International Migration Review* 44 (1): 202–26.

Landau, Loren B. 2018. "Friendship Fears and Communities of Convenience in Africa's Urban Estuaries: Connection as Measure of Urban Condition." *Urban Studies* 55 (3): 505–21.

Landau, Loren, and Iriann Freemantle. 2019. "Africa at the Gates: Europe's Lose-Lose Migration Management Plan." *AMMODI* (blog). January 28, 2019. https://ammodi.com/2019/01/28/africa-at-the-gates-europes-lose-lose-migration-management-plan/.

Larkin, Brian. 2008. *Signal and Noise: Media, Infrastructure, and Urban Culture in Nigeria*. Durham, NC: Duke University Press.

———. 2013. "The Politics and Poetics of Infrastructure." *Annual Review of Anthropology* 42 (1): 327–43.

———. 2017. "The Form of Crisis and the Affect of Modernization." In *African Futures: Essays on Crisis, Emergence, and Possibility*, edited by Brian Goldstone and Juan Obarrio, 39–50. Chicago: University of Chicago Press.

Le Cain, Blandine. 2017. "Affaire Theo: La police des polices privilégie la thèse de l'accident plutôt que celle du viol." *Le Figaro*, October 2.

*Le Monde*/AFP. 2017. "'Bamboula, ça reste convenable': Un syndicaliste de la police dérape, Le Roux le recadre," February 10.

*Le Monde/AFP*. 2005. "Le ministre de l'emploi stigmatise la polygamie." November 16.

*Le Nouvel Observateur*. 2013. "'Ni Noirs ni Arabes': Discrimination à la gare du Nord?" April 15.

*Le Parisien*. 2007. "Le Marché des 5 continents sème la zizanie." November 12.

Lefebvre, Henri. 1967. "Le droit à la ville." *L'Homme et la société* 6: 29–35.

———. (1974) 1991. *The Production of Space*. Oxford: Blackwell.

Lepoutre, David. 1997. *Coeur de banlieue*. Paris: Odile Jacob.

Lévi-Strauss, Claude. 1949. *Les structures élémentaires de la parenté*. Paris: Presses Universitaires de France.

———. 1962. *The Savage Mind (La pensée sauvage)*. London: Weidenfeld & Nicolson.

Levitt, Peggy. 2001. *The Transnational Villagers*. Berkeley: University of California Press.

Lewis, Mary Dewhurst. 2007. *The Boundaries of the Republic: Migrant Rights and the Limits of Universalism in France, 1918–1940*. Stanford, CA: Stanford University Press.

Lorcin, Patricia M. E. 2014. *Imperial Identities: Stereotyping, Prejudice, and Race in Colonial Algeria*. New edition. Lincoln: University of Nebraska Press.

Low, Setha M. 1996. "Spatializing Culture: The Social Production and Social Construction of Public Space in Costa Rica." *American Ethnologist* 23 (4): 861–79.

———. 2008. *On the Plaza: The Politics of Public Space and Culture*. Austin: University of Texas Press.

———. 2017. *Spatializing Culture: The Ethnography of Space and Place*. London: Routledge.

Lubkemann, Stephen. 2005. "The Moral Economy of Nonreturn among Socially Diverted Labor Migrants from Portugal and Mozambique." In *Migration and Economy: Global and Local Dynamics*, edited by Lillian Trager, 257–88. Lanham, MD: AltaMira Press.

MacGaffey, Janet, and Rémy Bazenguissa-Ganga. 2000. *Congo-Paris: Transnational Traders on the Margins of the Law*. Bloomington: Indiana University Press.

Mains, Daniel. 2011. *Hope Is Cut: Youth, Unemployment, and the Future in Urban Ethiopia*. Philadelphia: Temple University Press.

Malinowski, Bronislaw. 1922. *Argonauts of the Western Pacific*. London: G. Routledge & Sons.

Malkki, Liisa. 1992. "National Geographic: The Rooting of Peoples and the Territorialization of National Identity among Scholars and Refugees." *Cultural Anthropology* 7 (1): 24–44.

Mamdani, Mahmood. 2002. *When Victims Become Killers: Colonialism, Nativism, and the Genocide in Rwanda*. Princeton, NJ: Princeton University Press.

———. 2005. *Good Muslim, Bad Muslim: America, the Cold War, and the Roots of Terror*. New York: Three Leaves Press.

Manchuelle, François. 1997. *Willing Migrants: Soninke Labor Diasporas, 1848–1960*. Athens: Ohio University Press.

Mann, Gregory. 2006. *Native Sons: West African Veterans and France in the Twentieth Century*. Durham, NC: Duke University Press.

———. 2015. *From Empires to NGOs in the West African Sahel: The Road to Nongovernmentality*. Cambridge: Cambridge University Press.

Marcus, George. 1995. "Ethnography in/of the World System: The Emergence of Multi-sited Ethnography." *Annual Review of Anthropology* 24 (1): 95–117.

Marx, Karl. (1939) 1971. *The Grundrisse*. Edited and translated by David McLellan. New York: Harper & Row.

Masquelier, Adeline. 2005. "The Scorpion's Sting: Youth, Marriage and the Struggle for Social Maturity in Niger." *Journal of the Royal Anthropological Institute* 11 (1): 59–83.

Massey, Doreen. 2005. *For Space*. London: Sage.

Mauger, Léna. 2007. "Gare du Nord Terminus France: Symbole du malaise urbain, social et policier." *Le Nouvel Observateur*, April 26.

Mauss, Marcel. 1925. *Essai sur le don, forme et raison de l'échange dans les sociétés archaïques*. Paris: Librairie Félix Alcan.

Mazouz, Sarah. 2017. *La République et ses autres: Politiques de l'altérité dans la France des années 2000*. Lyon: ENS Editions.

Mbembe, Achille. 2000. "A propos des écritures africaines de soi." *Politique Africaine* 77: 16–43.

———. 2010. *Sortir de la grande nuit: Essai sur l'Afrique décolonisée*. Paris: La Découverte.

Mbodj-Pouye, Aïssatou. 2016. "Fixed Abodes: Urban Emplacement, Bureaucratic Requirements, and the Politics of Belonging among West African Migrants in Paris." *American Ethnologist* 43 (2): 295–310.

Meghelli, Samir. 2012. "Between New York and Paris: Hip Hop and the Transnational Politics of Race, Culture, and Citizenship." PhD thesis, Columbia University.

Mehta, Suketu. 1997. Gare du Nord. *Harper's Magazine*. August.

Meiu, George Paul. 2014. "'Beach-Boy Elders' and 'Young Big-Men:' Subverting the Temporalities of Ageing in Kenya's Ethno-Erotic Economies." *Ethnos* 80 (4): 1–25.

———. 2017. *Ethno-Erotic Economies: Sexuality, Money, and Belonging in Kenya*. Chicago: University of Chicago Press.

Melly, Caroline. 2017. *Bottleneck: Moving, Building, and Belonging in an African City*. Chicago: University of Chicago Press.

Menjívar, Cecilia 2006. "Liminal Legality: Salvadoran and Guatemalan Immigrants' Lives in the United States." *American Journal of Sociology* 111 (4): 999–1037.

Merriman, John M. 1991. *The Margins of City Life: Explorations on the French Urban Frontier, 1815–1851*. Oxford: Oxford University Press.

Messamah, Khelifa, and Jean-Claude Toubon. 1990. *Centralité immigrée: Le quartier de la Goutte d'Or: Dynamiques d'un espace pluri-ethnique: Succession, compétition, cohabitation*. Paris: L'Harmattan.

Mezzadra, Sandro, and Brett Neilson. 2010. "Borderscapes of Differential Inclusion: Subjectivity and Struggles on the Threshold of Justice's Excess." In *The Borders of Justice*, edited by Etienne Balibar, Sandro Mezzadra, and Brett Neilson, 181–204. Philadelphia: Temple University Press.

Miano, Léonora. 2017. *Marianne et le garçon noir*. Paris: Fayard.

Milliot, Virginie. 2013. "Pluralist Ambiance and Urban Socialisation: Ethnography of the Public Space in the Goutte d'Or Neighbourhood of Paris." *Ambiances: International Journal of Sensory Environment, Architecture and Urban Space* (online), Varia http://ambiances.revues.org/223.

Minian, Ana Raquel. 2018. *Undocumented Lives: The Untold Story of Mexican Migration*. Cambridge, MA: Harvard University Press.

Mitchell, Lisa. 2011. "To Stop Train Pull Chain" Writing Histories of Contemporary Political Practice. *Indian Economic & Social History Review* 48 (4): 469–95.

Moore, Sally Falk. 1987. "Explaining the Present: Theoretical Dilemmas in Processual Ethnography." *American Ethnologist* 14 (4): 727–36.

Morice, Alain and Swanie Potot. 2010. *De l'ouvrier immigré au travailleur sans papiers. Les étrangers dans la modernisation du salariat*. Paris: Karthala.

Morris, Rosalind. 2004. "Intimacy and Corruption in Thailand's Age of Transparency." In *Off Stage, on Display: Intimacy and Ethnography in the Age of Public Culture*, edited by Andrew Shryock, 225–43. Stanford, CA: Stanford University Press.

Mrazek, Rudolf. 1997. "'Let Us Become Radio Mechanics:' Technology and National Identity in Late-Colonial Netherlands East Indies." *Comparative Studies in Society and History* 39 (1): 3–33.

Muehlebach, Andrea. 2013. "On Precariousness and the Ethical Imagination: The Year 2012 in Sociocultural Anthropology." *American Anthropologist* 115 (2): 297–311.

Munn, Nancy. 1986. *The Fame of Gawa: A Symbolic Study of Value Transformation in a Massim (Papua New Guinea) Society*. Cambridge: Cambridge University Press.

Murphy, John P. 2011. "Protest or Riot? Interpreting Collective Action in Contemporary France." *Anthropological Quarterly* 84 (4): 977–1009.

Murphy, Libby. 2015. "A Brief History of 'Le Système D.'" *Contemporary French Civilization* 40 (3): 351–71.

Navaro-Yashin, Yael. 2007. "Make-Believe Papers, Legal Forms, and the Counterfeit: Affective Interactions between Documents and People in Britain and Cyprus." *Anthropological Theory* 7 (1): 79–98.

Ndiaye, Pap. 2008. *La condition noire: Essai sur une minorité française*. Paris: Calmann-Lévy.

Negroni, Angélique. 2007. "Scènes de violence à la Gare du Nord." *Le Figaro/Agence France Presse*, March 29.

Neveu-Kringelbach, Hélène. 2016. "The Paradox of Parallel Lives: Immigration Policy and Transnational Polygyny between Senegal and France." In *Affective Circuits: African Journeys and the Pursuit of Social Regeneration*, edited by Jennifer Cole and Christian Groes, 146–68. Chicago: University of Chicago Press.

Newell, Sasha. 2012. *The Modernity Bluff: Crime, Consumption, and Citizenship in Côte d'Ivoire*. Chicago: University of Chicago Press.

———. 2016. "Circuitously Parisian: Sapeur Parakinship and the Affective Circuitry of Congolese Style." In *Affective Circuits: African Journeys and the Pursuit of Social Regeneration*, edited by Jennifer Cole and Christian Groes, 269–301. Chicago: University of Chicago Press.

Newman, Andrew. 2015. *Landscape of Discontent: Urban Sustainability in Immigrant Paris*. Minneapolis: University of Minnesota Press.

Ngai, Mae M. 2014. *Impossible Subjects: Illegal Aliens and the Making of Modern America*. Princeton, NJ: Princeton University Press.

Noiriel, Gérard. 1996. *The French Melting Pot: Immigration, Citizenship, and National Identity*. Minneapolis: University of Minnesota Press.

———. 2007. *Immigration, antisémitisme et racisme en France, XIXe–XXe siècle: Discours publics, humiliations privées*. Paris: Fayard.

Nordman, Christophe J., and Laure Pasquier-Doumer. 2015. "Transitions in a West African Labour Market: The Role of Family Networks." *Journal of Behavioral and Experimental Economics* 54 (C): 74–85.

Novak, David. 2011. "The Sublime Frequencies of New Old Media." *Public Culture* 23 (3): 603–34.

Nyamnjoh, Francis B. 2011. "Cameroonian Bushfalling: Negotiation of Identity and Belonging in Fiction and Ethnography." *American Ethnologist* 38 (4): 701–13.

Open Society Justice Initiative. 2009. "Profiling Minorities: A Study of Stop-and-Search Practices in Paris." *Open Society Foundations.*

Ossman, Susan, and Susan Terrio. 2006. "The French Riots: Questioning Spaces of Surveillance and Sovereignty." *International Migration* 44 (2): 5–21.

Ouattara, Moussa. 2003. *Le grin: Rires et blagues à Bobo-Dioulasso (Burkina Faso).* Paris: L'Harmattan.

Papayanis, Nicholas. 1996. *Horse-drawn Cabs and Omnibuses in Paris: The Idea of Circulation and the Business of Public Transit.* Baton Rouge, LA: Louisiana State University Press.

———. 2004. *Planning Paris before Haussman.* Baltimore: Johns Hopkins University Press.

Parry, Jonathan and Maurice Bloch. 1989. "Introduction." In *Money and the Morality of Exchange,* edited by Jonathan Parry and Maurice Bloch, 1–32. Cambridge: Cambridge University Press.

Peabody, Sue, and Tyler Stovall, eds. 2003. *The Color of Liberty: Histories of Race in France.* Durham, NC: Duke University Press.

Perdonnet, Auguste. 1855. *Traité élémentaire des chemins de fer.* Paris: Langlois et Leclercq.

Perrot, Michelle. 1987. "Avant et Ailleurs." In *Histoire de la vie privée,* Vol. 4, edited by Philippe Ariès and Georges Duby, 15–18. Paris: Seuil.

Picon, Antoine. 2002. *Les saint-simoniens: Raison, imaginaire et utopie.* Paris: Belin.

Piot, Charles. 2010. *Nostalgia for the Future: West Africa after the Cold War.* Chicago: University of Chicago Press.

———. 2019. *The Fixer: Visa Lottery Chronicles.* Durham, NC: Duke University Press.

Ploquin, Frédéric. 2019. "Le 'J'accuse' de Jacques Toubon au préfet de police à Paris." *Le Journal de Dimanche,* April 13.

Poiret, Christian. 2010. "Le retour de la catégorie 'Noirs' dans l'espace public français." *Migrations Société* 131: 69–86.

Povinelli, Elizabeth. 2006. *The Empire of Love: Toward a Theory of Intimacy, Genealogy, and Carnality.* Durham, NC: Duke University Press.

Pratt, Mary-Louise. 1992. *Imperial Eyes: Travel Writing and Transculturation.* London: Routledge.

Préteceille, Edmond. 2011. "Has Ethno-Racial Segregation Increased in the Greater Paris Metropolitan Area?" *Revue Française de Sociologie* 52 (5): 31–62.

Price, Roger. 1975. *1848 in France.* Ithaca, NY: Cornell University Press.

Purseigle, Pierre. 2007. "'A Wave on to Our Shores': The Exile and Resettlement of Refugees from the Western Front, 1914–1918." *Contemporary European History* 16 (4): 427–44.

Quiminal, Catherine. 1991. *Gens d'ici, gens d'ailleurs: Migrations Soninké et transformations villageoises.* Paris: C. Bourgois.

Rabinow, Paul. 1989. *French Modern: Norms and Forms of the Social Environment.* Cambridge, MA: MIT Press.

Raissiguier, Catherine. 2010. *Reinventing the Republic: Gender, Migration, and Citizenship in France.* Stanford, CA: Stanford University Press.

Ralph, Laurence. 2014. *Renegade Dreams: Living through Injury in Gangland Chicago.* Chicago: University of Chicago Press.

Ratcliffe, Barrie M. 1991. "Classes laborieuses et classes dangereuses à Paris pendant la première moitié du XIXe siècle? The Chevalier Thesis Reexamined." *French Historical Studies* 17 (2): 542.

Razy, Elodie. 2007. "Les sens contraires de la migration." *Journal des africanistes* 77–2: 19–43.

Redfield, Peter. 2000. *Space in the Tropics: From Convicts to Rockets in French Guiana.* Berkeley: University of California Press.

Reed-Danahay, Deborah. 1993. "Talking about Resistance: Ethnography and Theory in Rural France." *Anthropological Quarterly* 66 (4): 221–29.

Reed-Danahay, Deborah, and Kathryn M. Anderson-Levitt. 1991. "Backward Countryside, Troubled City: French Teachers' Images of Rural and Working-Class Families." *American Ethnologist* 18 (3): 546–64.

Reynaud, Léonce. 1850. *Traité d'architecture.* Paris: Dunod, Éditeur.

Richer, Cyprien. 2008. "L'émergence de la notion de pôle d'échanges, entre interconnexion des réseaux et structuration des territoires." *Les Cahiers scientifiques du transport*, no. 54 (December): 101–23.

Rivière, Jean, and Sylvie Tissot. 2012. "The Media Construction of the Suburbs in France: Looking Back on the 2007 Presidential Campaign." Translated by Oliver Waine. *Metropolitics*, May 23.

Robcis, Camille. 2013. *The Law of Kinship: Anthropology, Psychoanalysis, and the Family in France*. Ithaca, NY: Cornell University Press.

Robledo, Manuela Salcedo. 2011. "Bleu, blanc, gris . . . la couleur des mariages: Altérisation et tactiques de résistance des couples binationaux en France." *L'Espace Politique: Revue en ligne de géographie politique et de géopolitique*, May 13.

Rogers, Susan Carol. 1995. "Natural Histories: The Rise and Fall of French Rural Studies." *French Historical Studies* 19 (2): 381–97.

Ross, Andrew Israel. 2019. *Public City/Public Sex: Homosexuality, Prostitution, and Urban Culture in Nineteenth-Century Paris.* Philadelphia: Temple University Press.

Rouch, Jean. 1956. "Migrations au Ghana." *Journal des Africanistes* 26 (1): 33–196.

———, dir. 1967. *Jaguar*. Les Films de la Pléiade.

Saada, Emmanuelle. 2003. "Citoyens et sujets de l'Empire français." *Genèses* 53 (4): 4–24.

———. 2012. *Empire's Children: Race, Filiation, and Citizenship in the French Colonies.* Translated by Arthur Goldhammer. Chicago: University of Chicago Press.

Sainati, Gilles. 2007. "De l'état de droit à l'état d'urgence." *Mouvements* 52 (4): 82–92.

Sanyal, Romola. 2014. "Urbanizing Refuge: Interrogating Spaces of Displacement." *International Journal of Urban and Regional Research* 38 (2): 558–72.

Sargent, Carolyn, and Dennis Cordell. 2003. "Polygamy, Disrupted Reproduction, and the State: Malian Migrants in Paris, France." *Social Science & Medicine* (1982) 56 (9): 1961–72.

Sargent, Carolyn, and Stéphanie Larchanché-Kim. 2006. "Liminal Lives: Immigration Status, Gender, and the Construction of Identities among Malian Migrants in Paris." *American Behavioral Scientist* 50 (1): 9–26.

Sauget, Stéphanie. 2009. *À La Recherche des Pas Perdus: Une Histoire des Gares Parisiennes au XIXe Siècle*. Paris: Tallandier.

Sayad, Abdelmalek. 1991. *L'immigration; ou, Les paradoxes de l'altérité*. Paris: Éditions universitaires.

———. 1999. *La double absence: Des illusions de l'émigré aux souffrances de l'immigré*. Paris: Seuil.

Schivelbusch, Wolfgang. 1987. *The Railway Journey: The Industrialization of Time and Space in the 19th Century*. Berkeley: University of California Press.

Schmid, Lucile. 2014. "Leçons de Calais." *Esprit* 410 (12): 9–11.

Schnapper, Dominque. 2007. *Qu'est-ce que l'intégration?* Paris: Gallimard.

Schneider, Cathy Lisa. 2014. *Police Power and Race Riots: Urban Unrest in Paris and New York*. Philadelphia: University of Pennsylvania Press.

Schreier, Joshua. 2010. *Arabs of the Jewish Faith: The Civilizing Mission in Colonial Algeria*. New Brunswick, NJ: Rutgers University Press.

Schulz, Dorothea. 2002. "'The World Is Made by Talk': Female Fans, Popular Music, and New Forms of Public Sociality in Urban Mali." *Cahiers d'études africaines* 4 (168): 797–830.

Scott, Joan Wallach. 2007. *The Politics of the Veil*. Princeton, NJ: Princeton University Press.

———. 2017. *Sex and Secularism*. Princeton, NJ: Princeton University Press.

Senghor, Richard. 2006. "Le surgissement d'une 'question noire' en France." *Esprit Janvier* (1): 5–19.

Shepard, Todd. 2008. *The Invention of Decolonization: The Algerian War and the Remaking of France*. Ithaca, NY: Cornell University Press.

———. 2018. *Sex, France, and Arab Men, 1962–1979*. Chicago: University of Chicago Press.

Siebecker, Édouard. 1867. *Physiologie des chemins de fer: Grandes compagnies, employés, public, portraits, anecdotes, conseils aux voyageurs*. Paris: J. Hetzel.

Silverman, Maxim. 1992. *Deconstructing the Nation: Immigration, Racism and Citizenship in Modern France*. London; New York: Routledge.

Silverstein, Paul. 2004a. "Of Rooting and Uprooting." *Ethnography* 5 (4): 553–78.

———. 2004b. *Algeria in France: Transpolitics, Race, and Nation*. Bloomington: Indiana University Press.

———. 2005. "Immigrant Racialization and the New Savage Slot: Race, Migration, and Immigration in the New Europe." *Annual Review of Anthropology* 34 (1): 363–84.

———. 2018. *Postcolonial France: The Question of Race and the Future of the Republic*. London: Pluto Press.

Simone, AbdouMaliq. 2004. "People as Infrastructure: Intersecting Fragments in Johannesburg." *Public Culture* 16 (3): 407–29.

———. 2009. *City Life from Jakarta to Dakar: Movements at the Crossroads*. London: Routledge.

Skinner, Ryan. 2015. *Bamako Sounds: The Afropolitan Ethics of Malian Music*. Minneapolis: University of Minnesota Press.

Smith, Daniel Jordan. 2017. *To Be a Man Is Not a One-Day Job: Masculinity, Money, and Intimacy in Nigeria*. Chicago: University of Chicago Press.

Smith, Étienne. 2006. "La nation 'par le côté': Le récit des cousinages au Sénégal." *Cahiers d'études africaines* 46 (184): 907–65.

Smith, Michael Peter. 2005. "Transnational Urbanism Revisited." *Journal of Ethnic and Migration Studies* 31 (2): 235–44.

SNCF Gare & Connexions. 2015. "Gare du Nord 2015–2023: Transformations." Dossier de presse, Mairie de Paris (June).

Soppelsa, Peter. 2012. "Urban Railways, Industrial Infrastructure and the Paris Cityscape, 1870–1914." In *Trains, Culture and Mobility: Riding the Rails*, edited by Benjamin Fraser and Steven Spalding, 117–44. Lanham, MD: Lexington Books.

———. 2013. "Paris's 1900 Universal Exposition and the Politics of Urban Disaster." *French Historical Studies* 36 (2): 271–98.

Sopranzetti, Claudio. 2014. "Owners of the Map: Mobility and Mobilization among Motorcycle Taxi Drivers in Bangkok." *City & Society* 26 (1): 120–43.

———. 2017. *Owners of the Map: Motorcycle Taxi Drivers, Mobility, and Politics in Bangkok.* Oakland: University of California Press.

Sorman, Joy. 2011. *Paris Gare du Nord.* Paris: Gallimard.

Soumahoro, Maboula. 2014. "Les enjeux de la célébration de l'histoire, des cultures et des populations noires en France." *Africultures* 98 (2): 180–85.

Soumaré, Diadié. 1993. "Quelle insertion pour les Soninké en France?" *Hommes & Migrations* 1165: 23–24.

Standing, Guy. 2011. *The Precariat: The New Dangerous Class.* London: Bloomsbury Academic.

Star, Susan Leigh. 1999. "The Ethnography of Infrastructure." *American Behavioral Scientist* 43 (3): 377–91.

Staum, Martin. 2003. *Labeling People: French Scholars on Society, Race and Empire, 1815–1848.* Montreal: McGill-Queen's University Press.

Stevens, Mary. 2009. "Still the Family Secret? The Representation of Colonialism in the Cité Nationale de l'histoire de l'immigration." *African and Black Diaspora: An International Journal* 2: 245–55.

Stoller, Paul. 1992. *The Cinematic Griot: The Ethnography of Jean Rouch.* Chicago: University of Chicago Press.

———. 1999. *Jaguar: A Story of Africans in America.* Chicago: University of Chicago Press.

———. 2002. *Money Has No Smell: The Africanization of New York City.* Chicago : University of Chicago Press.

———. 2016. *The Sorcerer's Burden: The Ethnographic Saga of a Global Family.* New York: Palgrave.

Stovall, Tyler. 2001. "From Red Belt to Black Belt: Race, Class, and Urban Marginality in Twentieth-Century Paris." *L'Esprit Créateur* 41 (3): 9–23.

———. 2006. "Race and the Making of the Nation: Blacks in Modern France." In *Diasporic Africa: A Reader*, edited by Michael Angelo Gomez, 200–218. New York: New York University Press.

Stovall, Tyler, and Georges Van den Abbeele, eds. 2003. *French Civilization and Its Discontents: Nationalism, Colonialism, Race.* Lanham, MD: Lexington Books.

Stuesse, Angela, and Matthew Coleman. 2014. "Automobility, Immobility, Altermobility: Surviving and Resisting the Intensification of Immigrant Policing." *City & Society* 26 (1): 51–72.

Surak, Kristin. 2013. "Guestworker Regimes: A Taxonomy." *New Left Review* 84: 84–102.

Surkis, Judith. 2006. *Sexing the Citizen: Morality and Masculinity in France, 1870–1920.* Ithaca, NY: Cornell University Press.

Tandjigora, Fodié. 2018. *L'immigration des diplômés maliens de France: Fuite des cerveaux ou quête de promotion sociale?* Paris: L'Harmattan.

Terzi, Cédric, and Stéphane Tonnelat. 2017. "The Publicization of Public Space." *Environment and Planning A: Economy and Space* 49 (3): 519–36.

Tetreault, Chantal. 2015. *Transcultural Teens: Performing Youth Identities in French Cites.* John Wiley & Sons.

Thomas, Dominic. 2013. *Africa and France: Postcolonial Cultures, Migration, and Racism.* Bloomington: Indiana University Press.

Ticktin, Miriam. 2011. *Casualties of Care: Immigration and the Politics of Humanitarianism in France*. Berkeley: University of California Press.

———. 2016. "Thinking beyond Humanitarian Borders." *Social Research: An International Quarterly* 83 (2): 255–71.

Timera, Mahamet. 1996. *Les Soninké en France: D'un histoire à l'autre. Hommes et Sociétés.* Paris: Karthala.

———. 2001. "Les migrations des jeunes Sahéliens: Affirmation de soi et émancipation." *Autrepart* 18 (2): 37–49.

Timera, Mahamet, and Julie Garnier. 2010. "Les Africains en France." *Hommes & Migrations* 1286–1287: 24–35.

Todd, Emmanuel. 2005. "Rien ne sépare les enfants d'immigrés du reste de la société." *Le Monde*, November 12.

Toledano, Alexander Michael. 2012. *Sharing Paris: The Use and Ownership of a Neighborhood, Its Streets and Public Spaces, 1950–2012*. PhD Thesis. University of California, Berkeley.

Tonnelat, Stéphane, and William Kornblum. 2017. *International Express: New Yorkers on the 7 Train*. New York: Columbia University Press.

Trager, Lillian. 2005. *Migration and Economy: Global and Local Dynamics*. Walnut Creek, CA: AltaMira Press.

Treps, Marie. 2017. *Maudits Mots: La fabrique des insultes racistes*. Paris: TohuBohu Éditions.

Trouillot, Michel-Rolph. 1995. *Silencing the Past: Power and the Production of History*. Boston: Beacon Press.

———. 2003. *Global Transformations: Anthropology and the Modern World*. New York: Palgrave Macmillan.

Tshimanga, Charles. 2009. "Let the Music Play: The African Diaspora, Popular Culture, and National Identity in Contemporary France." *Frenchness and the African Diaspora: Identity and Uprising in Contemporary France*, edited by Charles Tshimanga, Ch. Didier Gondola, and Peter J. Bloom, 246–76. Bloomington: Indiana University Press.

Tshimanga, Charles, Ch. Didier Gondola, and Peter J. Bloom. 2009. *Frenchness and the African Diaspora: Identity and Uprising in Contemporary France*. Bloomington: Indiana University Press.

Tsing, Anna. 2005. *Friction: An Ethnography of Global Connection*. Princeton, NJ: Princeton University Press.

Turner, Victor. 1969. *The Ritual Process: Structure and Anti-Structure*. Chicago: Aldine Pub. Co.

———. 1974. "Liminal to Liminoid, in Play, Flow, and Ritual: An Essay in Comparative Symbology." *Rice Institute Pamphlet–Rice University Studies* 60 (3).

van Gennep, Arnold. 1960. *The Rites of Passage*. Chicago: University of Chicago Press.

Vanderbeck, Robert M., and James H. Johnson. 2000. "'That's the Only Place Where You Can Hang Out:' Urban Young People and the Space of the Mall." *Urban Geography* 21 (1): 5–25.

Veracini, Lorenzo. 2013. "'Settler Colonialism': Career of a Concept." *Journal of Imperial and Commonwealth History* 41 (2): 313–33.

Vigh, Henrik. 2006. "Social Death and Violent Life Chances." In *Navigating Youth, Generating Adulthood: Social Becoming in an African Context*, edited by Catrine Christiansen, Mats Utas, and Henrik Vigh, 31–60. Uppsala, Sweden: Nordiska Afrikainstitutet.

———. 2008. "Crisis and Chronicity: Anthropological Perspectives on Continuous Conflict and Decline." *Ethnos* 73 (1): 5–24.

———. 2018. "Displaced Utopia: On Marginalisation, Migration and Emplacement in Bissau." *Identities* 25 (2): 192–209.

Vigh, Henrik, and Jesper Bjarnesen. 2016. "Introduction: The Dialectics of Displacement and Emplacement." *Conflict and Society* 2 (1): 9–15.

Von Schnitzler, Antina. 2016. *Democracy's Infrastructure: Techno-Politics and Protest after Apartheid.* Princeton, NJ: Princeton University Press.

Vora, Neha. 2013. *Impossible Citizens: Dubai's Indian Diaspora.* Durham, NC: Duke University Press.

Wacquant, Loïc. 2007. *Urban Outcasts: A Comparative Sociology of Advanced Marginality.* Cambridge: Polity.

Wakeman, Rosemary. 2004. "Nostalgic Modernism and the Invention of Paris in the Twentieth Century." *French Historical Studies* 27 (1): 115–44.

Weber, Eugen. 1976. *Peasants into Frenchmen: The Modernization of Rural France, 1870–1914.* Stanford, CA: Stanford University Press.

Weil, Patrick. 2005. *La France et ses étrangers: L'aventure d'une politique de l'immigration de 1938 à nos jours.* Paris: Gallimard.

Weiss, Brad. 2004. *Producing African Futures: Ritual and Reproduction in a Neoliberal Age.* Leiden, Netherlands: Brill.

White, Bob. 2008. *Rumba Rules: The Politics of Dance Music in Mobutu's Zaire.* Durham, NC: Duke University Press.

White, Hylton. 2012. "A Post-Fordist Ethnicity: Insecurity, Authority, and Identity in South Africa." *Anthropological Quarterly* 85 (2): 397–427.

White, Luise. 2000. *Speaking with Vampires: Rumor and History in Colonial Africa.* Berkeley: University of California Press.

Whitehouse, Bruce. 2012. *Migrants and Strangers in an African City: Exile, Dignity, Belonging.* Bloomington: Indiana University Press.

Wieviorka, Michel. 2008. "L'intégration: Un concept en difficulté." *Cahiers internationaux de sociologie* 125 (2): 221–40.

———. 2014. "A Critique of Integration." *Identities* 21 (6): 633–41.

Wilder, Gary. 2005. *The French Imperial Nation-State: Negritude and Colonial Humanism between the Two World Wars.* Chicago: University of Chicago Press.

World Bank. 2011. *Migration and Remittances Fact Book 2011.* Washington DC: World Bank.

Wright, Gwendolyn. 1991. *The Politics of Design in French Colonial Urbanism.* Chicago: University of Chicago Press.

Wylie, Laurence. 1957. *Village in the Vaucluse.* Cambridge, MA: Harvard University Press.

Xiang, Biao, and Johan Lindquist. 2014. "Migration Infrastructure." *International Migration Review* 48 (s1): S122–S148.

Zemouri, Aziz. 2013. "Quand la SNCF fait du (mauvais) zèle." *Le Point.* April 15.

Zola, Émile. 1890. *La bête humaine.* Paris: G. Charpentier et cie.

# INDEX

CPSIA information can be obtained
at www.ICGtesting.com
Printed in the USA
LVHW091751301020
670290LV00006B/1044

9 780520 304413